The Politics of Culture
in the Chávez Era

EDITED BY LISA BLACKMORE,
REBECCA JARMAN AND PENÉLOPE PLAZA

D1423835

Contents

The Politics of Culture in the Chávez Era
Edited by Lisa Blackmore, Rebecca Jarman, and Penélope Plaza
(University of Essex, University of Leeds, University of Reading)

Introduction: Charting Cultural Currents in Venezuela's Pink Tide

LISA BLACKMORE, REBECCA JARMAN, AND PENÉLOPE PLAZA

University of Essex, University of Leeds, University of Reading

From Honduras right down to Argentina, the turn of the twenty-first century was accompanied by a turn to the left in Latin American politics. This shift, announced by the election of Hugo Chávez and promptly followed by figures such as Luiz Inácio Lula da Silva, Néstor Kirchner, Tabaré Vásquez, Evo Morales and Rafael Correa, has given rise to countless studies of the political and operative configurations of the so-called 'pink tide' governments (Beasley-Murray, Cameron and Hershberg, 2009; Weyland, Madrid and Hunter, 2010; Beverley, 2011; Coronil, 2011). Analysing this turn to the left, scholars have assessed renegotiations of subject-state relations through populism, tracked the displacement of US hegemony in the region, and examined the viability of new South-South economic and diplomatic cooperation endeavours. A subject of significant contention, the Chávez era in Venezuela has been held up as a case study for the constitutive power of the 'posthegemonic multitude' (Beasley-Murray, 2010), the intervention of communal politics in statemaking (Ellner, 2004; Cicciariello-Maher, 2013) and the rebirth of leftist utopianism as a viable ideology that summons the tropes and discourses of nineteenth-century Independence movements in a twenty-first century setting (Coronil, 2011). It has also been criticised as a model of the centralisation of power and of authoritarian populism, which has unravelled into the economic crisis that beset Venezuela from approximately 2014 onwards (Levine, 2002; McCoy and Myers, 2004). Debates surrounding the complex configurations of power in the Chávez era have dominated contemporary Venezuelan scholarship. Yet this, in turn, is often embroiled in the same political polarisation that has seeped into virtually every aspect of the Venezuelan social fabric.

Amid the wave of publications that have attempted to account for the left turn in its regional and national contexts, far less attention has been paid to its impact on collective imaginaries, cultural policies, and aesthetic practices (see Smilde and Hellinger, 2011 and Zimmerman and Ochoa Bilbao, 2014 as exceptions). The reconfiguration of the left over recent years compels a reconsideration of cultural theories that enable us to examine how individual and collective imaginaries are negotiated and formed within, alongside or against the state in the intersecting terrains of politics and culture. This task, as Mabel Moraña (2008) has pointed out, entails recognising social, political, ideological and cultural phenomena as dynamic vectors which have the potential to anticipate and exist beyond the formal structures of the state and to impact national hegemony with equal, if not greater, force than formal politics. Put differently, cultural and aesthetic practices can be understood as:

> movilizaciones que atraviesan el ámbito colectivo sin estar todavía institucionalizadas, movilizaciones en las que los agentes, las agendas y las articulaciones entre los sectores sociales pueden ser caracterizadas como impulsos fluctuantes, espontáneos y discontinuos que actúan desde abajo. (Moraña, 2008: 122).

> actions that traverse the collective sphere without having yet been institutionalised, actions in which the agents, agendas and articulations between social groups can be understood as fluctuating, spontaneous and discontinuous thrusts that operate from below.

Conceiving of aesthetic and symbolic realms not as mirrors for political and social processes but as fault lines where the latter are heralded, represented and negotiated, thus establishes their critical and transformative capacities. At the same time, however, these interactions risk undercutting the idea that aesthetic and cultural practices also wield potential in rethinking reality when they remain divorced from ideological orders. Such is the argument made by Jacques Rancière in his ruminations on the politics of aesthetics in *Dissensus*. Rancière unearths a primary aesthetic gesture at the foundation of politics, which enacts a 'distribution of the sensible' and thus delimits modes of expression, representation and knowledge according to hegemonic practices. But he also acknowledges the dissensual potential of aesthetic practices as a means of rupturing normative distributions to induce 'the suspension of every determinate relation correlating the production of art forms and a specific social function' (2010: 138). In other words, aesthetic practices have the power to unfreeze the vectors that politics attempts to harness and marshal into rigid configurations of sensibility, thus rendering culture a forceful means of contestation that is divorced from partisan affiliation or ideological subscription. These dynamics make the field of cultural studies a fertile terrain in which to examine social tensions that are overdetermined by political allegiances, while acknowledging these as crucial points of reference in any discussion of 'pink tide' Venezuela.

Culture as a Socialist Mission?

The relationship between 'primary aesthetics' and 'aesthetic practices' is a lynchpin in assessing the intersections of politics and culture in the Chávez era (1999–2013), since it envisages a juncture at which a reconfiguration of positions and subjectivities may be possible (Rancière, 2010: 138). It also raises questions about how such reconfigurations are (re)inscribed and/or absorbed within dominant power structures at important historical junctures that precede the political period under consideration. The retrospective representation of the social upheavals of the Caracazo that erupted in Venezuela in 1989 exemplifies this tension between that which constitutes and that which exceeds the Bolivarian project as it is premised on narratives of historical transcendence. The street protests and looting have been construed as the rupture of existing hegemony, the emergence of a visible demand for a sea change in the relations between 'constituted' and 'constituent' power, and the empowerment of the masses beyond political identities or rigid cultural constructs (Beasley-Murray, 2010). Yet the subsequent inscription of this event and its visual imaginary into an official 'politics of memory' signals an absorption of multitudinary mobilisation and its subordination to the requirements of spectacular forms of historiography that were used to lay a foundation stone for the Bolivarian Revolution that was consolidated a decade after the Caracazo with Chávez's election to office. Since then, the state-led revisiting of the Caracazo through civic-military parades, commemorations, photographic exhibitions, and filmic re-enactments has sought to harness and represent historical events according to a Revolutionary telos against the neoliberal policies promoted during the final two decades of the period preceding the 1998 election of Chávez, denominated the 'Fourth Republic' (Vásquez 2008; Arroyo 2013; Blackmore 2014). This points to a domestic mode of what George Yúdice (2003) terms the performativity and 'expediency' of culture, albeit, in his case, one that applies to the global era of neoliberalism, globalisation and the instrumentalisation of culture as a resource to aid financial development (see also García-Canclini, 1989a: 182–183, 1989b: 87). The form of development associated with Bolivarian cultural production, however, is not economic but political. Here, culture is not a symbolic good put to economic ends, but one whose symbolic capital is mined to lay the affective and historiographical groundwork for the Chávez era.

A similar dynamic can be traced to the state-led Misión Cultura (Culture Mission). Echoing the nomenclature of the social welfare projects (*misiones*) that became a flagship of the Chávez administration, Misión Cultura was devised in 2008 as a long-term bilateral agreement, whereby Cuban officials would provide the transfer of skills needed to support local and community arts initiatives in Venezuela (Misión Cultura Corazón Adentro, 2016). Its wide-reaching remit entails generating and promoting socio-political and educational projects that foster community organisation and socialist society (Ministerio del Poder Popular para la Cultura, n.d.). Although it was initially promoted as a grassroots programme that would stimulate cultural groups already active in communities, Misión Cultura and its associated logo – a digital design that mimicked an official rubber stamp – soon became a framework for a wide range of state-led activities, such as dance and music ensembles, that perform in traditional cultural and educational institutions. At present, the Ministry of Culture and Misión Cultura have become indistinguishable. The use of the slogan '100% Revolución Cultural' raises the question of whether the latter's grassroots configuration and autonomy from the bureaucracy of culture have been subsumed into an apparatus of the state. In this sense, cultural participation and production might be said to have been captured as a form of political activism whose agenda is determined by the political establishment and designed to foment feelings of loyalty towards the government.

Yet not all such cultural projects that have interactions with the state may be taken as indicative of clientelistic relations that operate on a 'top-down' basis. For instance, elements of the street art scene have informed political campaigns and partisan branding, while also serving successfully as mechanisms with which groups have lobbied the state to direct funding to projects on the peripheries of formal cultural institutions. This has allowed for the expansion of community radio and television stations, like Catia TVe; hip hop festivals and graffiti collectives, like the Ejército de Liberación Comunicacional (Ejército de Liberación Comunicacional, 2008); and cultural centres operating in informal settlements, such as Tiuna El Fuerte and the Laboratorio de Artes Urbanas in Caracas. Such initiatives have drawn praise from sociologists and anthropologists for fostering cultural dynamism, community participation, and 'bottom-up' administration, as well as intervening in processes of state-making to transcend distinct state-society boundaries via the medium of alternative cultural practices (Fernandes, 2011; Schiller, 2011). Perhaps counterintuitively, independent editorials and art galleries have also flourished during the Chávez era, particularly as political polarisation has intensified. Having been denied access to state funding, these have found support among private enterprises and individual consumers. Caracas, in particular, has seen a growth in innovation and size among small-scale cultural institutions such as Los Galpones cultural centre and Lugar Común bookshop and publishers. Such initiatives have served to diversify the cultural field even as this is overshadowed by the predominance of state institutions.

These shifts in the places that are recognised as sites of cultural production have been accompanied by debates surrounding the ownership of culture in its various enunciations and forms of practice. In April 2016, when groups gathered at the Teatro Teresa Carreño, a grand cultural complex in central Caracas, to celebrate the programme's eighth anniversary, the vice president and culture minister reiterated a common message: 'We were taught that culture was everything that ordinary people didn't do; everything that was kept in museums and libraries, and in the places where ordinary people don't go', the minister told the audience (Marquina, 2016). The understanding was that now, however, 'popular' culture, understood as everyday practices, had been given a place on the grand stages traditionally reserved for 'high' and 'elite' forms of cultural production. This state-led privileging of the quotidian, and the traditional and the folkloric by implication, is not unique to Bolivarian Venezuela. According to Néstor García Canclini, the unsatisfactory advancement of neoliberal economic models in Latin America has encouraged political actors to rethink culture as a key element in articulating a political agenda. In this context, the state has been invested with symbolic legitimacy and consensus as the sole representative of national history, whose exclusive responsibility it is to protect and administer all forms of cultural traditions and heritage, leaving cultural modernity to the private sector, subjected to the dynamics of the global market (García-Canclini, 1989a: 182-183, 1989b: 87). This tendency to celebrate cultural expressions can thus be understood as an historical continuity as much as a political rupture in the region beyond Venezuela.

Marquina's sentiments are echoed in the programme set out in the polemical cultural legislation, the *Ley Orgánica de Cultura* (National Cultural Law), approved by decree in November 2014. Among various objectives, this seeks to protect and nurture Venezuelan cultural heritage and its practitioners. Although it enshrines a broad definition of culture, the law's subdivisions into categories such as 'Venezuelan culture', 'cultural identity' and 'communal culture' delimit culture in terms that privilege a specific notion of Venezuelan identity based on the nation's cultural traditions, racial diversity and folkloric customs (Kozak, 2013). The presence of concepts such as decolonisation, eco-socialism, and 'socialist ethics and aesthetics' (Kozak, 2013: 47, 302) align the law to values that are identifiably in line with the Bolivarian project, despite its legal binding to the 1999 Constitution. Thus the political deadlock of the cultural sphere in Venezuela can be broadly divided into those who operate alongside the cultural ideals of the state that are set out in the 2014 law, and those who mobilise against them (Torres, 2006; Jarman, 2014). In this polarised cultural scene, the leitmotif of a nation in ruins, not one that is future-facing, is leveraged by some of those who oppose the Bolivarian government and its endorsement of certain strands of cultural discourse.

Beyond Polarisation

To avoid the impasse created by polarisation it is vital to study and account for performative nexuses of politics and culture that stretch across a wide spectrum of positions. This approach reaches beyond restrictive political binarisms to alert to the possibility that, in spite of their ideological differences, both 'officialist' and 'oppositional' cultural strategies often converge, reductively and problematically, on a common ground that offers little room for critical manoeuvre. Wary of this deadlock, this interdisciplinary volume brings together scholars from the fields of cultural policy, media history, literature, film, anthropology, and cultural and heritage studies to focus on specific case studies that elucidate conflictive interfaces of politics and aesthetics, showing how cultural and aesthetic manifestations might resist or reinforce political hegemony, or otherwise challenge such categorisations.

The essays to follow offer original close readings of varied aesthetic manifestations and cultural activities, that encompass conventional cultural products, such as recent film and literature, as well as engagements with cultural imaginaries that play out in political protest, urban culture and grassroots heritage projects. A vital starting point to the task of charting cultural currents in the 'pink tide' is the broad overview of changes to cultural policy that have occurred during the Bolivarian Revolution conducted by Gisela Kozak (2013, 2015) and Manuel Silva-Ferrer (2013, 2014), whose chapters review the cultural policies developed in Venezuela between 1999 and 2013, a period spanning the two presidential terms of Hugo Chávez Frías and the advancement of the Bolivarian Revolution. During this period, the main objectives of the Bolivarian Revolution policies were to dismantle liberal democratic heritage and consolidate the Bolivarian Revolution as a new hegemonic block, supported by the state's control of oil revenues. Cultural policies were by no means separate from this macro-project, hence Kozak shows how the strategic guidelines of *Plan Socialista* (Socialist Plan) 2007–2013 and *Plan de la Patria* (Plan for the Fatherland) 2013–2019 brought to the fore questions about the autonomy of the cultural sector, national identity, and institutionality, as well as founding new conceptions of Venezuelan identity (*venezolaneidad*) which have become topics of heated contestation.

The Bolivarian Revolution emerged as a *sui generis* brand of mass mediatised populism, characterised as much by community television projects, as by the creation of new state channels (such as Vive and Ávila TV), and Chávez's own mode of live-televisual governance across the airwaves (see Frajman, 2014). The controversial closure of RCTV in 2007, Venezuela's oldest private television channel, is just one example of how mass media policies have mapped onto political conflicts over recent years, with opponents denouncing a power grab via the silencing or taming of opposition media outlets, such as the cable TV network *Globovisión* and daily broadsheet *El Universal*. Yet against the notion of the Bolivarian Revolution's 'communicational hegemony', Manuel Silva-Ferrer argues that after 1999 the audio-visual landscape underwent significant transformations that revealed novel scenarios in culture and communications, which have reshaped cultural consumption and negotiated power relations with the Bolivarian petro-state. The migration of audiences, readers and museum visitors from state-run spaces to privately run spheres of cultural production demonstrated by Silva-Ferrer can be read as a politicised expression of consumer preference that is at odds with the Bolivarian project. The modern mass media have indeed been instrumental in crafting the public imaginary of the Bolivarian Revolution, but the embrace of communication technologies has not worked to the detriment of an engagement of history and deep-rooted identity. As well as an emphasis on Afro-Venezuela heritage, the constitutional reforms of 1999 fostered increased visibility of indigenous communities within political spheres. Consequently, as Natalia Pérez Bonet explores, Venezuelan indigenous groups have worked to negotiate their identities among the dominant images of indigeneity reproduced by the national government. This has entailed forging their own space of representation and self-fashioning among the cast of indigenous heroes from the past, like Guaicaipuro, consecrated in official cultural heritage, and the 'Indian within' that government officials have claimed to carry within them as an embodied and eternal spirit of resistance. The politics of national identity in the Chávez era also encompassed the entangled imaginaries of decolonial rhetorics, which shuns both European colonialism and US imperialism, and the promise of a new mode of political subjectivity, emancipated from such legacies. As Don Kingsbury points out, since oil became the foundation for Venezuela's transformation into a petro-state in the twentieth century, oil has been integral to naturalising and signifying underdevelopment. In this context, making visible the alternate political subjectivities rooted in the Bolivarian Revolution, particularly those non-White, multitudinous, economically deprived ones, might be read as a means of resisting, as Kingsbury argues, the enduring coloniality of oil.

The representational ethos that accompanied shifts to insert the urban poor and traditionally disenfranchised into the forefront of the public sphere has also had implications for traditional modes of land tenure, notably in the political capital attached to the seizure of large farming estates that would effectively dispossess landowners (*latifundistas*), singled out as representatives of the historical social injustices that have kept large sectors of Venezuelan society in poverty and created push factors that over the twentieth century forced many to abandon the countryside for urban centres. Paula Vásquez unearths fault lines running through the promises of justice associated with policies of expropriation in her analysis of the hunger strike protest, repression and subsequent death of Franklin Brito, a Venezuelan farmer from Bolívar State who died in 2010 after his land was nationalised under Chávez's tenure. In Vásquez's reading, the political and symbolic manipulations that Brito's body underwent as it performed resistance in public spheres, sheds light on the affective terrains of the Bolivarian Revolution. She reveals how 'compassionate militarism' is paradoxically entangled with 'somatic culture' subjecting the sacred and political dimensions of the physical body in slow processes of annihilation.

During the Chávez era, the fates of a whole host of physical bodies (the former president's included) have been drawn into public discussions. From the transfer of Guaicaipuro's remains to the National Pantheon, via the exhumation of Simón Bolívar's bones, through to the memorial practices surrounding Chávez's own monumental internment at the military museum in Caracas, the intersection of illustrious figures and memory politics have become intertwined and contested. The recent transferral of the remains of iconic Venezuelan artist Armando Reverón (1889–1954) to the National Pantheon is a further case in point, yet this particular case study also reveals contradictions and tensions between state memorial practices and community politics at grassroots level. Drawing on long-term fieldwork and ethnography, Desiree Domec's chapter brings into focus the complexities of recovering El Castillete, Reverón's dwelling place and studio at Macuto, and a centrepiece in the cultural heritage and identity of this coastal community devastated by the mudslides that wrecked Vargas State in 1999. Domec examines how in the post-disaster landscape, El Castillete became a space for mis-encounters between community groups invested in the recovery of the ruined site and the inconsistencies of state oversight and management of the nation's cultural heritage. Indeed, as well as through the debris left by natural disasters, Venezuela's history of petro-modernity can also be traced through the architectural ruins left in the wake of periods of boom and bust. The instant modernity augured by the periodic exponential rise in oil revenues of the twentieth century created fertile ground for architectural projects to spring from the ground as material embodiments of the 'spectacles of progress' that Fernando Coronil associated with the 'magical state' (Coronil, 1997: 3). The contours of the urban landscape materialise, in this sense, the recent history of periods of rapid growth and their attendant developmentalist imaginaries, but also of moments of sharp decline and their material aftermath. By tracking the afterlives of El Helicoide and La Torre de David, two ambitious yet ultimately failed architectural projects in central Caracas, Lisa Blackmore defines them as 'phantom pavilions', that is, buildings originally conceived as microcosmic demonstrations of national development, which, as they lapse into curtailed ruins, shake the foundations of the association of the monumental buildings with unstinting progress, thus endowing the urban landscape with its appearance of makeshift modernity.

Alongside the culture of 'slumscrapers' like La Torre de David, and the governmental tolerance of citizen seizures of unoccupied buildings, the Chávez era also redimensioned the urban imaginary insofar as it redirected attention to the marginal communities whose ad hoc homes are arguably the most normative architectural typology in the country. In the early 2000s and through the 2010s, public discussions dwelt recurrently on informal architecture, whether through public outrage at the occupation by street hawkers of emblematic public spaces such as the Plaza Caracas at the Centro Simón Bolívar, or via official policies of fostering large-scale urban infrastructure in deprived areas, most dramatically embodied in the state-financed construction of the San Agustín cable car, which linked the 'informal' *barrio* to the 'formal' city. In her analysis of Mariana Rondón's internationally acclaimed film *Pelo malo* (2014), Rebecca Jarman probes the intersection of bygone state-funded social housing and urban marginality in Bolivarian Venezuela as these coalesce in the negotiation of sexual and spatial constructs. By exploring Rondón's 'queering' of the (in)famous Caracas neighbourhood, El Veintitrés de Enero, she asks if queerness is appropriated as a form of political protest, or whether queerness is, instead, taken as a premise that might nuance understandings of power and politics. Refusing to essentialise sexuality or territorially rooted subjectivities, *Pelo malo* attempts to foster a more intimate understanding of its inhabitants as a richly textured and conflicted community, as opposed to a collective historical protagonist united in revolutionary movement with the government.

Today, it is not just within the confines of the capital city or the national territory, however, that identity must be probed. The growing diaspora of Venezuelan citizens of different socioeconomic classes, who are leaving the country due to the precariousness of the current economic climate, means that aesthetic and cultural production stretches beyond territorial boundaries. As a result, any consideration of the politics of culture in the Chávez era must also attend to the practices of Venezuelans who have migrated elsewhere and whose engagement with national identity is mediated by geographical and cultural dis-location, not least in light of the fact that the Bolivarian Revolution itself emerged alongside the parallel rise of digital technologies through which social and political lives are increasingly lived out online. Attending to these issues, this book closes with an exploration of experiences of uprootedness, disenchantment, and nostalgia in Venezuelan literature produced in migration. Understood as a lament for the unfulfilled promises of democratic discourses, including most importantly that of national unity based on historical icons and economic prospects, María Teresa Vera Rojas identifies in Eduardo Sánchez Rugeles's collection of short stories, *Los Desterrados* (2012) new meanings of Venezuelan national identity from the perspective of the exiled subject.

The highly national context of the cases under discussion in this book does not mean that the methodologies used and questions raised are germane only to Chávez's Venezuela. Rather, as they depart from the contentious politics of recent times to reach back to the pre-Columbian past and the globalised present, these studies intersect with pressing inquiries about the enduring legacies of coloniality/modernity, the geopolitical tensions that continue to shape the world, and the deterritorialising impacts that globalisation and neoliberalism have exerted on local politics and narratives of belonging. In sum, then, the politics of culture in the Chávez era lays groundwork for transdisciplinary conversations, which as they cut across divides – whether of academic area, cultural medium, historical period, or national frontier – might just push discussions of Venezuela's current crisis beyond its polarised impasse and onto more fertile, critical terrains on which to study the tensions of the recent past as well as the structural and systemic factors in which they are bound up.

References

Arroyo Poleo, F. (2015) 'Reescrituras visuales del cuerpo nacional: políticas y poéticas de la memoria histórica en la Venezuela actual' in L. Duno-Gottberg (ed.) *La política encarnada, Biopolítica y cultura en la Venezuela bolivariana.* Equinoccio: Caracas, 177–214.

Beasley-Murray, J. (2010) *Posthegemony: Political Theory and Latin America.* University of Minnesota Press: London and Minneapolis.

Beasley-Murray, J., Cameron, M. and Hershberg, E. (2009) 'Latin America's Left Turns: An Introduction'. *Third World Quarterly* 30(2): 319–330.

Beverley, J. (2011) *Latinamericanism After 9/11.* Duke University Press: Durham and London.

Blackmore, L. (2014) 'Capture Life: The "Document-Monument" in Recent Commemorations of Hugo Chávez'. *Journal of Latin American Cultural Studies* 23(3): 235–250.

Ciccariello-Maher, G. (2013) *We Created Chávez: A People's History of the Venezuelan Revolution.* Duke University Press: Durham and London.

Coronil, F. (2011) 'The Future in Question: History and Utopia in Latin America (1989–2010)' in C. Calhoun and G. Derluguian (eds) *Business As Usual: The Roots of the Global Financial Meltdown.* New York University Press: New York, 231–292.

Ejército de Liberación Comunicacional (2008) 'No sabemos disparar' http://nosabemosdisparar.blogspot.ch [accessed 9 January 2018].

Ellner, S. and Hellinger, D. (eds) *Venezuelan Politics in the Chávez Era; Class, Polarization, and Conflict.* Lynne Rienner: Boulder and London.

Fernandes, S. (2011) 'Radio Bemba in an Age of Electronic Media: The Dynamics of Popular Communication in Chávez's Venezuela' in D. Smilde and

D. Hellinger (eds) *Participation, Politics and Culture in Venezuela's Bolivarian Democracy*. Duke University Press: Durham and London, 131–156.

Frajman, E. (2014) 'Broadcasting Populist Leadership: Hugo Chávez and *Aló Presidente*'. *Journal of Latin American Studies* **46**: 501–526.

García Canclini, N. (1989a) 'Políticas culturales para el fin de siglo' in *Las políticas culturales en América Latina: una reflexión plural*. Ediciones APPAC: Lima, 83–95.

García Canclini, N. (1989b) '¿Modernismo sin modernización?' *Revista Mexicana de Sociología* **51**(3): 163–189.

Jarman, R. (2014) 'Against Utopia: Fantasies of Emancipation in Ana Teresa Torres's Nocturama (2006)'. *Journal of Latin American Cultural Studies* **24**(1): 19–32.

Kozak Rovero, G. (2013) 'Políticas culturales del Estado en la Venezuela del siglo XXI (1999–2013)' in M. Bisbal (ed.) *Saldo en rojo: Comunicaciones y cultura en la era bolivariana*. Universidad Católica Andrés Bello: Caracas, 293–310.

Kozak Rovero, G. (2015) 'Revolución Bolivariana: políticas culturales en la Venezuela socialista de Hugo Chávez (1999–2013)'. *Cuadernos de Literatura* **19**(37): 38–56.

Levine, D. (2002) 'The Decline and Fall of Democracy in Venezuela: Ten Theses'. *Bulletin of Latin American Research* **21**(2): 248–269.

Marquina, J. (2016) 'Así celebraron ocho años de la Misión Cultura Corazón Adentro en el Teresa Carreño'. Alba Ciudad, 27 April. http://albaciudad.org/2016/04/fotos-mision-cultura-corazon-adentro-8-aniversario/ [accessed 9 January 2018].

McCoy, J. and Myers, D (eds) (2004) *The Unraveling of Representative Democracy in Venezuela*. Johns Hopkins University Press: Baltimore and London.

Misión Cultura Corazón Adentro (2016) Venezolana de Televisión, 25 April http://www.vtv.gob.ve/articulos/2016/04/25/mision-cultura-corazon-adentro-9-anos-mostrador-el-poder-creador-de-la-cultura-popular-7689.html [accessed 9 November 2015].

Ministerio del Poder Popular para la Cultura (n.d.) 'Competencias'. http://www.misioncultura.gob.ve/index.php/nosotros/competencias [accessed 9 November 2015].

Moraña, M. (2008) 'Negociar lo local: La "marea rosa" en América Latina o qué queda de la izquierda?' in M. Moraña (ed.) *Cultura y cambio social en América Latina*. Madrid: Veuvert, 113–134.

Rancière, J. (2010) *Dissensus: On Politics and Aesthetics*. Continuum: London.

Schiller, N. (2011) 'Catia Sees You: Community Television, Clientelism and the State in the Chávez Era' in D. Smilde and D. Hellinger (eds) *Participation, Politics and Culture in Venezuela's Bolivarian Democracy*. Duke University Press: Durham and London, 104–130.

Silva-Ferrer, M. (2013) 'Migraciones culturales en los 14 años de Hugo Chávez' in M. Bisbal (ed.) *Saldo en rojo: comunicaciones y cultura en la era bolivariana*. Universidad Católica Andrés Bello: Caracas, 274–292.

Silva-Ferrer, M. (2014) *El cuerpo dócil de la cultura: poder, cultura y comunicación en la Venezuela de Chávez*. Madrid and Frankfurt: Veuvert.

Smilde, D. and Hellinger, D. (eds) (2011) *Participation, Politics and Culture in Venezuela's Bolivarian Democracy*. Duke University Press: Durham and London.

Torres, A. T. (2006) 'Cuando la literatura entró en el siglo XXI' in B. González Stephan and C. Pacheco (eds) *Nación y literatura*. Fundación Bigott/Banesco/ Equinoccio: Caracas, 911–925.

Weyland, K., Madrid, R. and Hunter, W. (eds) (2010) *Leftist Governments in Latin America: Successes and Shortcomings*. Cambridge University Press: Cambridge.

Vásquez, P. (2008) 'Rituales de dignificación: moral y acción humanitaria en la política social de la revolución bolivariana venezolana'. *Estudios* **16**(31): 129–153.

Yúdice, G. (2003) *The Expediency of Culture: Uses of Culture in the Global Era*. Duke University Press: Durham and London.

Zimmerman, M. and Ochoa Bilbao, L. (2014) *Giros culturales en la marea rosa en América Latina* (2nd edition). Editorial La Casa: Puebla.

Preface

GEORGE A. YÚDICE

The Politics of Culture in the Chávez Era is a very welcome addition to the cultural studies and cultural policy bibliography on Latin America for several reasons. In the first place, this is the first comprehensive analysis of culture in the Chávez era. The book includes a thorough review of cultural and communicational policies, making an important contribution to the spate of cultural policy studies of the past 20 years. Much of this literature has dealt with cultural and creative industries, and especially their economic revenues. On the other hand, this edited volume focuses on the political uses of culture. Cases of censorship and the shutting of TV, radio and other arts and cultural institutions are rife. In this regard, the book shows the seamy side of the intervention of the Bolivarian Revolution into cultural industries.

But we also get another side of the story of state investment in already existing community culture. One of the most vibrant activist movements in Latin America is *Cultura viva comunitaria*, which lobbies states to recognise community cultural initiatives and invest 0.1 percent of national budgets to promote them. These initiatives do not follow any single model but, on the contrary, contribute to the vast cultural diversity of the hemisphere. The movement was inspired in part by Brazil's *Pontos de cultura* (Points of Culture) programme, which its director, at the time of its founding, characterised as follows: 'The Points of Culture make visible the living heritage of the communities, that's why the large platform that hosts them was named Cultura Viva (Living Culture), emphasising the idea that not only professionals produce culture but also people in their day-to-day activities. Autonomy, leadership and empowerment are the pillars of shared and transformative management in the Points of Culture' (Turino, 2010: 58). Thus, 'Leaders are created, identities are redrawn and traditional narratives are interrupted' (Turino, 2010: 63). Therefore:

> The programme does not seek a single nation, but different nations that imagine themselves heterogeneous and interactive. Because once the value of a community's point of culture is recognised, the next step is to connect it to other points of culture and create a network. Through the Points of Culture, these communities present a new way of seeing themselves and of being seen. (Turino, 2010: 121)

In 2013, the heads of state at that year's summit of the Iberoamerican General Secretariat, a regional UNESCO-like organisation consisting of Latin American countries, Spain, Portugal, and Andorra, created Iberculturaviva to strengthen the lobby for these initiatives. Venezuela is not part of Iberculturaviva and, as we see in this book, the community culture movement, embodied by the programme *Misión cultura*, has become a clientelistic appendage of the state, contrary to the spirit of the movement elsewhere in the region.

A third reason for reading this book is the fine-grained analysis of culture in one given 'Pink Tide' government. Its approach to culture is quite different from what one finds in the leftist governments of Argentina, Bolivia, Brazil, Ecuador and Uruguay of the new millennium, at least as far as cultural and creative industries and community culture are concerned. The collective imaginaries in these countries, as in other Latin American countries, pivot on diversity rather than the enshrinement of a given national culture, as one finds in Venezuela's National Cultural Law. Perhaps it would be fair to say that the cultural institutions of most Latin American countries have shown resilience in the face of attempts to reel them in to do the bidding of a particular government. And yet what is also of great interest in this book is the identification of forms of resistance even within programmes sponsored by the state. Most writing on Venezuela refers to a polar contest between the Chavista government and the opposition. But as we see in this book, not all resistance is attributed to the opposition. Moreover, as is argued in the introduction and in several chapters, both sides may end up deploying similar strategies.

There are explorations of diasporic cultural expressions for Cuba, the Dominican Republic, El Salvador, and Mexico. This book joins that scholarship on the literature and arts produced outside Venezuela, also examining life in translocal digital circuits. It is as complete a set of studies as one can get into one volume. Moreover, the studies are pitched in such a way that they not only illuminate Venezuelan culture but also serve to establish useful comparisons with the cultures of other countries.

Reference

Turino, C. (2010) *Ponto de cultura: o Brasil de baixo para cima* (2nd edition). Anita Garibaldi: São Paulo.

1

Cultural Policies and the Bolivarian Revolution in the Socialist Venezuela of Hugo Chávez (1999–2013)

GISELA KOZAK-ROVERO

Universidad Central de Venezuela

Introduction

The United Nations Educational, Scientific and Cultural Organization (UNESCO) defines culture as 'the set of distinctive spiritual, material, intellectual and emotional features of a society or social group, and that it encompasses, in addition to art and literature, lifestyles, ways of living together, value systems, traditions and beliefs' (UNESCO, 1972). Culture is our lifeblood: throughout history, it has connected individuals with the wider world in every corner of the globe. Many modern nation-states have passed legislation that protects the cultural practices deemed most important for their populations. In times of democracy, such policies designed to protect certain traditions and practices should not be confused with efforts to condition or channel the creative and social processes that feed into the circulation, production and transmission of what we know as culture. Indeed, the rich and fertile cultural terrains that often flourish at the margins or in defiance of dominant powers evidence the limitations of state control in this arena. These terrains have been cultivated by the creative and political actions of men and women in the fields of literature, visual arts, theatre, music and scholarship, and safeguarded by their defence of languages, political ideas or religious convictions. In democracy, the values that are attributed to the freedoms of speech, thought and creation guarantee diversity of cultural expression alongside the nation-state. As such, national cultural policies should recognise and support investigative research, conservation, funding, administration, creative production and distribution in the following areas: cultural heritage (*Protection of the World Cultural and Natural Heritage*),[1] literature and the written word, music, performing arts, plastic

---

Translated by Rebecca Jarman

1   According to the first article of this Convention, the following are considered to be 'cultural heritage':

arts, cinema and photography, radio and television, socio-cultural activity (*Recommendation concerning the International Standardization of Statistics on the Public Financing of Cultural Activities*),[2] gastronomy and cultural tourism, anthropology, history, sociology, cultural theory. This chapter offers an analysis of cultural policies in Venezuela since the rise of Hugo Chávez, with a focus on the following specific areas: (1) cultural institutions, legislation, cultural and public investment for culture; (2) creatives, cultural managers, cultural practitioners and intellectuals in Venezuela; (3) the new man, new woman: strategic objectives of the Bolivarian Revolution; (4) taking stock: the Bolivarian Revolution and its debts to cultural policy.

Cultural Institutions, Legislation, Cultural and Public Investment for Culture

In 1999, the numerous cultural institutions funded by the Venezuelan state included:

(a) Monte Ávila Editores (Monte Ávila Publishers)
(b) Biblioteca Ayacucho (Ayacucho Literary Collection)
(c) La Casa de Bello (Casa de Bello Historical Trust)
(d) Instituto Autónomo Biblioteca Nacional (the National Library system)
(e) Imprenta Nacional (National Publishing Office)

'monuments: architectural works, works of monumental sculpture and painting, elements or structures of an archaeological nature, inscriptions, cave dwellings and combinations of features, which are of outstanding universal value from the point of view of history, art or science; groups of buildings: groups of separate or connected buildings which, because of their architecture, their homogeneity or their place in the landscape, are of outstanding universal value from the point of view of history, art or science; works of man or the combined works of nature and man, and areas including archaeological sites which are of outstanding universal value from the historical, aesthetic, ethnological or anthropological point of view' (UNESCO, 2005).

2 The Recommendation concerning the International Standardization of Statistics on the Public Financing of Cultural Activities defines the following as socio-cultural activities:

7.0 Socio-cultural initiative, community cultural centres and promotion of amateur activities

7.1 Civic and professional associations

7.2 Other socio-cultural activities (ceremonies, social functions connected with religious, moral, ethical or philosophical beliefs)

7.3 Training outside the formal education system

7.4 Other activities necessary for socio-cultural activities. (UNESCO, 1980)

(f) Museums including the Museum of Modern Art, the Science Museum, the Fine Arts Museum, the Lía Bermúdez Museum, the National Art Gallery, the Alejandro Otero Gallery, the Zulia Museum of Contemporary Art, the Jacobo Borges Gallery, the Jesús Soto Gallery, the Arturo Michelena Gallery, the Trujillo Museum of Folk Culture, the Petare Gallery of Popular Culture, among others

(g) Festival Internacional de Teatro (International Festival of Theatre)

(h) Centro Nacional de Cinematografía (National Centre of Cinematography)

(i) Compañías Nacionales de Teatro y Danza (National Theatre and Dance Companies)

(j) Movimiento de Teatro Penitenciario (Prison Theatre Movement)

(k) Complejo Cultural Teresa Carreño (Teresa Carreño Centre for the Arts)

(l) Consejo Nacional de la Cultura (National Council for Culture)

(m) Fundarte (Foundation for Culture and Arts)

(n) Centro de Estudios Latinoamericanos Rómulo Gallegos (Rómulo Gallegos Centre for Latin American Studies)

(o) Centro Cultural La Estancia (La Estancia Arts Centre)

(p) Sistema Nacional de Orquestas y Coros Juveniles e Infantiles de Venezuela (Venezuelan National System of Youth Orchestras and Choirs)

(q) Premio Internacional de Novela Rómulo Gallegos (International Rómulo Gallegos Prize for Literature)

(r) Festival de Teatro de Oriente (Festival of Oriental Theatre)

(s) Cultural Management Committees for public universities

(t) Televisora Nacional Canal 5 (National Broadcasting Channel 5), Venezolana de Televisión and Radio Nacional de Venezuela (National Venezuelan Radio)

(u) Schola Cantorum choral system

(v) Cultural centres across the nation

(w) Public spaces such as squares, promenades and boulevards

(x) Cinemas and theatres

   (i) National bookshop franchise Kuai Mare

   (ii) Culture Management Committees under regional and municipal governance

   (iii) Consejo Nacional de la Cultura (National Council for Culture)

   (iv) Archivo General de la Nación (General National Archive)

   (v) Vicente Emilio Sojo Foundation

   (vi) Baroque and Renaissance Chamber Orchestras

   (vii) Magazines including *Imagen*, *Nacional de cultura* and *Encuadre*, among others

(viii) Contemporary theatre and dance groups that received subsidies from the state.

The revolutionary government has preserved the titles of some institutions and has renamed others. Significantly, in 2005, the government created the Ministerio del Poder Popular para la Cultura (Ministry of Popular Power for Culture), under the direction first of architect Francisco Sesto, which set up a series of cultural platforms that oversaw activities related to cinema and audiovisual culture, literature and literacy, intellectual history, patrimony and heritage, music and the performing arts, and visual arts (Minsterio del Poder Popular para la Cultura, 2010).

Other important additions to the cultural sphere since 1999 include state-run culture councils, the Misión cultura (Mission for Culture), designed to foster community arts and consolidate a 'national identity', the Bachelor of Arts in Education and Cultural Development, and the Ministerio del Poder Popular de Asuntos Indígenas (Ministry of Popular Power for Indigenous Affairs), charged with the protection of indigenous cultures. These cultural institutions created by the Bolivarian Revolution would fill vacuums in the structures of state power or function in parallel with pre-existing institutions. For example, the main political objective of the state-run publishers El Perro y la Rana (The Dog and the Frog) is to decentralise the production of texts and offer publishing facilities in every Venezuelan state, in contrast to the central state-run publishers Monte Ávila (Mount Ávila) and Biblioteca Ayacucho (Ayacucho Library). The Distribuidora Nacional (National Book Distributor) has a similar function in the distribution of texts throughout the entire country. La Villa del Cine was conceived as a small film studio that would lend its services to national and international filmmakers. The Museo de Arquitectura (Museum of Architecture) set out to revise the discipline's historical key moment's, while the Fundación Red de Arte (Arts Network Foundation) would sell the work of Venezuelan artists. The Centro Nacional de Historia (National Centre for History) merits special mention as an example of an institution created to run in parallel with another already in existence, when the latter refused to cooperate with the ideological demands of the Revolution. In this instance, I am referring to La Academia Nacional de la Historia (the National Academy of History), a longstanding and prestigious national institution from which numerous important historical documents have been confiscated. The history behind UNEARTES (University of the Arts) is comparable: rather than invest in pre-existing universities and academies, a new institution was created that would work with the ideological bend of the government. Television channels such as Ávila, Vive, Colombeia and TVes, and the radio station ALBA FM were afforded the same role of advocating revolutionary politics: their schedule of cultural programmes leans consistently to the left with little room for debate, while their presenters promote the state and attack the political opposition. A similar claim may be made of the series of national magazines: A Plena Voz (Out Loud), La Roca de Crear (Bedrock of Creation), Así Somos (This is Us), Se Mueve (We Move), Arte de Leer (The Art of Reading), Memorias de Venezuela (Memories of Venezuela), Buen Vivir (Wellbeing) and La Revuelta (The Mix). Memorias de Venezuela, for example, is the informative, public-facing publication pertaining to the Centro Nacional de Historia and is responsible for the promotion of an official version of Venezuelan history that justifies the Bolivarian Revolution. A Plena Voz is a cultural magazine whose content favourable to the Revolution limits its capacity to fulfil its founding function: to disseminate knowledge of Venezuelan culture in all its variety and plurality.

In terms of financial management, the state has made significant investments in the cultural sector, although much of this is not accounted for in the official budget. The amount designated for cultural enterprises has not officially increased above the median figures prior to 1998. For specific projects, such as the Mausoleo del Libertador (the mausoleum for Simón Bolívar), the government transferred money from other areas while seeking additional credit and special expenditure. Up until 2013 El Sistema benefited from contributions from other ministries, including investments made by el Despacho de la Presidencia y Seguimiento de la Gestión del Gobierno (the President's Office). These examples illustrate the discrepancies in public investment in arts and culture in Venezuela in line with studies done by Carlos Enrique Guzmán Cárdenas (2011), who notes that the official amount designated for culture has not exceeded 0.53 percent of the national budget.

Financing for the cultural sector is largely determined by the oil-rent distribution policies that are typical of the Bolivarian Revolution. One example is the sustained and high-level support offered to El Sistema and to the national cinema industry that has accompanied smaller-scale investments in the mass production of magazines, CDs and audiovisual material. To this could be added a number of public events, from small community activities to large-scale poetry festivals, classical music concerts and international academic conferences, funded by state organs that favour traditional, folkloric, indigenous and urban cultures, different manifestations of youth culture, and many different forms of street art. However, one salient problem is a lack of reliable and systematic research into the public consumption of state-funded culture. As things stand, we are unable to quantify the impact of state policies that include the mass-production of free or low-cost cultural materials and the frequent intervention of government platforms at a grassroots level. Nor can we testify to an increase in audience numbers that might correspond to fourteen years' worth of massive investment in cultural production. Three notable exceptions to this dearth of scholarship are the studies on national reading habits carried out by the Centro Nacional del Libro (National Book Centre), the statistics on Venezuelan viewing audiences collected by the Centro Nacional de Cinematografía (National Centre of Cinematography), and the number of children and adolescents participating in El Sistema, collated by the same institution.

In this vein, the Ministry of Culture has published a limited amount of data corresponding to the impact of the 'memory and folklore' policy between 2005 and 2012. Yet these figures, available on the ministry's website, do not offer a detailed overview of cultural consumption in Venezuela comparable to, say, the 'Survey of Cultural Consumption from the Poverty Project' ('Estudio de Consumo Cultural del Proyecto Pobreza', UCAB, 2010) undertaken by the Universidad Católica Andrés Bello. This broad, systematic and rigorous study yields results that are not favourable to the government, but that only cover a period up to 2008. Their figures suggest, for example, that at the time of the survey 85 percent of the participants claimed that they did not frequently visit museums and art galleries; 91 percent did not attend classical music concerts and 75 percent did not attend popular music concerts; 69 percent never visited bookshops and 74 percent never visited libraries. These percentages represent the lower economic strata of society, who also happen to be the main targets of the state's cultural policies.

Unfortunately, we do not have access to data that reflect the consumption of state-produced culture corresponding to the period between 1999 and 2013. The creation of the new Ministry of Culture in 2005 did not generate any formal analyses of cultural consumption except, as already mentioned, in the field of literature and literacy. Still, it is worth analysing the figures that we do have because they give us some idea about the impact of state policies on the population's reading habits. Despite significant state investment, including the provision of books to traditional academic and professional public sectors, statistics suggest that levels of national readership remain largely unaffected. The following paragraphs will only take into account the impact of state-produced books, leaving aside for the moment other kinds of cultural material. The 'Estudio de Consumo Cultural del Proyecto Pobreza' by UCAB mentioned above indicated that, in 2008, 48 percent of the population were in the habit of reading. A more recent survey by the CENAL, the National Book Centre, entitled 'Estudio del Comportamiento Lector, Acceso al Libro y la Lectura en Venezuela 2012' ('Study of Readership Behaviour, Access to Books and Reading in Venezuela 2012', CENAL, 2012) demonstrates that 10,503,780 people (50 percent of the literate population) read at least one book per year. This indicates a slight rise in readership of 2 percent.

If we compare the CENAL study with research published in 2013, such as 'Venezolanos comelibros' by Lisseth Boon and Jesús Alberto Yajure (2014), and 'El libro; entre cuentos y cuentas' by Carlos Delgado Flores (2013), we note that Venezuela has tripled the number of titles published per person in the country: this increased from four titles per year in 2004 to twelve in 2012. According to the Centro de Estudios del Libro de América Latina y del Caribe (Centre of Latin American and Caribbean Book Studies), the Venezuelan state publishes the second highest number of books in Latin America. Venezuelan readership is 2 percent above the Latin American average and there has been a demonstrable growth in interest in historical and socio-political books among the reading public. But despite the massive distribution of free or low-cost materials by the national government via the Platform of Literature and Literacy, 80 percent of those interviewed by CENAL claim not ever to have acquired a government publication. Correspondingly, the most popular genre is self-help books, and the most popular form of fiction is the novel. Both of these genres are predominantly catered for by the private sector. State intervention has not substantially changed reading habits since 1998. In any case, the greatest number of readers can still be found among professional and educational sectors. Of the 10,503,780 self-proclaimed readers, half read only four books per year. In the best-case scenario offered, one quarter claim to read more than ten. Finally, the variety and availability of titles available has decreased alarmingly. In 2008, Venezuela imported US$422 million worth of books. In 2011 this dropped to US$93 million. The reduction corresponds to the increasingly strict currency controls imposed by the state.

We should also add that the educational and cultural organs of the state have no efficient mechanisms in place for measuring the impact of government-produced textbooks on the literacy skills of school-aged children. Nor are there reliable national or international data available on how these millions of books improve education, cultivate ideas or build social relations. The clearest example of such policies that oversee the production and distribution of books but neglect to assess their tangible social benefits can be found in the case of El Perro y la Rana, the revolutionary literary publisher *par excellence*. El Perro has published hundreds of titles in different collections that are sold at heavily subsidised prices. Although its priority in publishing new authors is commendable, the decentralised strategies that oversee the distribution, sales, and circulation of the work of young poets, narrators and essayists mean that the function of El Perro y la Rana is primarily symbolic. It is a publisher whose work has a negligible impact on the Venezuelan readership.

Furthermore, the range of books produced by the government is extremely limited. While state currency controls mean that it is very costly to import books, the government publishing strategy is largely haphazard while displaying marked ideological bias. This serves to alienate publishers that are not aligned with the Revolution and, perhaps more importantly, undermines competition with the private sector that promotes the work of non-officialist authors at non-subsidised prices. It is also important to note that there is no official programme in place that allows libraries, for example, to guarantee a wide range of reading material for subscribers. Those authors who do not identify with the Revolution are therefore denied the opportunity to promote their work and seek potential readers with the help of state support and finance, which in theory corresponds to the entire population regardless of political allegiance.

Within a legal framework, the 1999 Constitution contains a number of articles that guarantee the development of culture. In the fourth chapter, 'De los Derechos Culturales y Educativos' ('On Educational and Cultural Rights'), and in the Preamble, the creation and distribution of cultural products is enshrined as a fundamental freedom in a pluricultural nation where the essential notion of diversity must be respected. Despite this, however, the Law of Culture that was designed to enshrine these constitutional values was not approved until November 2014. This law does not do justice to the constitutional article, but defines Venezuelan culture in restrictive and traditionalist terms as 'cultures that create nationhood' (indigenous, afro-descendant, popular rural and urban creole cultures) without taking account of the burgeoning realms of information technology and media communications, the transnational culture industry (publishers, music, radio, public television channels, etc.) and the contributions of successive waves of immigrants who have settled in our country. Other laws pending definitive legislation include the Ley de Fomento y Protección al Desarrollo Artesanal (Law of Promoting and Protecting Artesanal Development) and the Ley de Protección Social del Artista Venezolano (Law of Social Protection for Venezuelan Artists), which form part of the Simón Bolívar Socialist Plan (2007–2013) and the 'Plan de la Patria' (2013–2019), and do not necessarily correspond to the values set out by the current Constitution.

Creatives, Cultural Managers, Cultural Practitioners and Intellectuals in Venezuela

The current dynamics of the cultural sphere in Venezuela have engendered complex process of exclusion and self-exclusion on the grounds of political beliefs. These, in turn, have reorganised the entire conception of cultural creation, distribution and transaction and modified cultural enjoyment began to depend on personal political ideas. The state bodies that finance cultural production require ideological affiliation, or at least some amount of political discretion, on behalf of their beneficiaries. This is particularly notable in the areas of music, dance and popular culture, and less so in literature, publishing, visual arts, theatre, intellectualism and cultural journalism. Cinema is a somewhat unusual case given that the creation of Villa del Cine and the state funding of production and distribution have, in fact, been fruitful: the number of films made in Venezuela has increased in recent years, although the work of those not aligned with the Revolution is deemed unworthy of state support, as confirmed in a remark made several years ago by the former Minister for Culture, Francisco Sesto (2007). Furthermore, Venezuelan cinema has lost its tendency towards cutting political critique that was once a defining feature. The present-day situation also includes witch hunts and mandatory participation in the revolutionary political proselytism that burdens all state-employed bureaucrats, and those in the cultural sector in particular. This means that the artists, policy-makers, writers, thinkers and technicians who are openly dissident must carry out their work without state support. If nothing else, this situation has spawned a degree of autonomy for cultural actors in the political camp of the opposition, while prompting recognition of the harsh conditions faced by those whose work challenges the government.

In Caracas, theatre companies such as the Grupo Actoral Ochenta, SKENA and Hebu Theatre have enjoyed successful performances in private auditoria such as the Trasnocho cultural arts centre. Independent arts centres such as Los Galpones and other private galleries have opened up new spaces for the visual arts marginalised by the government's museum network. Two notable organisations in this regard are the musical movement Movida Acústica Urbana and its highly original work in remastering and remixing popular traditional Venezuelan music, and the Ateneo de Caracas that moved to a new headquarters following the general occupation of such spaces across the country. In the capital and in other regions, independent cultural centres have received some support from town councils and municipal governments ruled by the political opposition, although this is of course dependent on the resources and priorities of those in power. In Caracas, generous amounts of support have been pledged by the Cultural Management Committee of Chacao and their corresponding offices in other areas, including Baruta, Sucre, and El Hatillo. In the publishing world, private initiatives such as Editorial Alfa (Alfa Books), Editorial Libros Marcados (Noted Books), Libros de El Nacional (El Nacional Books) and Lugar Común (Commonplace), among others, have channelled interests in Venezuelan politics, history and literature that have grown in recent years. These organisations have also offered partial solutions to the difficulties posed by the importation of foreign books on an individual basis, given the currency controls maintained by the state.

To be sure, there has not been any cultural landmark in the independent cultural arena that has not been met or trumped by officialist culture. For example, the government has financed a Centro Nacional de Historia to counterbalance the Academia Nacional de la Historia, which does not toe the party line, and the autonomous public universities that have resisted ideological domination. The Centro Nacional is supposedly designed to rescue a national historic memory that was wilfully suppressed by 'official history' in the pre-Chávez era. Yet the public universities of Venezuela have, at least in living memory, been governed by leftist intellectuals and have thus given rise to entire generations of historians whose work revisited Venezuelan history privileging the disenfranchised social perspectives championed by Marxism in Latin America. It is simply untrue to claim that, prior to 1999, Venezuelan intellectuals cultivated a national history that was racist, superficial, bourgeois and anti-popular, or one that corresponded unquestioningly to the educational and cultural policies of the imperialist right-wing government that was then in power: the social democratic party, Acción Demoncrática, and the social Christian party COPEI, which alternated in government between 1958 and 1998, are located at the centre of the ideological spectrum and have little in common with the military dictatorships in the Southern Cone or the communist regime in Cuba. As such, the multifaceted private and public education systems in Venezuela before the election of Hugo Chávez were not determined by a single line of thought.

In the world of publishing, there is the Platform of Books and Reading, which is comprised of: Monte Ávila, El Perro y la Rana, Biblioteca Ayachucho, the Librerías del Sur bookshop franchise (Bookshops in the South), the Casa Nacional de Letras Andrés Bello (Andrés Bello National Centre for Literature), Imprenta de Cultura (Cultural Press), Distribuidora Venezolana de la Cultura (Venezuelan Distributer of Culture), and the Centro Nacional del Libro. In all these endeavours, state actors are responsible for the selection of books to be published, and also manage editing, distribution and sales. So far, this is all in keeping with the traditional policies of state-run cultural organs before the new millennium. The problem arises when a government like the current one attempts to introduce an initiative like the stagnant Plan Revolucionario de Lectura (Revolutionary Reading Plan), which included fragments of speeches by the late President Hugo Chávez, and the late President of Cuba, Fidel Castro. Such initiatives are not driven by a desire to encourage free intellectual debate but with the aim of ideological coercion, albeit in revolutionary terms. In addition, the narrow range of El Perro y la Rana and Monte Ávila collections of political, historical and social writings do not reflect the diverse nature of politics and political beliefs in contemporary Venezuelan society. Although Monte Ávila has continued to publish Venezuelan literature, its flagship collection is Milenio Libre (Free

Millennium), which is dedicated to publishing the great works of the radical international left. Monte Ávila has an excellent reputation, earned over the course of several decades, and has created two literary programmes, Biblioteca Básica de Autores Venezolanos (Classic Collection of Venezuelan Authors) and Autores Inéditos (Unpublished Autors), which have had a positive impact despite irregular distribution and marketing strategies that did not adequately showcase their authors or permit easy access to their texts. Fortunately, and in so far as can be expected, the Biblioteca Ayacucho has managed to retain its prestige as a publisher of Latin American thought and culture, although it is not the most privileged of state literary institutions.

Within the remit of the performing arts, highly renowned theatre groups such as Skena and Grupo Actoral Ochenta have lost state funding. This highlights a political strategy to divide the cultural spheres of popular urban and traditional music, highly notable in state commissions and public events. The scheduling restrictions for soap operas and musicals on public television has meant that many actors, directors and musicians have been forced to change careers or, alternatively, offer performances in private theatres. This cultural migration is exacerbated by the partisan bias of television channels such as TVES, Vive TV, Colombeia, and Ávila TV, which, as already mentioned, follow the lead of cultural, educational and communicational policies in deepening ideological segregation. In all this, perhaps the most worrying development is the decline of independent cultural centres that are targeted by the Revolution in its bid for hegemony: in these areas, the choice is between keeping a low profile and self-censorship.

Likely the case study that best evidences the consequences of state cultural policy, particularly where it demonises the so-called cultural 'elitism' that existed prior to 1999, can be found in the treatment of national museums. The Sistema Nacional de Museos (National Foundation of Museums) is made up of: Galería de Arte Nacional (National Art Gallery), Museo de Arte Contemporáneo (Museum of Contemporary Art), Museo de Bellas Artes (Museum of Fine Art), Museo de Ciencias (Science Museum), Museo Alejandro Otero (Alejandro Otero Museum), Museo de la Estampa y del Diseño Carlos Cruz-Diez (Carlos Cruz-Diez Museum of Graphic Design), Museo Arturo Michelena (Arturo Michelena Museum), Museo de Arte Popular (Museum of Popular Art), Museo de Arquitectura (Museum of Architecture), Museo de la Fotografía (Museum of Photography), Museo de Ciencia y Tecnología (Museum of Science and Technology), Museo de Coro (Coro Museum), Museo de Calabozo (Calabozo Museum). María Elena Ramos's *La cultura bajo acoso* (2012) offers a detailed analysis of revolutionary cultural policy while providing a worrying account of the state of museums in twenty-first century

Venezuela. Ramos's account highlights the way in which these different museums have been subject to homogenisation, evident not only in the disappearance of individual branding and in the streamlining of artistic interests and academic investigation, but also in the administrative centralation of the Sistema Nacional de Museos that has, by all accounts, curbed the autonomy of these institutions. According to Ramos, the negative attitudes that are now typical in the everyday running of museums, such as the rejection of individual retrospectives or exhibitions, the undermining of curators and the disdain for the staff entrusted with the custody and preservation of the collections, were prompted by decisions made by former minister Farruco Sesto that instrumentalised cultural production for ideological ends and undermined the pedagogical and patrimonial purpose of museums. It also seems pertinent to add in passing that, in addition to its usual activities, the Museo Alejandro Otero has also served as a refugee camp for those left homeless by landslides and flooding, with the attendant problems of accommodating the refugees in a space that is inadequate for social housing and the deprivation of access to cultural patrimony for other Venezuelan citizens. Ramos's analysis also notes that not even the inauguration of new museums or the new headquarters for the Galería de Arte Nacional can counterbalance the problems of access that the artistic patrimony of Venezuela has suffered following the state decision to remove the collections of each museum in the thrust towards centralisation being undertaken at all levels of governance. During the leadership of former minister Pedro Calzadilla there was a brief period of ceasefire between the government and the national museums, accompanied by a recognition of the importance of restoring individual retrospectives and exhibitions. However, Calzadilla also supported the use of national museums during the commemorations of the twentieth anniversary of Chávez's failed coup d'état in 1992. By way of example, Ramos lists the following events: Testimonios de un Tiempo Político (Testimonies of a Political Time, Museo de Bellas Artes); El Camino de la Revolución (The Revolutionary Path, Museo Jacobo Borges); Exposición Temática sobre el 4-F (4-F Multimedia Exhibition, Museo Alejandro Otero), among others. This strongly suggests an instrumentalist vision of culture propagated by the current government that speaks of 'socialist ethics and aesthetics'.

The New Man, New Woman: Strategic Objectives of the Bolivarian Revolution

The Bolivarian government is supported by several prominent Venezuelan artists hailing from different disciplines. Some of these artists have much experience and have made significant contributions to national culture, while others are young and still forging their artistic visions. But beyond qualitative judgments, these artists, writers and cultural practitioners have not achieved the same kind of artistic innovation seen in Soviet poetry, cinema and design that emerged during the first years of the Bolshevik Revolution. Nor has Bolivarian Socialism generated anything like the creative boom that fed the Cuban ballads and the Mexican murals, which later became national cultural symbols and could be read as popular expressions of a society in revolution. Under Bolivarian Socialism, the notion of 'innovation' is devalued by odes to Chávez written by twenty-somethings (indeed, some of these showing great potential as young poets), musical tributes to leftist folk singer Alí Primera, local radio shows hosted by young presenters who venerate the Chinese cultural revolution, and murals and graffiti that are paid for by the state. Such approaches appear to be fed by nostalgia for the past, a nostalgia for the 1970s fused with indigenous cultures, a touch of Afro politics and a sprinkling of Che Guevara. Inner-city youth movements like Tiuna El Fuente are, in this sense, more genuinely innovative. Featuring street dance, hip-hop and urban sports like boxing and basketball, their videos like Petare Será otro Beta (Petare will be something different) demonstrate some cultural impetus instead of capitalising on an aesthetic that means nothing to the popular sectors that are supposedly the Revolution's protagonists. Equally, programmes on Ávila TV that feature Venezuelan youth cultures in dialogue with global movements that celebrate slum cultures and urban living are more challenging than the crude political instrumentalisation of culture that is found in exhibitions about the 1992 coup led by a young Chávez.

Much more visible and, indeed, more successful than leftist cultural nostalgia or the political manipulation of artistic movements is 'El Sistema', with the talented conductor Gustavo Dudamel at its helm and at the service of the government, and with its highly publicised worldwide tours and gifted musicians which, until recently, represented a showcase for Bolivarian cultural policy. In truth, El Sistema has functioned for at least 40 years, and has garnered the support of all the intervening governments since it was set up by the maestro José Antonio Abreu in the 1970s. Interestingly, Abreu was also the director of the Consejo Nacional de Cultura when Carlos Andrés Pérez was president and almost toppled by the 1992 putsch.

In the midst of all this, according to Fidel Barbarito, who is, at the time of writing, the incumbent Minister of Culture, a new socialist aesthetics will give cohesion to the values attributed to the so-called New Man and the New Woman. What are the values that are claimed to support the principles, the practice and the legitimacy of culture in contemporary Venezuela? The following strategic objectives are set out in the Proyecto Nacional Simón

Bolívar Primer Plan Socialista (2007–2013) (National Simón Bolívar Project First Socialist Plan):

(a) New socialist ethics: this proposes the re-formation of the Venezuelan nation, rooted in the values and beliefs of an advanced socialist humanism that is intertwined with the legacy of Simón Bolívar's historical thought.

(b) Supreme social happiness: the construction of an inclusive social structure, inspired by a productive, humanist and endogenous social model, will engender egalitarian living conditions, or what Bolívar termed 'supreme social happiness'.

These objectives seek to establish a new hegemonic order, where hegemony is used by government ministers, the current president and the late Chávez in accordance with the definition given by Marxist thinker Antonio Gramsci to mean the configuration of a national culture that rests on moral standards that are antithetical to the values of the capitalist system. In this scheme of thought, the propagation of cultural policies is tantamount to the formation of the New Man and the New Woman who will reject the principles of capitalism that are unjust, unequal and exploitative of human beings. The Bolivarian state thus seeks to determine how Venezuelan men and women adhere to the notion of belonging to a nation that is defined in strictly communitarian terms. It goes without saying that all societies, partisan rule notwithstanding, develop around a legal paradigm that determines our actions, and that we all form part of an economy that structures, limits or stimulates different ways of living. In all corners of the world, we eat, breathe, love and interact following the complex processes of social and symbolic practices that pertain to the region, the nation, the educational system and the local family traditions in question. It is here, in this pliable dimension of the social fabric, that Bolivarian Revolution seeks to intervene. Although the Constitution of the Bolivarian Republic of Venezuela may well consecrate the pluralist nature of the nation, this pluralism is understood in the narrow terms of the cultural regional diversity that props up state versions of nationality, especially when this is of indigenous and Afro origin, but not in terms of the cultural hybridity and transculturation processes that have taken place organically and throughout history.

The Venezuelan version of modernity that has arisen with the waves of national and international migration, a system of mass education, the exploitation of oil and the growth of the state in both public and private realms is dismissed as an historical error by the current government. According to Bolivarian Socialism, modernity in Venezuela brought with it the spread of racism, consumerism, alienation, elitism and pro-imperialism, with the result that these toxic ideologies have penetrated lifestyles, eating habits and ways of dressing, and have also infected universities, museums, cinema, sexual preferences, the media and national literature. The state's obsession with the creation of parallel institutions is supplemented by a systematic polarisation of social groupings, from families, trade unions, and religious institutions to businesses, political parties, and cultural organisations. The path chosen towards an understanding of the past has been one of total rejection. Rather than foster critical debate on the multiple influences and contradictions in Venezuelan cultural assimilation, the strategy has been to denounce these processes entirely. The cultural achievements attributable to previous governments or related to figures pertaining to the opposing sectors of the Bolivarian Revolution have been systematically disqualified as elitist. Popular culture has been condemned for its connection to global capitalism and the mass culture originating in North America, specifically cinema, music and television

When Nicolás Maduro was elected by a margin in 2013, notably half the population rejected the new social order that had been imposed by the state, despite its considerable investments in communication, culture and education. This resistance held, in part, thanks to the rent-seeking model of modernisation that saw frustrated desires for social mobility and economic prosperity channelled into popular culture. For almost a century, the Venzeuelan state has obtained the majority of its income from the sale of its crude oil to the US. Until 1975, these funds were secured by the taxes imposed on major international companies. After this date, when President Carlos Andrés Pérez nationalised the oil industry, the Venezuelan state came to control an enormous amount of wealth. The state became a key actor in distributing this wealth via public welfare policies and intervention in the economy. Oil has thus been the protagonist of Venezuelan modernity and has intervened significantly in the country's cultural landscape. The sons and daughters of immigrant oil workers, the expansive – if precarious – education system, the importation of international popular culture, egalitarian and independent discourses, members of the opposition and, we can imagine, no small part of those who support the government are among those who reject the notion of a singular national culture, an authentic 'national identity' to be salvaged and orchestrated by the state. Clearly, the restrictive application of cultural policies has not helped the present government in challenging the rent-seeking cultural model engendered by modernisation, which has limited the effect of state propaganda. An understanding of the capitalist ideology that drives popular culture is vital to any analysis of the current situation in Venezuela with regards to the cultural, education and communicational policies of the state.

Taking Stock: The Bolivarian Revolution and its Debts to Cultural Policy

The memory and folklore section of the Ministerio del Poder Popular para la Cultura offers numerous examples of inefficient application of governmental cultural policies. Here, problems include repeated failures to carry out official projects included in the national budget, a deficiency of technological platforms, a shortage of qualified staff and difficulties in the importation of cultural supplies. These phenomena are all related to the interventionist stance of the government which creates problems in all domains of state activity. With its centralised planning strategies, inspired by 'actually-existing socialism' in the twentieth century, the Bolivarian Revolution has debilitated local councils and municipal governments, especially those ruled by the political opposition. This, in consequence, has exhausted regional budgets and has curbed the political capacity of local authorities. The establishment of cultural platforms at national, regional, and municipal levels, alongside the multiplication of state organisations and the Misión Cultura, was meant to decentralise and reapportion political power. Yet the presence of political sectarianism and the highly ideological determination of the cultural agenda has curbed this endeavour, with the help of biased cultural actors and the unfair distribution of resources.

The obvious targets of the government's public policies are the urban and rural popular sectors. Symbolically, the state has ensured that the entire nation understands its role in twenty-first-century Venezuela. Both the Misión Cultura, largely managed by Cubans, and the National System for Popular Culture exert loyalty to the Plan Socialista Simón Bolívar: 'The National System for Popular Culture includes all public and private bodies that influence cultural policy and adhere to the values of the System while accepting the political strategies of the Proyecto Nacional Simón Bolívar' (Ministerio del Poder Popular para la Cultura, 2011).

Those artists, cultural practitioners and policy-makers who do not openly support such official policies are excluded from the system, which leads to self-censorship, silence, or reluctant adherence, calling into question constitutional values such as freedom of speech and thought, the freedom to create, and the ideals of political pluralism. It is perfectly plausible that the state could, for example, promote a musical instrument like the cuatro (a Venezuelan stringed instrument) alongside the violin or the piano. Yet the relativist and traditionalist understanding of national culture, exemplified by the Proyecto de Ley Orgánica de Cultura, means that such policies overlook the diverse nature of culture in the twenty-first century, while also entering into conflict with state strategies that encourage the use of information technology and social media in social, educational, political and cultural interactions that are approved by the government. Similarly, state intervention debilitates the autonomy of artists, cultural practitioners and policy-makers, who are obliged to obey state policy instead of acting as non-partisan cultural ambassadors.

The prejudices against cultural modernity are evident in the government's obsession with the notion of developing a cultural industry, a term that is normally used as a synonym for Hollywood or in reference to capitalist modes of cultural production. All production within the remits of design and graphics, public service radio and television, cultural tourism and national cinema is industrial de facto, regardless of whether it is overseen by Villa de Cine or by Warner Brothers. This anti-modern thrust is also manifest in the government's disavowal of the economics of cultural production, which is understood only in terms of social investment and not as an opportunity to create employment and prosperity via cultural development. The restrictions imposed by state ideology defy another aspect of official Venezuelan cultural policy: the roles of public service television and radio in fostering debate surrounding the ethics and aesthetics of historical values and heritage, rather than responding exclusively to the interests of the government in power. The numerous community radio stations and television channels that showcase a selection of cultural programmes also project the political visions of the government to their viewers via the transmission of carefully edited documentaries and reports. The argument that such practices are necessary to counterbalance the 'right-wing media' overlooks the fact that the socialist media are publically funded and, in their usage of public resources that by right belong to everybody, evidence the authoritarian tendencies of the Venezuelan government. In this sense, low ratings are caused not only by a refusal to recognise that half the population has not invested in the revolutionary project but also by the failure to analyse the output and impact of financial investment in cultural sectors.

Not only is the state's evaluation of Venezuelan culture in terms of 'national identity' at odds with the context of globalisation but, given the evangelical character of the government in a country marked by polarisation, it also generates resistance and suspicion. In Venezuela, like in all nation-states, there are many different cultural practices and value systems that serve different functions for different sectors, regardless of whether these share the same territorial borders and the same system of law and order. The Bolivarian Revolution refuses to acknowledge the fact that, even if the 1980s did see the exacerbation of socio-economic inequalities during a prosperous time for the oil-rich nation, the logics of racism, elitism, conservatism and classism did not penetrate all areas of national life prior to the rise of the *chavista* government, which now calls for the systematic purification of the nation-state. The state's promise to represent society in its diversity remains unfulfilled, given that the past exclusions of popular urban, rural and indigenous sectors cannot be counterbalanced with a systematic attack on other cultural heritages, registers and ways of thinking. Perhaps more importantly, Venezuela has also been denied a place in the global cultural landscape, which is not restricted to the Caribbean or Latin America but includes the world in its entirety.

References

Boon, L. and Yajure, J. A. (2013) 'Venezolanos comelibros'. *Últimas Noticias*, 'El Domingo', 24 March, 1-3.

Centro Nacional del Libro (2012) *Estudio del comportamiento lector, acceso al libro y la lectura en Venezuela 2012*. Centro Nacional del Libro: Caracas.

Delgado Flores, C. (2012) 'El libro: entre cuentos y cuentas'. SIC: 41-43.

Instituto de Investigaciones Económicas y Sociales de la Universidad Católica Andrés Bello (2010) 'Estudio de Consumo Cultural en Venezuela 2010'. SIC, 24 March.

Ministerio del Poder Popular para la Cultura (2011) *Sistema Nacional de las Culturas Populares*. Ministerio del Poder Popular Para la Cultura: Caracas.

Proyecto Nacional Simón Bolívar (2011) *Primer Plan Socialista-PPS-2007–2013*. Partido Socialista Unido de Venezuela: Caracas, 29 March.

Ramos, M. E. (2012) *La cultura bajo acoso*. Artesanoæ Editores: Caracas.

Sesto, F. (2007) 'Fabiola y nuestros errores'. *Aporrea*, 24 October. [WWW document]. URL http://www.aporrea.org/actualidad/a43136.html [accessed 30 December 2014]

UNESCO (1972) *Convention Concerning the Protection of the World Cultural and Natural Heritage*. UNESCO: Paris.

UNESCO (1980) *Recommendation concerning the International Standardization of Statistics on the Public Financing of Cultural Activities*. UNESCO: Paris.

UNESCO (1982) *Declaración de México sobre Políticas Culturales*. UNESCO: Paris.

UNESCO (2005) *Protection of the World Cultural and Natural Heritage*. UNESCO: Paris.

2

Hegemony in a Global Age: Mutations of the Communicational Landscapes in Contemporary Venezuela

MANUEL SILVA-FERRER

Free University Berlin

Introduction

Most of the studies carried out in recent years in the field of media and communications in Venezuela focus their attention on processes determined by the relationship of the media to state power, a decisive factor in the transformations at work in the sphere of culture and communications at the beginning of the twenty-first century. But this chapter takes a different direction. I seek to observe how these transformations are not limited to a struggle between a repressive state apparatus, on the one hand, and resistance from the masses on the other. As such, I return to the cultural turn produced in Latin America of the late 1980s that enabled cultural studies to relate the analysis of cultural messages and structures to strategies of consumption. I do so in order to understand how the media, more than a strictly commercial or ideological phenomenon, represent 'a cultural phenomenon through which many people [...] experience the creation of the meaning of their lives' (Martín Barbero, 1995a: 183).

An analysis of these circumstances involves consideration of how the distinctive elements of this specific national case study interact with wider global contexts. Hence, this chapter, while not bypassing the important role played by the state in the most recent reshaping of the Venezuelan cultural field, will approach communications less from the standpoint of political power, and more from the perspective of cultural politics. I will examine a set of transformations related to what could be defined as the 'cultural elements of culture'.

The Centrality of the Margins

The start of the twenty-first century marked a turning point in the discourse of mass communications in Venezuela. This sought to transform the way

Translated by Eleonora García Larralde and Rebecca Jarman.

in which the popular classes were represented by the media. Alongside the intense political debates and transformations that have taken place in different social and cultural arenas, this is reflective of the significant historical shifts experienced by the country since the beginning of the 1980s. It is also indicative of the historical role played by the popular classes in the transformations of national imaginaries that are produced at the site of contact between mass media and political power.

The *telenovelas* (soap operas) produced in Venezuela during the 1950s consolidated a popular discourse that was identified with the masses. This formed part of a media trend driven, above all, by the concept of modernisation as the transformation of the geographic landscape and the pursuit of social mobility that was experienced in the transition from rural life to that of an urban existence. In Latin America, this idea was much influenced by the New Deal, and then by the policies of the Washington Consensus in the context of the cold war, when the expansion of capitalism was linked to social progress (Franco, 2002). The 1980s were also characterised by new political doctrines for socio-economic deliverance, now with the advancement of the neoliberal project. The first major challenge to this ideology in the media was posed in 1992, when the series *Por estas calles*, written by Ibsen Martínez, captured the atmosphere of decadence and decomposition that led to the fall of Carlos Andrés Pérez's government (1989–1992). *Por estas calles* was an inflection point in the narrative sphere of the popular, as it developed a new frame of reference by assuming the standpoint of the popular classes. This cast the poorest sectors as the protagonists of a story that was, crucially, narrated from their perspective and not from that of an outsider. This represents a development similar to that which Beatriz Sarlo identifies in Argentinean literature of the 1920s as: 'a new pact in reading with the involvement of new sectors of the public, [that] will open up the possibility of addressing that social space in a more intimate way incorporating personal and biographical dimensions' (Sarlo, 1988: 179).

This shift marked the beginning of an important change to the discursive practices of television and marketing companies. In brief, it permitted the social and racial diversification of media protagonists and models of consumption. In this context, television newscasts surprised audiences with their casting of dark-skinned presenters, and the producers and directors of *telenovelas* – highly influenced by contemporaneous developments in Brazil – expanded their referents of racial representation. The *telenovela Negra consentida* (2004), written by Valentina Párraga, is a case in point. It was marketed by its producers as a 'love story between two worlds of different colours and tastes'. Generally speaking, it represented an attempt gradually to incorporate into the world of television productions the diverse racial spectrum that characterised national cultural heterogeneity. However, the programme was not devoid of the offensive racial stereotypes that are pervasive in Venezuela's highly segregated society, nor was it unmarked by the influence of the aesthetic models pertaining to dominant popular/modern/western global cultures. It was, then, no mean feat that for the first time, in 1998 (and then again in 2005), a dark-skinned woman won the Miss Venezuela pageant, the highest-rated show on Venezuelan television. From then on, the presence of dark-skinned women has become commonplace in a contest that had been historically dominated by lighter-skinned women.

In this regard, a strategic instrumentalisation of differences and inequalities in state television and publicity was the logical outcome for a populist government that sought to capitalise on the contradictions and de-synchronisations of a nation characterised by asymmetries. But this was not fortified with an analysis of the root causes of such fragmentation, nor was it accompanied by a set of proposals designed to overcome these problems. The only aim of this strategy was to sustain the connection between the state media and the masses. The marginal sectors of society, considered a pre-modern, rural, poor 'other' even as they formed a majority in national demographics, were given new aesthetic and ideological qualities in the sphere of the mass media. This, in turn, encouraged the popular classes to identify with the experiences and events that constitute new national imaginaries in Venezuela.

Crucial to observe here is how the margins have become central in the space of Venezuelan communications; or, put differently, from a postcolonial perspective, how what Walter Mignolo calls the dark side of modernity has been given a degree of visibility in the mainstream media. This might be understood as a discursive reaction to the crisis and decentralisation of the modern project (Mignolo, 1995: 94), whereby the mass media – especially state-run media – have engaged in highly politicised exchanges among the peripheries at a time when this latest phase of globalisation drives different social relations and forms of cultural mapping.

Communicational Hegemony? Tactical Movements among Audiences

The mutations that have occurred over the last eighteen years in the cultural and communicational landscapes of Venezuela have also produced transformations in the habits of television audiences. One of the most significant of these shifts has been the mass migration of the viewing public from terrestrial television to pay television via cable or satellite. This trend in consumption has arisen in response to the monopolisation of public space that has been exerted by the government, whose strategy when it came to power was to align all communication channels – both public and private – to its political project.

The first real sign of this shift came in 2007 with the government-imposed closure of Radio Caracas Television (RCTV), then one of the two most important television stations in the country. Its closure was rejected by the public, as demonstrated in the numerous high-profile protests that followed the announcement. Subsequently, there was an increase of up to 40 percent in the use of digital media as a way to access alternative sources of information (Correa, 2009: 254-255). There was also an increase in paid subscriptions to private television and what would become the beginning of a progressive decline in terrestrial television audiences. Venezuelan scholar Marcelino Bisbal estimates that almost two million viewers turned to pay TV, calculating the overall spread of this trend as almost 70 percent (Bisbal, 2010).

The primary cause of this migration is a widespread public rejection of the politicisation of television and of the conflictive nature of the content broadcast on terrestrial networks. Secondary causes include the economic restrictions placed on private television companies that negatively affected their investment potential and, thus, the quality of their programming. The combination of an official proselyting programming strategy and the use of anachronistic aesthetics and thematic codes has meant that public television is out of sync with the cultural norms of contemporary audiovisual media. This means that the massive communicational apparatus created by the government, far from hegemonising and subjugating the masses, instead generated a strong feeling of rejection among the public. This ultimately translated into significantly low audience numbers and partially accounts for the failure of official attempts to create a 'communicational hegemony' that is adequately reflected in the quantifiable studies of social scientists.

In sum, these efforts to construct an alternative discourse to that imposed historically by commercial global television has failed in developing a strategy to modify the role traditionally assigned to the sphere of communications in Latin America. The aim was to deflect processes of cultural modernisation and globalisation, thus breaking the affective links between the masses and the commercial phenomena of advertising and consumption. But this has not been realised. The fact is that those who were targeted by such policies, typically from low-income sectors, contribute to the audience numbers that have legitimised commercial radio and television as the last point of access to globalisation in Latin America. In doing so, they have called upon their function of 'opening doors to the illusion of belonging', 'allowing the rhythm of modernity to flow', and 'globalising the viewer, by insisting that their country corresponds to international reality (making them familiar) with the diversity of the landscape', as argued by Carlos Monsiváis (2000: 211-227).

The Decline of Venezuelan *Telenovelas*

The historical role of television, particularly television melodrama, in contributing to processes of cultural modernisation and in the construction
of national imaginaries (as identified by Carlos Monsiváis) hit a stumbling
block in Venezuela at the start of the twenty-first century. At that point,
the domestic production of *telenovelas* was severely affected by changes in the
national economy and by the increasingly unequal terms of exchange between
local and global markets. Several existing studies have demonstrated how
this current stage of technological globalisation has ushered in new trends
in the production of melodrama and in the marketisation of media cultures.
Such trends mark the end of the financial certainties enjoyed by the Latin
American entertainment industry for at least half a century (Martín-Barbero,
1995b; Mato, 1999, 2002, 2005). In the case of Venezuela – one of the foremost
exporters of *telenovelas* on the continent – the effects of globalisation were
compounded by domestic political clashes that, together, produced a series
of dramatic upheavals in the melodrama business. The closure of RCTV that
was instigated by the government in 2007 was a sign of a fundamental crisis
in the sector. This was exacerbated by economic instability, leading to a sharp
decline in income from advertising, and, correspondingly to a reduction in
local media production across the board. This decline was coupled with a fall
in ratings, following the flight of audiences to paid television subscriptions,
and culminated in a growing tendency to relocate the production of melodrama from Venezuela to affiliates of national television companies based in
the United States, predominantly in Miami (Mato, 2002), a city that, in recent
years, has become a critical geographical co-ordinate for the Latin American
cultural industry (Yúdice, 2002: 239-250).

The immediate outcome of this scenario was that, notwithstanding the tradition of Venezuelan melodrama of over half a century, by 2010 there were
no local *telenovelas* on terrestrial television in prime-time slots. Not only did
this have a negative effect on national production companies and their many
employees, but it also meant that, in the global competition to capture local
markets, the country imported much more cultural content than it exported.
Consequently, despite the gloss of irony that still coats much critical analysis
of the *telenovela* as a cultural product, the industrial decline of Venezuelan televised melodrama marks the end of an important cycle in its cultural history.
It has been demonstrated that, in the second half of the twentieth century,
Venezuela emerged as a regional leader in the production of media content
whose most tangible legacy was its contribution to the construction of Latin
American imaginaries and identities. Simultaneously, this reveals paradox-
ical results for a populist government whose nationalist strategies have led
to a flight of Venezuelan capital, and with it the loss of many jobs, while

promoting massive imports of similar foreign products for mass domestic consumption.

The Rebirth of Venezuelan Music

The Law of Social Responsibility for Radio and Television that came into effect in Venezuela in 2005 to regulate the messages transmitted by audiovisual media had a significant impact in the arena of radio broadcasting. Following its implementation, those radio stations whose scheduling consisted mainly of music programmes were obliged to set aside at least 50 percent of daily airtime for traditional Venezuelan music, and another 10 percent for music from Latin America and the Caribbean. This measure resulted in an increase in local record producers and radio shows, due also in part to the departure of transnational music companies from the Venezuelan scene. This, in turn, was a consequence of the economic restrictions that impeded their day-to-day operations, of the rampant production of pirate goods, and of a reduced consumer market. We can observe two main outcomes in this area: (1) as a result of these protective measures, the once powerful local commercial radio sector was forced to modify its programming strategy, historically dominated by advertising and transnational record industries; and (2) the important field of Venezuelan music received renewed recognition, despite the fact that, like other forms of national culture that had global market potential, this was systematically rendered inaccessible to commercial interests.

The implementation of this law was met with debates surrounding the definition of the traditional music that was to be broadcast by legal obligation. At this stage in the process of globalisation, where might we find a precise definition of tradition and folklore? Are these the traditions of Hispanic or indigenous origin that disappeared in Latin America with the imposition of the modern nation-state? Or are they the expressions of regional folklore that have been obliterated by the modernisation of culture with the expansion of the mass media? Is tradition simply that which does not circulate in commercial media? These questions aside, the issue became far less complex in practice. Ultimately, more importance was given to emphasising particular characteristics of a nationalist bent, as opposed to the revitalisation of endangered traditions. So it follows that it was not difficult for the programming managers of radio stations to circumvent the question of defining traditional music by proposing their own interpretation of the concept, without relying on UNESCO specialists. Thus, in compliance with the law, traditional Venezuelan music was refashioned by radio broadcasters as a hybrid of folkloric music of multiple origins and historical contexts (*joropos*, *tonadas*, *gaitas*, etc.), as Venezuelan classical music, as old pop music produced nationally, and as the reinterpretation of all the above by a younger generation of musicians.

Despite its many failures, the policy for the protection of national music did reap some positive results, even if only temporarily. All told, it facilitated the emergence of a small-scale independent record industry, whose most noteworthy contributions were the fusions created by musicians trained in Venezuela's expansive network of classical institutions. These combined popular arrangements with instrumental scores that ranged from orchestral to electronic, exploring the ample scope of possibilities offered by different genres of musical interpretation. This trend in the local market coincided with the incorporation of several Venezuelan performers into the global scene of classical music. This, along with the vast publicity campaign generated by the Venezuelan youth orchestra system (El Sistema) and the numerous musicians who currently occupy senior roles in orchestras worldwide, has guaranteed an important place for the country on the world map of classical music.

These interactions between the local and the global reveal several of the ways in which the processes of globalisation act upon different spheres of culture, and, moreover, the numerous factors that can impede full integration into the global market. Fundamentally, very little Venezuelan musical production has entered the global marketplace, despite the existence of set distribution networks like those associated with the genre of world music. At a national level, these experimentations in tradition and folklore with classical music have been distributed by new media, on social networks and among specialised audiences. On the contrary, the latest recordings of Venezuelan orchestras and performers commissioned by Deutsche Grammophon and other major classical labels of global reach are of limited availability in the country. This shows how inequalities in commercial and cultural flows are determining factors in forging connections between peripheral audiences and metropolitan artists, and metropolitan audiences and peripheral artists and, above all, in facilitating exchanges between the two. As García Canclini has pointed out, such 'tangential globalisations' reveal that, in instances of unequal competition, 'globalisation is and is not what it promises' (García Canclini, 1999: 12).

In the case of Venezuelan music, it would seem that the alternative to navigating the complex exchanges between flows of global commerce and the restrictive cultural and economic politics of the protectionist nation-state is to exit the domestic stage and become a global actor at the cost of participation in local circuits. This predicament is one inherent in the peripheral condition, as described by George Yúdice, who notes that the financial resources of Latin American companies are usually insufficient to cover the standard costs of transnational production and distribution. This situation stunts the development of such enterprises and obstructs their insertion into global circuits. As a result, a significant portion of national musical production is handed over to large consortiums, who market such products outside their place of origin and encourage the most successful artists to settle in the various cosmopolitan capitals of show business (Yúdice, 2002: 235-260).

Although the main characteristic of globalisation is to intensify contact and exchanges between different societies, the scenario described here is unfolding in the opposite direction. In Venezuela, the management of culture is torn between the public sphere, governmental projects and entrepreneurial strategies. In a Latin American context, García Canclini attributes this phe-nomenon to the recent development of national cultural policies that align with 'pre-globalised' strategies designed to protect cultural production and distribution (1999: 144). These are policies that have set out to challenge the hegemony of large entrepreneurial groups. To them, the majority of grassroots cultures, as they exist in pre-industrialised form and are of lim-ited distribution and small profit margins, have been nothing more than a hindrance in the effort to appropriate and homogenise national cultural markets.

Sisyphean Punishment and Venezuelan Cinema

Venezuelan cinema has a reputation in Latin America for its limited reach and its stagnated development. It has been deemed incapable of advancing the interests of a coherent cinematic collective, at both intellectual and indus-trial levels. The historical factors that have prevented the development of a meaningful corpus of Venezuelan films are, in large part, the result of the subaltern and peripheral condition of the national filmic industry. These, in turn, correspond to the limitations that are typical in dependent economies, and also are indicative of the limited and inconsistent efforts of the state in supporting the development of minimal domestic film productions. Therefore, when examining the recent evolution of cinema in Venezuela, it is necessary to reconsider two large sectors of the industry that run parallel but have had divergent outcomes:

(a) The first consists of the distribution and exhibition sectors of the film business that are affiliated with the big players of globalised enter-tainment, whose development has evolved in tandem with that of the metropolis. These were sectors that were successful in capitalising on the oil boom of the first decade of the twenty-first century with a sub-stantial increase in the number of movie screens and, as a result, in the number of spectators.

(b) The second is the production sector, consisting of a mix of directors, artists, technicians, and critics, allied with small entrepreneurs, uni-versities and, above all, with the state. An increase in investment in

this sector resulted in an increase to this group's activities. Despite
the relatively successful box office performance of certain films and
the prizes garnered at international festivals, however, this sector
has not managed to produce a cogent or ground-breaking body
of work.

To understand this duality, one has to bear in mind that of all the artistic
enterprises linked to industrial production, film-making in particular is conditioned by the investment climate and is highly susceptible to shifts in the
economy and the legal frameworks that sustain it. This is perhaps because
filmmaking is the most costly of the arts. This situation is even more evident
in countries where the state plays a determining role not only in the legislation of the media sector but also as a direct promoter and financier of filmic
production. Consequently, it is of no coincidence that the economic boom in
Venezuela that took place between 2003 and 2008, and the modification of
the Law for Cinematography in 2005, served to produce a burst of filmic production that later went into a steep decline with the economic crisis that is
ongoing at the time of writing.

The Persistence of Americanisation

It is important to note that the rapid economic expansion that occurred
between 2003 and 2008 as a result of the steep rise in oil prices and other
commodities triggered an increase in the construction of shopping malls
in Venezuela. Thanks in part to the deterioration of the urban landscape, these became places of refuge for the country's business elites
and for the film-screening industry and its actors. This period of economic growth saw an increase in the number of screens available for the
purpose of commercial distribution, growing from 253 to 481 between
1999 and 2013. Such numbers had already been bolstered when regu-
lations on the price of cinema tickets were lifted in the mid-1990s. This
attracted investments to the sector and permitted improvements to an
infrastructure that was two decades out of date, leading to an exponential
increase in audience numbers and in the number of films screened in the
country.

The number of films premiered in the country thus grew from 130 in
1999 to 171 in 2013. The production of Venezuelan films grew at a comparable rate: three films premiered in 1999 and 21 in 2013. The total number
of cinema attendances also grew from 13,461,028 in 1999 to 29,875,751 in
2013 (Silva-Ferrer, 2014: 253). But these increases did not translate into a
qualitative improvement of the sector, which remains bound to the North
American film industry that dominates the programme of films shown in

the country. Far behind this is the number of European productions that are screened, distributed by the same North American companies or by festivals organised independently with the support of some European embassies and film institutions. In last place are Latin American films including those from Venezuela. This shows how the increase in Venezuelan film production is not met with an increase in audience numbers. For the first decade of the twenty-first century these represented an average of just 2.52 percent, in relation to 97.47 percent for foreign films, most of these from North America (Silva-Ferrer, 2014: 254).

Parallel to this expansion of the commercial sector, aligned with global film distribution circuits, is the Cinemateca Nacional, or the state-led initiative to create a national network of community cinemas. This project was first begun during the second half of the 1990s, with a limited amount of success and very few resources. The idea was to create alternative spaces for film screenings in every municipality of the country. The construction of nineteen commercial-standard cinemas was projected for 2009, along with a decent number of community cinemas (official numbers estimate 170) that would function in small venues with video projectors and mobile screens. The aims of this initiative were commendable, but the results were somewhat negligible and the project has proved mostly unsustainable. This has several explanations. First, its programming was challenging for audiences generally unfamiliar with auteur cinema, and was later undermined by its explicit political agenda. Second, the plan did not take into consideration the changes effected on the communicational landscape with the rise of 'new media' and new online forms of cinematographic distribution. Nor did it account for the difficulties to be encountered in opening spaces of this kind in places with limited prospective audiences. Survival is already difficult for the few cinemas on the independent scenes of Caracas, Maracaibo and Barquisimeto, all university cities with a potential audience in the educated middle classes. For obvious reasons, then, similar projects in rural areas of the country were met with failure. It should be noted that even the consumption of films for the purposes of entertainment, as well as intellectual stimulation, form part of a cultural trend that, perhaps like no other, is subject to the technological advances of globalisation that have changed the norms of production and the reception of media products.

In Venezuela, these difficulties are also linked to the fact that, as already mentioned, tendencies in the consumption of film have been determined in the last three decades by the incorporation of cinemas in shopping malls. This has made of the cinematographic experience a hybrid of commerce and culture, leaving far behind a sense of nostalgia for the old and well decorated grand theatres and the political will of anachronistic cultural policies. In this new cultural architecture of Latin America, as Beatriz Sarlo states, 'people no longer move around the city' but in 'a replica of the city of services in miniature, where all urban extremes have been liquidated', in a sort of 'spatial capsule conditioned by the aesthetics of the market' (Sarlo, 1994: 14-15). So, in spite of efforts to develop 'pre-globalised' cultural policies, or the offer of alternative films that is not sustained by real demands from the population, the small Venezuelan film industry is still bound to the process of americanisation within the framework of globalisation. Thus, it is fair to observe that Hollywood films and actors, alongside *telenovela* actors, are still defining the entertainment business, the routes towards globalisation and, more broadly, the very idea of what modernity means for significant segments of the population.

Films Commissioned in the Service of the Revolution

The first two decades of the twenty-first century have seen a continuation of the crisis that has affected the quality and stability of Venezuelan film since the last part of the twentieth century. This is a period in which very few of the works produced had the capacity to adapt to the narratives and thematic structures of various filmic genres in a way that would attract significant audience numbers and ensure that the financial and creative efforts of the industry remained profitable. It was, according to film critic Rodolfo Izaguirre (1997), 'an outward-facing cinema', far more preoccupied with dramatising the problems of development than it was with dramatising the problems of the people. In this manner, productions from recent decades have been characterised mostly by the absence of any innovation in expressive or conceptual proposals. The results have been very irregular and do not offer a solid base from which to interpret the complex reality of the country in the artistic form of cinema.

The production of Venezuelan film had an upsurge in 2006, when the state's prioritisation of the industry was evidenced by an increase in investment, the reform of the Law of Cinematography (2005) that taxed the commercial sector of the media to finance film production, and the implementation of quotas for these films' screening and distribution. These changes culminated in 2006 with the creation of film distributor Amazonia Films, and the centre for film studies and film production La Villa del Cine. Both institutions were integrated into the government's mass media apparatus that oversaw the resurgence of films produced in the country. This resulted in one of the most prolific periods – at least in quantitative terms – in the entire history of Venezuelan film, with the production of some 75 feature films and 300 documentaries for cinema and television during the first decade of the twenty-first century.

Since its creation, the Villa del Cine has become the hub of cinematic creation in the country, alongside the Centro Nacional Autónomo de Cinematografía (National Autonomous Centre for Cinematography, CNAC) that provides autonomous funding for film production, and, as we will see, the emergence of a grassroots *barrio* cinema. The Villa del Cine was principally oriented towards formulating a new subjectivity that sought to convey the epistemologies of national history and individual stories from different perspectives and conditions. This was particularly evident in its manifest interest in promoting the values and characters deemed iconic by the Bolivarian Revolution, achieved by revising the national epic, and by re-evaluating certain aspects of popular traditions and cultures that were considered priorities in the government's cultural political strategy. So much was implied by the Minister for Culture, Francisco Sesto, who addressed a letter to film-maker Franco de Peña after he had publically questioned the mechanisms for the institution's selection and production of projects. He stated:

> [Listen carefully, because this is important] La Villa produces whatever it, that is to say, whatever its authorities, its managers, its board of directors, deems adequate for that particular moment.

> [*Continuing in another letter*] We don't have any moral or legal obligation to take your opinions into consideration. We adhere to our own criteria and our sense of responsibility when taking on commitments for La Villa and deciding on the role it has to play in the development of national film. At the end of the day, we designed this apparatus, right? (Letters from Francisco Sesto, Minister of Culture, to Franco de Peña. *Diario El Universal*. Caracas, 2 May 2007)

The statements are explicit. La Villa del Cine produces what the Revolution wants it to produce, and in that respect, the idea that 'we designed this apparatus' is uncontested. Among the productions deemed appropriate by the cultural authorities are those that contribute to the revision of history and to the perpetual uncovering of the traumas associated with colonisation The most salient examples of this post-colonial cinema are two mediocre productions by Román Chalbaud: *El Caracazo* (2005) and *Zamora: tierra y hombres libres* (2009); and the most elaborate, *Miranda regresa* (2007) and *Taita Boves* (2010), both by historian and film-maker Luis Alberto Lamata.

All of these productions are characterised by their meagre efforts to develop an auteur cinema that would promote an alternative local historiography, and by their forced attempts to forge links between the past and

the political struggles of the present. Motivated by this objective, directors have drawn parallels between situations, characters and slogans that
are separated by 150 years, leading to the conflation of the protagonists
of nineteenth-century colonial conflicts with the struggles for power in
the midst of the twenty-first. Thus, in one scene from *Miranda regresa*, the
protagonist declares in a prophetic tone of voice:

> I sparked the fire, kid. I made a plan. It might not happen today or tomor-
> row, but that doesn't matter. I know that it won't take years. I know that
> in the centuries to come, Venezuela will be truly independent. That in
> centuries to come, America will be free. That's my story, and I promise
> it will carry on …

Zamora: tierra y hombres libres can be placed in the same genre of future-facing
epic films. With a good dose of creative freedom, its scriptwriter, Luis Britto
García, imagines that the protagonists had access to the Communist Party
manifesto in the year that it was published in Paris while a war between *caudillos* raged in Venezuela, a country whose historical burdens were among the
greatest of nineteenth-century Latin America. At one point, Zamora's German
travelling companion comments:

> Cheer up Ezequiel, look at what's arrived from those tremendous Ger-
> man kids – he unfolds a copy of *Die Revolution – proletarians forced to sell
> labour are a commodity like any other* […] *Workers of the world unite!*

From then on, our hero – whose main problem in 1848 was the redistribution
of land, as it was during the entire Federal War (1859–1863) – becomes not
only an instigator for the small-time traders who he represented, but also for
the slaves and the small number of artisans in the rural, semi-feudal Caracas of the mid-nineteenth century. Once the peasants are converted by the
mechanisms of the film into the 'working class', they are impelled to organ-
ise as 'independent producers', as the Chávez government would propose in
its time, and in each of the *caudillo*'s interventions are summoned by the call:
'revolution, revolution, revolution'.

Azotes de Barrio Take Over Cinema

Another transformation in the sphere of the media in contemporary
Venezuela is the emergence of the movement known as *cine de barrio*.
This is comprised of a small number of amateur films made with minimum
technical resources and freedom from strict directorial input. More than
anything else, the movement seeks to address the problems of day-to-day life

that are associated with urban poverty, for example violence, unemployment, precariousness, drugs, and police corruption. They do so by reproducing the narrative formulas of genre film and by incorporating the aesthetics of homemade videos. Against the logic of commercial television, the success of films such as *Volver al pasado* (2009) by Yosmar Istúriz or *Azotes de barrio en Petare* (2006) by Jackson Gutiérrez, shot in the *barrios* of Caracas with actors from the same communities, demonstrate that popular audiences are most interested in seeing their own realities depicted on screens.

It is worth noting that the Venezuelan public was already familiar with a filmic tradition concerned with violence and urban marginality, though one that, for better or worse, was produced by professional artists and film-makers who were driven by commitments that were social and, more-over, political. The *cine de barrio* is a different phenomenon. It is a marginal cinema made by its protagonists from the margins. Although it is a commu-nity experience, it is not exempt from the influence of commercial interests (the local press estimates that street vendors sold about 20,000 copies of *Volver al pasado*). Thus, the phenomenon speaks less to the industrialised Brazilian movement of 'new film from the margins' and more to the rise of new actors and forms of communications boosted by new media. The propagators of the *cine de barrio* seek to reformulate their own identities from a marginal position, in dialogue with the discourses of official policies.

The fact that new media technologies have simplified the processes of film production has allowed for the emergence of a genuinely popular cinematog-raphy in Venezuela. This enables novice film-makers to produce all kinds of movies with small video cameras or even on their mobile phones. This cur-rent phenomenon is characterised not only by a lack of interest in developing an auteur genre, but also by its capacity for wide distribution via social net-works, the different channels that operate on the internet and in the circulation of pirated copies. This latter form of distribution represents an important part of the country's informal cultural economy, dedicated to selling films and ille-gal software, that feeds back into the circulation of content on new media, in this 'contradictory movement of globalisation and fragmentation of cul-ture, which is, in turn, a de-localization and revitalisation of what is local' (Martín-Barbero, 2002: 94).

A Short Introspective Journey down Memory Lane

Beyond the success of Lorenzo Vigas's *Desde allá* (2015) at the Venice Festi-val, and at San Sebastián for Mariana Rondón's *Pelo malo* (2013), as discussed in Rebecca Jarman's contribution to this volume, perhaps one of the most interesting Venezuelan films of the past two tumultuous decades is *Postales de*

Leningrado (2007). This is a filmic autobiography made in postmodern mode that takes an introspective journey down memory lane. This film was directed by Mariana Rondón, the daughter of a *guerrillero* active in the 1960s, who tries to recover fragments of her past as it was affected by the clandestine struggle. The story is narrated by two children who describe, from different times and places, their process of assimilating and comprehending subversive life, all the while playing at being invisible.

What distinguishes this film from others that seek to reconstruct history is that, while it makes use of historical images and documents, its aim is not to fabricate a story by seamlessly interweaving elements from the past and the present that will contribute to the revision of 'national memory' or to discover a hidden 'collective memory'. On the contrary, it treads a solitary path to a more intimate place where power, ideas, desire and feelings come together to create a personal map of memory. It is a bank of images that, as defined by Henri Bergson (1911), are much more than mere representation, and much less than a concrete object. It is between one place and another where existence comes to life.

With this approach, the film does not return to the past in search of History with a capital H, but rather it travels to history in search of dispersed elements from an intimate past. This narrative strategy becomes a therapeutic exercise in regressive memory that brings to light the repressed events that form the underside of modern oil-producing Venezuela. The story is organised as a patchwork of memories of absence, split families, postponed celebrations, secrets, silences and, above all, fear. This is narrated from the perspective of two children who have learnt to live in uncertainty with the constant presence of danger. The real identity of their parents is unknown to them, and they fear that they might leave for Leningrad, a fantastic place where snow falls, and from where the children receive postcards as signs of life. 'Because parents who reach Leningrad', says Teo to his cousin, 'never come back'.

These games of fear, present throughout the film, allow the director, in her dual capacity of narrator and protagonist, to question the heroism conferred by some sectors of the utopian left on the numerous guerrilla groups active in Latin America during the 1960s. So too she scrutinises the frivolousness of university solidarity movements and 'Marxist reading groups' and the irrationality of disciplinary guerrilla courts created to exercise 'popular will'. In this vein, Teo's uncle does not sound so reactionary when he says, 'you are my brother, and I love you, but I just don't get this revolution of yours that leaves my kids with empty stomachs on New Year's Eve'.

These comments, however, do not point in a single direction. To achieve this balance, the director incorporates a set of archival images that document the training of military groups designed to combat the guerrillas and, later, reconstructs the chants sung as part of the military indoctrination that took place in the context of the cold war:

> I want to eat / a fridge / filled with meat / with guerrilla meat / *guerrillero*! /
> I will kill you! / and your meat / I will eat you! / and your ear! / I will eat you!

The film is unique in that its evocations of fear are sedated by the narrative perspective of its child protagonists. There are no dramatic outbursts, and the use of suspense and bloodshed is limited. The subversive elements of the film that include incarceration, torture, psychiatric detention, the identification of corpses and the grandmother's madness all stem from the children's imagination and form part of their games. This is accentuated by the use of a 1960s pop aesthetic, whose multiple perspectives and semiotic heterogeneity are clearly of a postmodern bent. This integrates fictional material, documentaries, cartoon characters, edited photos, animated drawings, and a soundtrack that includes versions of insurgent antifascist Italian songs such as *Bella Ciao,* as well as the classic Cuban song *Hasta siempre comandante* by Carlos Pueblas, interpreted in the style of hip-hop.

Yet the introspective and playful character of the film does not detract from its attempts to create a dialogue with the complex situation of the present moment. This is evident when the grandfather chastises the children as he sees them marching ('Don't do that, soldiers don't think') or when the commentator on military exercises announces that 'no country has established peace without spilling blood'. The most insightful of these transversal connections, marked as notes in the margin of the main filmic text, is a brief and serendipitous conversation between two *guerrilleros* that takes place in the background and could easily go unnoticed. Nonetheless, it reveals much about a fleeting moment, once insignificant and now crucial in modern Venezuelan history, which saw a convergence between the Communist Party of Venezuela and contingents of the Venezuelan army. It is the missing part of a jigsaw puzzle for social scientists intent on constructing a genealogy of *chavismo,* seeking to locate the source of the confluence between the military and the Marxist *guerrilleros,* subsequently embraced by the Bolivarian ideology:

> – At the meeting point some army guys are going to join us for a military-civilian exercise.
> – Army guys? Us under their command?
> – Shit, look at us, we're in bad shape …
> – We're in really bad shape, but with the army you never know …
> – … Besides, we won't be able to talk about Lenin or Marx, just Bolívar.

– And what will the Russian comrades say?
– Hell, if one of those Russians ever shows up here, we'll just tell them what happened, and that's it.

This vast archipelago of memories and provocations is created according to the arbitrary criteria of a child. As it jumps between reality and fiction, between past and future, it pays witness to the heterogeneous temporalities attributed to the diverse historical trajectories of Latin America. Above all, and in the midst of fierce political debates in Venezuela, the author does not pass judgment. Rather, she tells the story that is engraved in her memory, as someone who relives and reconstructs her dreams and most intimate recollections. This is a film free of ideological commitments, militant discourses, and pedagogical pretensions. It is reaffirming, and bears no resentment.

Closing Remarks

During the last two decades, the media and communications sector has played a central role in the multiple transformations underway in Venezuelan society and culture. These transformations are not only bound up with the authoritarian turn of the Bolivarian Revolution and the profound economic crisis that is ongoing in the country, but also with changes in the sphere of communications on a global scale. This phenomenon is directly related to the emergence of new information technologies and their implication in the conflicts over the delineation of political, cultural and national identities and terrains. In this context, the efforts of state powers to establish a 'communicational hegemony' have resulted in failure, as this chapter has argued. In the gradual transition from a party-led democracy to an authoritarian regime, this failure is most clearly demonstrated in the migration of stakeholders and audiences. This trend in the field of the media is replicated across society and culture in the mass retreat to the private realm that has typically been the response to the government's attempts at 'hegemonisation'. Nevertheless, this movement of retreat and resistance has contributed to the decline of the free press, with lamentable consequences for the whole system of communications in Venezuela.

Amid these struggles, the desire to redefine national narratives has generated important changes in the discursive representation of the popular classes. This, in turn, has effectuated a broader sense of ethnic and social diversity in the media, duly representative of the country's cultural heterogeneity. This process has encouraged the popular classes to identify with concepts of the nation, while also serving to forge highly politicised and dynamic exchanges between cultural and political actors during this latest stage of globalisation. As a result of the convergence of these events, the production of national television has declined, affecting above all the production of *telenovelas* that, for half a century, were the showpiece of national Venezuelan culture on the global media stage.

These exchanges between the local and the global in the television business find correlation in other sectors of the national cultural industry, notably in music and publishing. In this way, we have seen how local political and economic factors determine the internal dynamics of culture and its new forms of production and reception. This is compounded by the nationalist, state-led cultural policies that evolve in constant contact with the mechanisms of global markets, together creating the challenges and paradoxes that bear upon efforts of integration from the margins into global circulation.

References

Bergson, H. (1911) *Matter and memory*. George Allen and Unwin: London.

Bisbal, M. (2010) 'El 65% de los venezolanos no ve cadenas'. *Tal Cual*, Caracas, 17 May 2010, p.5.

Cabrujas, J. I. (2002) *Y Latinoamérica inventó la telenovela*. Alfadil: Caracas.

Correa, C. (2009) 'La trama de la libertad de expresión en Venezuela' in M. Bisbal (ed.) *Hegemonía y control comunicacional*. Alfa: Caracas, 241-270.

Franco, J. (2002) *The Decline and Fall of the Lettered City: Latin America in the Cold War*. Harvard University Press: Cambridge.

García Canclini, N. (1999) *La globalización imaginada*. Paidos: Buenos Aires.

Izaguirre, R. (1997) 'En el cine venezolano, la lengua es el asalto'. *Congreso Internacional de la lengua española*. Zacatecas. www.congresodelalengua.es/zacatecas/plenarias/cine/zaguir.htm [accessed 15 June 2008].

Martín-Barbero, J. (1995a) *Pre-textos. Conversaciones sobre la comunicación y sus contextos*. Universidad del Valle: Santiago de Cali.

Martín-Barbero, J. (1995b) 'Memory and Form in the Latin America Soap Opera' in R. C. Allen (ed.) *To be Continued ... Soap Operas Around the World*. Routledge: London, 276-284.

Mato, D. (1999) 'Telenovelas: trasnacionalización de la industria y transformaciones del género' in N. García Canclini (ed.) *Industrias Culturales e integración latinoamericana*. Grijalbo: México, 229-257.

Mato, D. (2002) 'Miami in the Transnationalization of the Telenovela Industry: On Territoriality and Globalization'. *Journal of Latin American Cultural Studies* **11**(2): 195-213.

Mato, D. (2005) 'Markets and representations of transnational identities. The transnationalization of the Telenovela Industry, territorial references and the production of markets and representations of transnational identities'. *Television & New Media* **6**: 423-444.

Mignolo, W. (1995) *The Darker Side of Renaissance: Literacy, Territoriality, and Colonization*. University of Michigan Press: Ann Arbor, MI.

Monsiváis, C. (2000) *Aires de familia. Cultura y sociedad en América Latina*. Anagrama: Barcelona.

Sarlo, B. (1988) *Una modernidad periférica: Buenos Aires 1920–1930*. Ediciones Nueva Visión: Buenos Aires.

Sarlo, B. (1994) *Escenas de la vida posmoderna: intelectuales, arte y videocultura en la Argentina*. Ariel: Buenos Aires.

Silva-Ferrer, M. (2014) *El cuerpo dócil de la cultura. Poder, cultura y comunicación en la Venezuela de Chávez*. Iberoamericana/Vervuert: Madrid/Frankfurt am Main.

Yúdice, G. (2002) *El recurso de la cultura*. Gedisa: Barcelona.

3

The Indian Within: Negotiating Indigenous Identity among Dominant Images of Indigeneity in Venezuela

NATALIA GARCÍA BONET

University of Kent

Introduction

The myth of *mestizaje* has played a crucial role in the construction of Latin America's national identities, prompting the creation of a unique aesthetic based on cultural and racial mixing, which concealed references to racial and ethnic diversity within nations. In the specific case of Venezuela, the notion of *crisol de razas* (racial melting pot) dominated the political scene. This definition of Venezuela implied that all citizens were a mixture of black, white (Spanish) and indigenous blood. These narratives simultaneously rendered contemporary indigenous groups invisible and transformed the heroic indigenous past into a subdued element of the all-encompassing descriptor *criollo* (creole), which became synonymous with a distinct Latin American identity. In this sense, although contemporary indigenous groups had been rendered invisible by the dominant ideologies of nationalism, the image of the Indian, especially through its most epic incarnations, like that of Cacique Guaicaipuro, played an important role in the construction of Venezuelan national ideology.

Hugo Chávez rose to power in 1998, with the largest electoral margin of the last 40 years, and one of the discursive pillars of his self-proclaimed Bolivarian Revolution was the recognition of previously neglected minority groups, especially indigenous and African descendant populations. As such, alongside the innovative laws on indigenous rights incorporated into the 1999 Constitution of the Bolivarian Republic of Venezuela (Constitución de la República Bolivariana de Venezuela, RBV), indigenous communities were positioned at the centre of political discourse. Under the new government, indigenous groups that had been silenced by the syncretising rhetoric of *mestizaje*, seemed to have found a space for recognition.

Yet the 'new' political discourse about indigeneity continues to be permeated by tropes that reduce indigenous identity to a trait: an ingredient of Venezuelan distinctiveness grounded in the past. Guaicaipuro, and the other heroic *indios* ('Indians') who fought against the Spanish Empire in the sixteenth century, have become a preferred symbol of resistance in the revolutionary rhetoric of the twenty-first century. Moreover, indigeneity – understood as the embodiment of the spirit of resistance – has been claimed to reside within the bodies of government officials. Both Hugo Chávez (in office 1998–2013) and Nicolás Maduro (in office 2013–) have publicly identified themselves as indigenous whilst appearing partly dressed in indigenous attire. This recognition of the 'Indian within' constructs an image of Venezuelan creoles as hybrids, within which the identities of Spanish, black (African) and indigenous co-exist in perpetual tension. However, this mosaic construction of creole identities has also placed contemporary indigenous groups in the complex position of representing an essential component of that very same identity that defines their exclusion. Drawing on this paradox, this chapter explores how Venezuelan indigenous groups negotiate their identity among dominant images of indigeneity reproduced by the national government, how they forge their own space between the indigenous heroes from the past and the 'Indian within'.

The Myth of *Mestizaje*

Postcolonial Latin American nation-states were constructed in parallel to their European counterparts but maintained a mimetic relationship with them. The 'European elsewhere' (Taussig, 1997) remained the model to replicate; yet it also represented a distorted mirror in which a singular Latin American identity was to be reflected. The first of these distortions was related to the fact that the governments of the emergent nations had to deal with a rather mixed population; the typical Latin American citizens differed considerably from the European model (Wade, 1997). The new states were placed in the complex position of trying to emulate their European neighbours while, at the same time, having to build something distinct from them. As such, the emergent postcolonial states needed to construct a new and different identity, one that represented their definite emancipation from colonial bonds (Krauze, 2011).

This delicate balance, of trying to mimic Europe while constructing something different, led some Latin American intellectuals, at beginning of the twentieth century, to create a unique aesthetic based on cultural and racial mixing, which was epitomised by the myth of *mestizaje*. Through works such as *Ariel* (1900) by José Enrique Rodó and *La raza cósmica* (1925) (The Cosmic Race) by José Vasconcelos, an idealised image of Latin Americans was created, which transformed the violent process of racial and cultural mixing that took place in the American colonies into the origin myth of Latin American nations: *mestizaje*. This new mixed identity seemed to imply that *mestizaje* had happened once and for all, and that Latin American citizens represented the homogenous product of this mixture, at the same time as it concealed references to nations' racial and ethnic diversity (Metz, 2010).

In the Venezuelan context, the notion of *crisol de razas* (racial melting pot) was often invoked by Arturo Uslar Pietri – one of Venezuela's most emblematic writers and modernisers – on his television show *Valores humanos* (Human Values) in 1953 (Amodio, 1999). As such, it formed part of a wider project of modernisation that tended to associate the nation's internal ethnic diversity with poverty and 'backwardness', a discourse common to other Latin American contexts (Escobar, 1995; Rival, 1996). All of these narratives presented indigenous populations as representatives of the nation's past (Wade, 1997), thus pertaining exclusively to the period before the constitution of the nation-state and inevitably dissolved in the all-encompassing identity of the creole formulated thereafter. As a consequence of these representations, contemporary indigenous groups were rendered invisible (Mato, 2008) and the creole became synonymous with the one and only Latin American identity (Wade, 1997).

However, in spite of the invisibility endured by indigenous peoples as a product of the hegemonic myth of *mestizaje*, during the most part of the twentieth century, 'invisible Indians' featured in the first chapters of Venezuela's history textbooks. The image of Cacique Guaicaipuro, for example – who according to official history was the chief of both Caracas and Teques indigenous groups, and led the resistance against the Spaniards during the sixteenth century – has featured prominently in history textbooks, as well as in a wide range of iconographic contexts; from statues and paintings, to mass reproduction on the cover of a very popular brand of school notebooks: Cuadernos Caribe. Later, during the Bolivarian Revolution, the importance of his image reached a new level when it was included on the ten-bolivar banknote. The role played by Guaicaipuro – and other heroic Indians – in the construction of Venezuelan national identity has been extensively discussed by García Gavidia (2003), who notes that the exaltation of indigenous resistance played an important role in drawing the limits of the emergent Latin American nations.

Besides representing an important figure in Venezuela's heroic history, the image of Guaicaipuro took on a religious and magical personification as one of *Las tres potencias* (the three powers) of the María Lionza cult (Taussig, 1997; Wade, 2005). These three powers are embodied in the figures of María Lionza (usually represented as a white woman), the Indian Guaicaipuro, and a black man: El Negro Felipe (Felipe the Black Man). The three powers of the Maria Lionza cult, however, are not dissolved into a homogenous identity, but represent, instead, the tensions created by the co-existence of these three strong powers within the body of creoles. The María Lionza cult, and the notion of the three powers can thus be seen as a metaphor for the Venezuelan nation

(Taussig, 1997). According to this imaginary, *mestizaje* does not necessarily imply a process of whitening that erases subaltern groups, but rather a mosaic in which those different identities co-exist, creating tensions within the individual (Wade, 2005).

In this reading, the blood of Guaicaipuro and the other Indians who fought against the Spanish Crown is still alive, though latent, in the contemporary creole. According to Wade (2005) these *potencias* provide creoles with different traits, which remain dormant or woke, and are triggered in specific circumstances. These can be considered as immiscible substances that inhabit the body of contemporary Venezuelans and, thus, define their character. As such, indigeneity is not rendered invisible, as much as it is hidden inside the body of creoles. The Indian element – epitomised by the blood of Guaicaipuro – provides the creole with a spirit of resistance. This imaginary has been openly embraced by the Revolution's leaders, who, by identifying themselves as direct descendants of Guaicaipuro, draw links between indigenous resistance to colonial powers and the Revolution's ongoing battle against foreign intervention. The reduction of indigeneity to a trait of creole identity conceals the problems faced by contemporary living indigenous populations. Simultaneously, the exaltation of the indigenous past perpetuates the 'petrification of the Indians' (García Gavidia, 2003), their position as monuments of the past and as symbols of a resistance that still lives on within the body of Venezuelans.

Indigeneity as Perennial Resistance

The term indigeneity often serves to encompass people from different countries, ethnic groups and backgrounds. In this sense, it works as a sort of meta-category, rooted in the notion of a shared history of oppression and asymmetric power relationships with the state (Hodgson, 2002; Metz, 2010). In spite of its status as an umbrella term, indigeneity cannot be considered a neutral category. On the contrary, it has a specific history related to the conquest of the Americas and the following process of colonisation: 'There were no indigenous peoples prior to the 1494 Treaty of Tordesillas when, by Papal decree, the globe was divided between Portugal and Spain' (McIntosh *et al.*, 2002: 23). The colonial history of 'indigeneity', then, loads the term with special significance for the people who use it, for whom it represents more than a bureaucratic category (McIntosh *et al.*, 2002), since as Niezen points out: 'What [the] indigenous share is some form of subsistence economy, a territory or homeland, a spiritual system predating the arrival of missionaries, and a distinctive language. Most importantly they share the destruction and loss of these things' (Niezen in Metz, 2010: 291).

Indigenous people are compelled to construct their history in terms of both continuity and disruption, having undergone a history of colonisation and oppression while also having managed to 'survive' it (Metz, 2010). Moreover, the pending threat over indigenous identity is not exclusively relegated to their past. Indigenous groups are often linked to discourses of vulnerability and need of protection; they are placed in a fragile and interstitial position that mirrors their marginal, eternally unresolved, incorporation into the nation. Indigeneity, as the product of a specific relationship with the state, becomes indivisible from the dominant discourses that shape the imaginary about indigenous peoples. In this sense, indigenous identity is partly constructed by the different narratives reproduced by non-indigenous actors, thus transforming indigenous self-identification into a process of 'becoming Indian as well as being Indian' (Jackson, 1995: 3). These discourses, in the case of Venezuela, define indigeneity in terms of both vulnerability and resistance.

The idea that cultures, especially indigenous cultures, need protection arises from the concept of acculturation, 'understood (in its narrower acceptation) as resulting from exogenous factors related to the colonial expansion of "civilised" or "developed" societies at the expense of more "backward" ones, a process inevitably leading to cultural impoverishment and the social mutation of the colonised' (Santos Granero, 2009: 478). This notion of acculturation transforms cultures into 'things' that can be lost for ever and tends to equate processes of contact to cultural erasure and loss (Urban and Sherzer, 1991). As such, any form of adaption or assimilation seems to imply a change in the ethnic identity of the group which is being assimilated into mainstream society (Ramos, 1998).

The notion that indigenous cultures need to be protected – sheltered from the assimilation forces of the 'west' – suggests that indigenous groups are vulnerable to these foreign forces. This notion of vulnerability forms part of the patronising idea that compares, through discursive resources, indigenous people to children (Ramos, 1998) and at the same time attributes them with a series of idealised traits (cf. Wade, 1997; Ramos, 1998; Kuper, 2003). These ascribed characteristics place indigenous people in opposition to dominant (western) cultural practices, constructing a 'rhetoric of authenticity' (Chanok, 2000: 22), which makes of indigeneity a stable reference for the ever-changing and, therefore, contaminated lifestyles of the 'west'. Moreover, this rhetoric renders 'modern societies' the only ones with the ability to innovate without risking cultural death (Moore, 2011). This protective attitude towards indigeneity and the yearn for 'genuine' experiences – both of which exist outside of the limits of the 'west' – responds to a disenchantment with modernity that is created by modernity itself (Bendix, 1997).

Disillusionment with modernity and the fear of the destructive expansion of the 'west' places indigenous people in an eternal position of resistance, as if they represented the last bastion of authenticity against the unquestionably 'western' forces of globalistion (Kuper, 2003). This type of discourse assimilates modernity into hegemonic society, while attributing traditional or popular culture to the subaltern. This constructed dichotomy between modernity and tradition not only reflects an idealised notion of indigenous people as the last combatants in a battle against modernity; it also contributes to reifying difference, turning indigenous groups into the only true 'others' (Wade, 1997). In this sense, indigenous people are both idealised and exoticised, or indianised (Ramos, 1998), and this radicalised difference acts as an 'aesthetic fascination' (Urban and Sherzer, 1991:11) that – in a similar manner to idealisation – justifies the protective attitude towards indigenous communities.

Indigenous Movements in Latin America

During the last two decades of the twentieth century, Latin American countries underwent a process of 're-indianisation' (Jackson and Warren, 2005; Metz, 2010). Indigenous groups that had been rendered invisible, or even considered to be extinct (Amodio, 2007), have re-emerged in the public sphere, forming indigenous organisations and demanding recognition. This phenomenon relates to wider global movements towards the rights of indigenous peoples, such as the 1989 and 2003 International Labour Organization's (ILO) and C169 Indigenous and Tribal Peoples Convention; the United Nations International Year of the World's Indigenous People (UN); two subsequent UN Decades of Indigenous People; and other successful mobilisations in the region (Jackson and Waldren, 2005). These mobilisations on the rights of indigenous peoples demanded consensus on a working definition of indigeneity, which has long been the subject of debates within academia (see Béteille, 1998; Ramos, 1998; Kuper, 2003; Barnard, 2006, among others), yet international organisations such as the UN, the ILO, the World Bank and the European Union have established similar criteria (Metz, 2010). This relative consensus has promoted the internationalisation of indigeneity, which 'has come to also presuppose a sphere of commonality among those who form a world collectivity of indigenous peoples' (Merlan, 2009: 303). According to this criterial definition of indigeneity (Merlan, 2009), one of the conditions for claiming an indigenous identity is to be the descendant of a colonised population. This defining feature has helped the claims of Latin American indigenous groups, who share an undeniable history of colonisation.

Besides a history of colonisation and asymmetric power relationships, other accepted criteria of indigenous identity include having a distinct culture and practising a series of traditions which help to differentiate indigenous groups from dominant society (Metz, 2010). In Latin America, equating indigenous identity to a distinct culture conveyed, on the one hand, a revalorisation of indigenous traditions, as well as an acknowledgement of multiculturalism in the previously considered homogeneous nation-states (Yashar, 2005; Amodio, 2007). The same process also constructed a sense of continuity between contemporary indigenous peoples and past indigenous groups who suffered the processes of conquest and colonisation. Indigenous people were thus identified with a position of continuous resistance, of having maintained a set of distinct values and traditions, despite the fact that those values and traditions were under constant threat from outsiders. This definition makes of 'authentic' indigenous culture something that always needs to be recovered and revalued, but never reinvented.

The process of revalorisation of indigenous culture that started during the last three decades in Latin America needed to establish links with an indigenous past, and thus account for the temporary disappearance of indigenous groups during an important part of the nations' republican history. In this sense, academics committed to the indigenous cause often invoked the notion of ethnic shame (see Amodio, 2007 and Monsonyi, 2008b) to account for that period of silence and concealment of indigenous identity, as well as for the process of assimilation that led to indigenous groups strategically identifying themselves as *mestizos* (mixed) or *criollos* (creoles) (Metz 2010; Gow, 2007). However, the process through which these previously invisible groups have gained visibility is not as direct as it may seem. In the case of Venezuela, dominant discourses have managed to incorporate this new indigenous salience while maintaining some aspects of its concealment.

Culture, especially indigenous culture, entails a symbolic capital (Bourdieu, 1999) that is often utilised by national governments to claim legitimacy and historic continuity (García Gavidia, 2003). In contemporary Venezuela, the position of indigenous people – constructed in terms of both subalternity and resistance – has been extrapolated to the realm of national politics. As will be explained below, the constant threat over indigenous cultures, as well as indigenous people's inherent ability to resist it, have been appropriated by the official discourse reproduced by the *chavista* government. The revolutionary government, then, continually presents itself as the target of assimilation forces embodied by the global market and the expansion of an inherently US American form of neocolonialism. For this appropriation to be effective, however, government officials needed first to present themselves as partly indigenous, thus exploiting the symbolism that relates indigeneity to purity and resistance, and representing themselves as the heirs of the nation's heroic past.

As was mentioned above, anti-colonialist discourses have been part of Latin American nationalisms since their constitutive moments. Moreover, the exaltation of the indigenous past has also been a recurrent feature of the construction of national identities. However, the appropriation of the symbolism of subalternity and resistance in contemporary Venezuelan politics has prompted the emergence of a new form of *indio permitido* (permitted Indian) (Hale and Millaman, 2004; McNeish, 2008) – one that not only represents the aforementioned qualities, but is also a strong supporter of the Bolivarian Revolution. By claiming an indigenous identity, therefore, the government has not only appropriated the symbolism related to indigeneity, but has simultaneously reshaped the meaning of 'legitimate' indigeneity, thus connecting it discursively to the Bolivarian Revolution.

The Bolivarian Revolution's 'Permitted Indian'

In a public act in Amazonas in 2013, the then Venezuelan vice president, Jorge Arreaza stated: 'Aquel miembro de un pueblo indígena que no tiene la claridad de estar con la Revolución Bolivariana es prácticamente un traidor a su pueblo, a su comunidad' ('Any member of an indigenous group who does not have the clarity to support the Bolivarian Revolution is practically a traitor to his/her own people, to his/her own community') (Medina, 2014). This statement is framed in the wider political discourse in which indigenous people embody the resistance against foreign forces; yet in this particular case, 'foreign forces' are incarnated by the opposition party. In this sense, what the statement suggested was that one of the requirements for people to be able to claim a legitimate 'indigenous' identity would be to identify oneself as *chavista*.

In 2013, a non-governmental organisation (NGO) named Laboratorios por la Paz (Peace Laboratories) published a document entitled *Diagnóstico sobre el derecho a la asociación indígena en Venezuela* (Diagnosis on the Right to Free Association for Indigenous Peoples in Venezuela), which comprised a very general survey about indigenous organisations' rights to free association. Throughout the document there are many references to the demands of traditional indigenous organisations such as *consejos de ancianos* (councils of elders) to be acknowledged, without having to establish an indigenous *consejo comunal* (communal council) – a form of grassroots organisation created by the Chávez government in 2006 as part of a 'New Geometry of Power' (Wilde, 2017). The document also recounts different conflicts between competing communal councils (usually two or more councils formed in the same indigenous community) and how its members often attempt to discredit their rivals by accusing them of having links to the opposition coalition, the Mesa de la Unidad Democrática (MUD, Table of Democratic Unity).

In one of my many visits to a Pemón indigenous community of the La Gran Sabana (The Great Savannah), located in southeast Venezuela, I spoke to a former *capitán* (captain), who had occupied the position for over eighteen years. Pemón *capitanes* (captains) are the local civil authorities who represent the community *vis à vis* external institutions and the Venezuelan state. The former *capitán* told me about the relationship between the *capitanía* (captaincy) in his community and one of the main indigenous organisations of Bolívar State, which is supposed to act as an autonomous entity and serve as a voice for other indigenous groups in the area. However, according to the *capitán*, in its relationship with indigenous communities, the organisation had become a representative of the government, and, more specifically, of the government's party: Partido Socialista Unido de Venezuela (Venezuelan United Socialist Party, PSUV):

> The only thing they care about is power. They have completely forgotten how to work with the communities and when someone criticises them in any way they go and accuse them of being part of the opposition. That was what happened when they donated bikes to the community. Elbano [a community member] went and told them that the bikes were great, but that the community needed something more concrete, something that would last, because those bikes were going to break down eventually; and just because of that they went around telling everyone that Elbano was with the MUD [opposition coalition].

This fear of being accused of belonging to the opposition party stems from a concern that this association would then lead to a stoppage in the provision of governmental funds and exclusion from some of the government's special welfare programmes (*misiones*). Episodes such as this one attest to the construction of a new form of 'legitimate' indigeneity, which once more implies that legitimate indigenous communal councils are those that are openly aligned with the Bolivarian Revolution.

I am not suggesting that these discursive transformations have influenced the ways in which indigenous people perceive themselves in everyday life. However, they do prescribe how indigeneity is presented officially, and the way claims and demands are formulated *vis-à-vis* the government. Supporting the Bolivarian Revolution, incarnated by the figure of Hugo Chávez, has become a synonym of belonging to the Venezuelan nation, as demonstrated by PSUV slogans like '*Todos somos Chávez*' (We are all Chávez) and '*Chávez es el pueblo*' (Chávez is the people). This exhortation to identify with Chávez and the Revolution in order to claim adscription to the nation becomes more problematic when it is extended to indigenous people, whose incorporation into the nation remains precarious.

The Indian within the Revolution

Indigeneity, as an essential ingredient of creole identity, is often represented as the spirit of resistance. In the narrative of Venezuelan official history, indigenous people are the protagonists of the resistance against the Spanish Empire, and have become a symbol of resistance against foreign forces in contemporary political discourses. During a public act in September 2008, Hugo Chávez, announced the expulsion of the United States' Ambassador from Venezuela, in an act of solidarity with Bolivian President, Evo Morales, who had taken similar measures:

> Váyanse al carajo, yanquis de mierda, que aquí hay un pueblo digno, yanquis de mierda. Váyanse al carajo cien veces; aquí estamos los hijos de Bolívar, de Guaicaipuro y de Tupac Amaru. Este pueblo está resuelto a ser libre. (Go to hell, damned Yankees, because here there is a proud people. Go to hell a hundred times, damned Yankees. We here are the sons of [Simón] Bolívar, of Guaicapuro and of Tupac Amarú. We are resolved to be free.)

This speech reveals the symbolic capital attached to indigenous heroes of the past. By placing indigenous identity in the past, Chávez made it common to all Latin Americans through the implication that all are heirs to Guaicaipuro and Tupac Amarú. However, the metaphoric extension of indigeneity in the speech is not applicable to all Latin Americans, or indeed to all Venezuelans. The 'proud people' that Chavez invoked are only those who oppose the American Ambassador's presence in the country, those who share the Bolivarian Revolution's political stance and can have a legitimate claim as heirs of the indigenous heroes of the past.

The construction of this form of Bolivarian indigeneity is facilitated by the role the Revolution has played in the promotion of indigenous rights. By the beginning of the 1990s, most Latin American countries had included in their constitution a set of laws and amendments concerning the rights of indigenous people (Lee Van Cot, 2003). However, even though Venezuela was one of the countries to ratify the 169 ILO Convention in 1989, it had advanced very little in this direction. Indigenous groups were seldom mentioned in legislation, apart from a brief reference to their imminent incorporation into the 'life of the nation' in the 1961 Constitution (Lee Van Cot, 2003). It was not until Chávez's election in 1998 that the incorporation of legislation concerning the Venezuelan indigenous population started to be considered. In 1999, the newly elected government proposed a radical constitutional reform, which attempted to mark a clean break from Venezuela's previous practices of governance (McCoy, 2000) by transforming the relationships between the government and minority groups such as indigenous and African descendant populations. This considerable delay in the implementation of indigenous rights in Venezuela, which occurred almost a decade later than the rest of Latin America, brought about important opportunities for the Chávez government and for indigenous groups.

The 1999 Constitution gave the government the opportunity to prove its intentions to truly transform the nation and redeem the rights of those groups that had been neglected by previous governmental practices. The transition from one of Latin America's most backward set of laws on indigenous rights to one of the most innovative ones thereby served the government's rhetoric of a radical revolutionary break from the past. On the other hand, indigenous groups which had been rendered invisible by previous governments found for the first time a space in which to discuss their needs and a public forum to claim their rights in the Asamblea Constituyente (Constituent Assembly), which allocated three of the 121 seats to indigenous delegates (Lee Van Cot, 2003). Although small, this representation constituted a considerable improvement on past indigenous participation in public affairs.

The creation of the Constituent Assembly prompted the mobilisation of indigenous organisations from all over the country. At the same time, indigenous groups took this opportunity to make themselves visible, occupying public spaces and presenting themselves in traditional attire: 'Indians singing and dancing in traditional costumes, maintained a constant presence in the courtyard outside the assembly throughout the deliberations' (Lee Van Cot, 2003: 59). This strategic use of indigeneity, based on emphasising alterity through the use of traditional clothing and performing traditional dances, represents one of the ways for indigenous people to position themselves in front of the government while at the same time asserting their identity.

After months of negotiation and the constant presence of indigenous groups in the capital, the 1999 Constitution was approved, with the inclusion of a series of collective rights for Venezuela's indigenous populations, such as the reformulation of the Presidential Decree no. 283 for Educación Intercultural Bilingüe (EIB, Intercultural Bilingual Education). First proclaimed in 1979, during the government of Luis Herrera Campins, the EIB provides the basis for the implementation of bilingual education programmes taught in Spanish and an indigenous language, with an emphasis on indigenous culture. The government has made the first efforts to implement the EIB through state-run Escuelas Bolivarianas (Bolivarian Schools) located in indigenous territories.

Other intercultural education initiatives created independently from the national government have had to go through a more complex process to negotiate their position. A specific example of this is the Universidad Indígena de Venezuela (Indigenous University of Venezuela, UIV), which I visited in 2012.

The 1999 constitutional reform represented one of the first steps towards the creation of the UIV. Nevertheless, during the first nine years after its creation, the institution did not receive recognition from the Venezuelan government, which was withheld until the UIV included in their academic programme the Bolivarian curriculum, which stresses an official narrative of national history, that emphasises the achievements of Simon Bolívar and other heroes of Venezuelan Independence (Monsonyi, 2008a). In 2010, however, a series of episodes led to negotiations with the government, and, by 2015 official recognition for the UIV – with a set of new conditions and modifications – had almost been granted. The negotiating table was set by one of the UIV's indigenous coordinators, who attended an official act, featuring President Hugo Chovez, at the Teresa Carreño Theatre – one of Caracas's most important theatre venues, which is often used for official acts. He told me the story of what happened there during my visit to the UIV:

> I went there wearing a *guayuco* (loincloth), because how else would he [Chávez] recognise me? And in a moment of silence, when I knew I was going to be heard, I screamed '*Viva Chávez*' and the cameras caught me. That is when they asked me what I was doing there, and what I wanted, and I said: 'I want Chávez to recognise the Indigenous University of Venezuela'.

The 'theatrical' characteristics of this way of exercising power (Balandier, 1994), in which decisions are taken in front of an audience, is a common practice in Venezuelan politics; every Sunday during his terms as president, Chávez would hold his lengthy television show *Aló Presidente*, in which he granted loans and solved different issues presented by ordinary people. Moreover, the indigenous coordinator's strategy engaged in the game of visibility and invisibility that the Chávez government needed to play. In this sense, the UIV's coordinator had adopted an image that suited the dominant national narratives: by wearing a *guayuco* (loincloth), he fitted the stereotype of the traditional indigenous subject while, by lending his support to the Bolivarian Revolution, he played out the role of the 'good revolutionary' (Rangel, 1976).

The coordinator's chosen attire, the *guayuco*, and his chosen words to account for it – 'how else would he recognise me?' – echo an anecdote narrated by Santos Granero (2009) in which Chemmel, a Yanesha from the Peruvian Amazonia, wears his traditional garments in front of a congress audience and then changes into 'western' clothing. Santos Granero recounts that after seeing Chemmel wearing 'western' clothes, a Chilean friend of his 'asserted, a bit puzzled, "I would have never recognised him"' (Santos Granero, 2009: 477). In both of these cases, wearing indigenous attire represents a way of guaranteeing recognition, of being recognised as an 'other' in formal contexts, whether a congress, presidential act, or otherwise. The UIV coordinator's clothing embodied his strategic choice to perform in a particular 'situation', acting within those 'historical locations where crucial and political contexts are enacted' (Rubenstein, 2002: 76). To gain official recognition for the IUV, its coordinator needed first to be recognised as 'indigenous' by the Venezuelan government.

The coordinator was reproducing an image of indigeneity that, as explained above, dominates official acts and representations of indigenous people, an image that incorporates elements associated with traditional indigenous culture and the aesthetics of the Bolivarian Revolution. A red loincloth for the men, and a skirt or dress (made with red fabric) for indigenous women, is a recurrent feature in televised governmental events.

When I conducted fieldwork in 2015 in La Gran Sabana, my research on intercultural education programmes prompted by the national government led me to attend many official acts organised by the school district. These acts featured performances of the official representation of indigeneity and of the official representation of the state. When the end of school year was approaching, the red fabric used to create costumes for the children to wear in school presentations was in high demand all around Santa Elena de Uairén, one of the biggest towns in the municipality. One of my informants, who made different types of craftwork to sell to tourists, such as hammocks, baskets, and other traditional objects, assured me that she knew how to make 'authentic' indigenous clothing and showed me different photographs of this officialised version of indigenous dress.

Official acts and events function as spaces where different images of indigeneity are crystallised and combined to create the aesthetics of the official indigenous subject, which relies significantly on establishing links between the Revolution's present and Venezuela's indigenous past. Individuals like the UIV coordinator and Chemmel have the ability to enter and exit those spaces, acting according to specific historical or political contexts. During my research it became apparent that this official representation of indigeneity did not always coincide with the definition used by people in their everyday lives. While this contrast escapes the scope of this chapter, it is nevertheless important to point out that even though individuals have the ability to enter and exit the stage of officialdom, decisions made in the realm of national politics have very real effects in their daily lives.

Guaicaipuro and Contemporary Indigenous Groups

As noted earlier, indigenous people feature in Venezuelan primary school history textbooks as the first heroes of the resistance against the Spanish

Empire. This resistance is celebrated every year on 12 October, the day Columbus arrived on the American continent, as the 'Día de la Resistencia Indígena' (Day of Indigenous Resistance). The name of this celebration, however, is the result of a series of discursive transformations throughout the years. For the best part of the twentieth century, Venezuelans celebrated 12 October as 'El descubrimiento de América' (Discovery of America) or as 'El día de la raza' (Race Day). In the late 1980s and early 1990s, motivated by shifts in indigenous rights occurring in the rest of Latin America, the festivities acquired a more politically correct tone and were renamed 'El encuentro entre dos mundos' (Encounter between Two Worlds).

The Day of Indigenous Resistance came into being after Chávez's election and the constitutional reform of 1999 (Angosto, 2008) as part of a shift in official historical narratives that moved the focus from the actions of Spanish conquistadors onto those of indigenous people. After their initial appearance as heroes of the resistance against the Spanish invasion, Indians feature, albeit in stereotypical terms, in the historical constructions of colonial times, specifically to describe the different forms of *mestizaje*: a sort of scientific formula, according the nomenclature of the time. After this, indigenous people seemed to disappear almost entirely from the narration of Venezuela's Republican history only to re-emerge much later with Chávez's rise to power and the birth of the nation's Quinta República (Fifth Republic).

This re-emergence of indigenous people is somewhat dependant on their previous invisibility as political subjects, as if the Indians had been 'created' alongside the new Republic: a 'new Indian' to mirror the 'new man' that Chávez claimed the Revolution would bring into being (Kozloff, 2008). The new discourse of the nation opened a space for the 're-indianisation' of Venezuela and at the same time used the official narratives about indigenous people to construct a historical link with the territory and give the Bolivarian Revolution a sense of continuity. 'The Revolution started 500 years ago', claimed Chávez in one of the acts organised to celebrate the Day of Indigenous Resistance in 2003 (see Angosto, 2008). This assertion, which linked indigenous resistance against the Spanish, the nineteenth-century battles for independence and the twenty-first century Bolivarian Revolution, was accompanied by the promotion of the heroic acts of Indians who appeared alongside other, more 'traditional' heroes from the official history of Venezuela (ibid.).

According to Fernando Coronil, the identification of the ruler and the state in Venezuela makes of every president a magician able to invoke the 'the invisible powers of oil money' (Coronil, 1997: 2). While Chávez often showcased this ability in his weekly television show, his biggest act of prestidigitation was to collapse the historical past into the present, thus creating 'an eternal present […] in which past wars fought over the independence of the country, for example, are experienced as "eternal" sources of the spiritual strength of the Venezuelan people' (Zúquete, 2008: 108). The figure of Guiacaipuro has represented one of the ingredients of this fusion. The positioning of Guaicaipuro as one of the heroes of independence took on a rather literal form, when in 2001 his symbolic remains were placed in the National Pantheon, next to those of Venezuela's emancipator, Simón Bolívar.

The cult around the figure of Guaicaipuro has led Fernando Angosto (2008) to coin the term 'Guaicaipurism' to refer to the Revolution's parallel discourse to Bolivarianism, which makes use of indigenous epic struggle against the Spanish Empire to justify the Revolution's struggles in the present. According to Angosto, 'Guaicaipurismo is a crucial complement to Bolivarianism as a source of symbolic and narrative production that supports and expresses the collective political identity that takes form as Chavismo' (2015: 90), thus allowing a bottom-up identification. However, I argue that this exaltation of the figure of Guaicaipuro represents one of the discourses underpinning the Bolivarian Revolution's 'permitted Indian'. Guaicuaipuro both represents and comes to replace all contemporary indigenous peoples. The discourse that establishes a direct connection between the Revolution and the heroic Indians of the past manages at the same time to dissolve indigeneity. After all, if we are all Indians, nobody really is.

Beyond representing a form of emancipation for previously silenced and neglected indigenous populations, the figure of Guaicaipuro is invoked as a way to establish an identity of blood and territory with a contemporary Venezuelan population. The discourses of 'Guaicaipurism', then, insert indigenous people into Venezuelan official history narratives as evidence of the construction of a new diverse and multicultural state (Amodio, 2007) and of a process that Chávez called 'paying the historic debt' to the nation's indigenous people (Angosto, 2008). At the same time, though, they make indigenous peoples' struggles one with that of mainstream society – softening the edges of the nation's internal contradictions in a sort of historical *mestizaje*.

Conclusion: Between Visibility and Invisibility

The 1999 constitutional reform represented an attempt to make a clean break from previous governments. Chávez had risen to power with the largest electoral margin in the last 40 years, and his popularity was partly sustained by the idea that there was a mismatch between the government and civil society (Lee Van Cot, 2003) and that this rupture should be mended through radical political reform. In this process of deconstructing the relationship between the government and society to rebuild it, a series of gaps were created, small fissures that allowed Venezuelan indigenous groups to mobilise and gain terrain in the political sphere. However, this newly elected government also needed to construct a national narrative to give a sense of cohesion to the country. This national narrative had a space for indigenous people; however, this space was reserved for an 'ideal Indian'.

Despite the important legislative transformations in indigenous rights included in the 1999 Constitution, the new spaces provided for indigenous people are still regulated by nationalist discourses. Those discourses contribute to the shaping of indigenous identity while at the same time generating counter-narratives and creative strategies to cope with them. While contemporary indigenous groups and indigenous organisations struggle to gain recognition and make demands related to their specific and pressing needs, the national government maintains a narrative in which indigenous groups are the heroes of the past who fought against the Spanish Empire, and the ingredient of the national identity that makes Venezuelan creoles distinct.

These contradictions mirror the 'chameleonic nature of *mestizaje*', which can either represent a homogenising, and whitening, force which erases subaltern identities, or one that embraces those subaltern identities to pit itself against the 'west' (Wade, 2005: 253). The latter formulation was evinced by Nicolás Maduro, at a public act in Amazonas, during his 2013 campaign to succeed Chávez as president, where he declared: 'Yo siento aquí el espíritu de Aramare, el espíritu de Guaicaipuro y yo soy su heredero. Yo soy Maduro, el indio brazo duro heredero de Guaicaipuro' (I feel the spirit of Aramare and Guaicaipuro, and I am their heir. I am Maduro, the strong armed Indian, heir to Guaicaipuro) (*El Universal*, 2013). Through this claim, the then candidate and now President of Venezuela managed to conceal, once again, the problems faced by contemporary indigenous groups behind the epic images of the past.

In contemporary Venezuelan politics, the recognition of special rights for indigenous people seems to run parallel to a discourse that denies the special circumstances experienced by indigenous populations. In its attempt to prove their commitment to indigenous people and other previously silenced minorities, the Bolivarian Revolution has assimilated the discourses of resistance and subalternity that historically belonged to them. When all Venezuelans share in the history of segregation and oppression, which was historically experienced by indigenous people, there is no longer a justification for according special rights to indigenous groups. Moreover, the idea that this history belongs not to a minority, but to all citizens, vindicates the government's wary attitude towards foreign regimes.

The self-representation that indigenous people are compelled to stage – presenting themselves as a combination of authentic indigenous subjects who have maintained their culture and traditions throughout the years, and political activists who strongly support the Bolivarian Revolution – makes them into hybrid subjects, to match the hybridity of political figures. As government officials make themselves partly indigenous, they simultaneously force indigenous groups to blend into the undifferentiated poll of Venezuelan citizens, where they must claim their rights following the procedures established by the government and by asserting their alliance to the Revolution. In this sense, the recognition of indigeneity as an ingredient that is latent in every Venezuelan citizen represents a strategic move by the government to claim political legitimacy and ratify its commitment to minority groups. Yet, at the same time, it represents a way to dissolve difference and to undermine indigenous identity.

In sum, instead of atonement to previously neglected indigenous populations, the Bolivarian Revolution awoke the 'Indian within'. During the 2012 campaign in the run up to the presidential elections, the last in which Chávez participated, the opposition candidate, Henrique Capriles Radonski, visited indigenous communities and appeared wearing a traditional indigenous crown. At one of his campaign rallies, a vexed Chávez declared: 'Yo que soy medio indio, porque sí tengo sangre india y negra, soy una mezcla de los indios de la sabana y los negros que vinieron del África a ligarse con nosotros en estas tierras, ni yo me atrevo a ponerme esa sagrada corona de los caciques aborígenes' ('I am half Indian, because I do have indigenous and black blood and am a mixture of the Indians of the savannah and the blacks who came from Africa to mix with us in these lands, but even I wouldn't dare put on that sacred crown of indigenous chiefs'). Chávez's response reflects the indignation produced upon witnessing the opposition making use of a discourse that the government had previously appropriated for itself.

References

Amodio, E. (1999) 'El mito del crisol: razas, etnias e historia' in L. Meneses, J. Briceño and G. Gordones (eds) *Hacia la antropología del siglo XXI*. CONICIT CONAC: Mérida, 31–37.

Amodio, E. (2007) 'La república indígena. Pueblos indígenas y perspectivas políticas en Venezuela'. *Revista venezolana de economía y ciencias sociales* **13**(3): 175–188.

Angosto, L. (2008) 'Pueblos indígenas, guaicaipurismo y socialismo del siglo XXI en Venezuela'. *Antropológica de la Fundación La Salle de Ciencias Naturales* **LII** (110): 9–33.

Angosto, L. (2015) *Venezuela Reframed: Bolivarianism, Indigenous People and Socialism of the Twenty First Century*. Zed Books: London.

Balandier, G (1994) *El poder en escenas: de la representación del poder al poder de la representación*. Paidos: Barcelona.

Barnard, A. (2006) 'Kalahari Revisionism, Vienna and the "Indigenous Peoples" Debate'. *Social Anthropology* **14**(1): 1–16.

Bendix, R. (1997) *In Search of Authenticity: The Formation of Folklore Studies*. University of Wisconsin Press: Madison.

Béteille, A. (1998) 'The Idea of Indigenous People'. *Current Anthropology* **39**(2): 187–192.

Bourdieu, P. (1999) 'Rethinking the State: Genesis and Structure of the Bureaucratic Field' in G. Steinmetz (ed.) *State/Culture: State-formation after the Cultural Turn*. Cornell University Press: London, pp. 53–73.

Coronil, F. (1997) *The Magical State: Nature, Money, and Modernity in Venezuela*. University of Chicago Press: London.

Escobar, A. (1995) *Encountering Development*. Princeton University Press: New Jersey.

Gow, P. (2007) '"Ex-Cocama": Transforming Identities in Peruvian Amazonia' in C. Fausto and M. Heckenberger (eds) *Time and Memory in Indigenous Amazonia*. University Press of Florida: Gainesville, 194–215.

Hale, C. and Millaman, R. (2004) 'Rethinking indigenous politics in the era of the '"indio permitido"'. *NACLA Report on the Americas* **38**(2): 16–21.

Hodgson, D. (2002) 'Introduction: Comparative Perspectives on the Indigenous Rights Movement in Africa and the Americas'. *American Anthropologist* **104**(4): 1037–1049.

Jackson, J. (1995) 'Culture, Genuine and Spurius: The Politics of Indianness in the Vaupés, Colombia'. *American Ethnologist* **22**(1): 3–27.

Jackson, J. and Waren, K. (2005) 'Indigenous Movements in Latin America, 1992–2004: Controversies, Ironies New Directions'. *Annual Review of Anthropology* **34**: 549–573.

Kozloff, N. (2008) *Revolution! South America and the Rise of the New Left*. Palgrave Macmillan: Basingstoke.

Krauze, E. (2011) *Redentores: ideas y poder en América Latina*. Debate: Mexico D.F.

Kuper, A. (2003) 'The Return of the Native'. *Current Anthropology* **44**(3): 389–402.

Lee Van Cot, D. (2003) 'Andean Indigenous Movements and Constitutional Transformation: Venezuela in Comparative Perspective'. *Latin American Perspectives* **30**(1): 49–69.

Mato, D. (2008) 'Panorama regional' in D. Mato (ed.) *Diversidad cultural e interculturalidad en educación superior: Experiencias en América Latina*. IESALC-UNESCO: Caracas, 21–82.

McCoy, J. (2000) 'Demystifying Venezuela's Hugo Chavez'. *Current History* **99**(634): 66–71.

McIntosh, I. *et al.* (2002) 'Defining Oneself, and Being Defined as, Indigenous: A Comment on J. Bowen (AT 16,4) and M Colchester (AT 18,1)'. *Anthropology Today* **18**(3): 23–24.

McNeish, J. (2008) 'Beyond the Permitted Indian? Bolivia and Guatemala in an Era of Neoliberal Developmentalism'. *Latin American and Caribbean Ethnic Studies* **3**(1): 33–59.

Merlan, F. (2009) 'Indigeneity Global and Local'. *Current Anthropology* **50**(3): 303–333.

Metz, B. (2010) 'Questions of Indigeneity and the (Re)-Emergent Ch'orti' Maya of Honduras'. *Journal of Latin American and Caribbean Anthropology* **15**(2): 289–316.

Monsoyi, E. (2008) 'Universidad Indígena de Venezuela' in D. Mato (ed.) *Diversidad cultural e interculturalidad en educación superior: experiencias en América Latina*. IESALC-UNESCO: Caracas, 427–438.

Monsonyi, E. (2008) *El Indígena venezolano en pos de su liberación definitiva*. El Perro y La Rana: Caracas.

Moore, H. (2011) *Still Life: Hopes, Desires and Satisfactions*. Polity Press: Cambridge.

Ramos, A. R. (1998) *Indigenism: Ethnic Politics in Brazil*. University of Wisconsin Press: Madison, WI.

Rangel, C. (1976) *Del buen salvaje al buen revolucionario: mitos y realidades en América Latina*. Monte Ávila Editores: Caracas.

Rival, L. (1996) 'Formal Schooling and the Production of Modern citizens in the Ecuadorian Amazon' in B. Levinson, D. Foley and D. Holland (eds) *The Cultural Production of the Educated Person*. State University of New York Press: New York.

Rubenstein, S. (2002) *Alejandro Tsakimp: A Shuar Healer in the Margins of History*. University of Nebraska Press: Lincoln.

Santos-Granero, F. (2009) 'Hybrid Bodyscapes: A Visual History of Yanesha Patterns of Cultural Change'. *Current Anthropology* **50**(4): 477–512.

Taussig, M. (1997) *The Magic of the State*. Routledge: London.

Urban, G. and Sherzer, J. (1991) 'Introduction: Indians, Nation-States, and Culture' in G. Urban and J. Sherzer (eds) *Nation-States and Indians in Latin America*. University of Texas Press: Austin, 1–18.

Wade, P. (1997) *Race and ethnicity in Latin America*. Pluto Press: London.

Wade, P. (2005) 'Rethinking *Mestizaje*: Ideology and Lived Experience'. *Journal of Latin American Studies* **37**(2): 239–257.

Wilde, M. (2017) 'Contested Spaces: The Communal Councils and Participatory Democracy in Chavez's Venezuela'. *Latin American Perspectives* **44**(1): 140–158.

Yashar, D. J. (2005) *Contesting Citizenship in Latin America: The Rise of Indigenous Movements and the Postliberal Challenge*. Cambridge University Press, New York.

Zúquete, P. (2008) 'The Missionary Politics of Hugo Chávez'. *Latin American Politics and Society* **50**(1): 91–121.

Newspapers

El Universal (2013) *Seguidores de Maduro en Amazonas claman por mejoras eléctricas*. El Universal, 6 April. [WWW document]. URL http://www.eluniversal.com/nacional-y-politica/elecciones-2013/130406/seguidores-de-maduro-en-amazonas-claman-por-mejoras-electricas [accessed 7 July 2016].

Medina, F. (2014) *El abrazo que asfixia*. El Universal, 23 June. [WWW document]. URL http://archivo.derechos.org.ve/derecho-de-los-pueblos-indigenas/el-universal-el-abrazo-que-asfixia [accessed 7 July 2016].

4

Oil's Colonial Residues: Geopolitics, Identity, and Resistance in Venezuela

DONALD V. KINGSBURY

University of Toronto

Venezuela has been an oil country since the early twentieth century. Of course, oil contours the economies, the geography of town and country, the reasons for and technologies of warfare, the limits and prerogatives of sovereignty, and the exploitation and desecration of environments and their inhabitants in all late modern states. However, it does so unevenly. If all of modernity is soaked to its bones with oil, Venezuela's position within that modernity is different from producer and consumer states like Canada, Norway or the United States. For Venezuela oil is linked to a deformed republican project. It has become perhaps *the* dominant signifier of underdevelopment.

In Venezuela, oil occupies an important place in the discursive universe of underdevelopment, one that has historically produced a self-defeating political subject among elites in Venezuela and which exacerbates already marked anxieties of vulnerability, dependency and modernisation. These anxieties are internalised and reproduced in what I describe – adapting the work of Aníbal Quijano to what Fernando Coronil suggestively described in terms of a 'global division of nature' in the modern world system (Coronil, 1997: 29-42) – as the coloniality of oil. Coloniality naturalises, hides and rewrites maldevelopment as underdevelopment. It obscures historically rooted processes through which the developed world of the North Atlantic has actively hindered economic growth and political independence in the South. The seemingly neutral category of underdevelopment in turn suggests the developing world need only catch up (Coronil, 2011: 246; Escobar, 2012: 6). Coloniality is a uniquely capitalist power formation, aimed at controlling labour and resources, but its influence spreads beyond the immediate relations of production, colonising the epistemological frameworks, assumptions and lifeworlds at the very core of modernity (Quijano, 2014: 285). More than simple racism, then, coloniality's articulation of race, development, and common sense form a matrix that shores up the profoundly unequal power relations of the prevailing global political economy.

In Venezuela, coloniality unfolds most obviously in concerns around the resource curse – in which abundance of a highly valued commodity dooms

Previously published in BLAR Volume 35, Issue 1 [04 September 2016].

a country to corruption, inequality and underdevelopment (Karl, 1997; Schubert, 2006; Naím, 2009). This curse is not merely academic. It is the topic of street corner debate, shaping the symbolic and material substance of daily life. It dominates headlines, it is a constant presence and reference in speeches, and it marks the landscape in the banners and massive public works projects of the state oil company, Petróleos de Venezuela, SA (PDVSA, Venezuelan Oil). As Coronil (1997) suggests, this symbolic and physical ubiquity has resulted in a situation in which oil forms the 'transcendent and unifying agent of the nation' such that, 'Venezuela [has] two bodies, a political body made up of its citizens and a natural body made up of its rich subsoil' (Coronil, 1997: 5). Throughout much of the twentieth century, this elite anxiety surrounding oil, race and capitalist modernity posed these two bodies on either side of an internal and antagonistic frontier. Venezuela was thus defined by oil, but also by the national project to transcend its status as a petrostate. The dialectic of this elite discourse is, finally, tragically self-defeating. The logic of coloniality – of race, place and development – results in a subject lacking faith in its ability to one day no longer 'drow[n] in the devil's excrement', as one statesman famously concluded (Pérez Alonso, 2011). This constituent pessimism of the subject – of entangled bodies drowning in oil – is the dialectic at the heart of the coloniality of oil in modern Venezuela.

This dialectic cannot be resolved. In a world system structured by coloniality, development is a forever fleeting horizon. The political sequence that begins with the *caracazo* (the explosion in Caracas) – a spontaneous uprising in response to neoliberal shock therapy in February 1989 that saw up to 3000 people killed in the subsequent government crackdown – breaks from this tragic history in a constituent refusal of colonial logics of domination and development. The electoral success of anti-systemic candidates such as Hugo Chávez in 1998 are thus catalysing symptoms of a decolonising moment in which the obsession with oil and development as the core of the national project are replaced by experiments in *autogestión* (self-management) and the self-valorisation of Venezuela's once-excluded majorities. These processes, I argue in this chapter, gesture towards a Venezuela beyond the coloniality of oil.

The chapter proceeds in three sections that trace the coloniality of oil and offer glimpses of its aftermaths in Venezuela. The first section provides a brief overview of the petroleum industry and its role in Venezuelan political economy. The second introduces the coloniality/modernity perspective and refracts this critical tradition through the civilisational anxieties of developmentalist elites in the petrostate. Here we can appreciate the extent to which political economy is as much about social reproduction as it is concerned with capital accumulation. In the conclusion, I explore potential departures from the failed dialectic of development in the late twentieth and early twenty-first centuries. From submission to refusal to construction, then, this chapter tracks the formation of and resistance to the coloniality of oil.

Political Economy and Oil in Venezuela

Oil established the vertical and horizontal vertices of national sovereignty and identity in Venezuela in the early twentieth century. The country emerged from the protracted wars of independence in 1830 as one of the poorest in Latin America: deeply indebted and with its infrastructure in ruins as elites focused more on lucre than reconstruction. The rest of the nineteenth century was defined by civil wars and fragmented sovereignty, reflecting in many ways the sorts of struggles between liberal and conservative parties, peasants and landlords, and industrialisation and agriculture witnessed throughout the region. It was thus only after the seizure of power by Cipriano Castro at the head of his armies in 1899, and then the consolidation of centralised control by his protégé Juan Vicente Gómez after 1908, that one could begin to speak of a Venezuelan nation-state in the modern sense of the term.

Gómez took over 'a country almost completely without the types of organisations or entities that could mobilise effective demands or pressures on the government' (Bautista Urbaneja, 2013: 2). As a result of this inheritance, he was able to use his position as broker between powerful foreign oil concerns and the Venezuelan subsoil to concentrate tremendous financial, political and military power in the executive branch. Without local industry of any significance and with the military power of the oligarchs and *caudillos* neutralised, a pattern developed in Venezuela whereby one's proximity to the state rather than one's control over labour power determined wealth and status (Coronil, 1997: 4; Cartay, 2005: 8). In this system of rentier capitalism the state charged foreign oil companies for access to the national subsoil and then selectively distributed rents to its allies. There is, in other words, no moment of so-called primitive accumulation by a future capitalist class so central for the self-image of the western modernity. In a more direct, perhaps Weberian register, rentier capitalism impeded the formation of a domestic bourgeoisie with eyes for local reinvestment opportunities. In similar fashion, Venezuela has consistently underperformed in the construction of a productive and financial architecture capable of absorbing increasingly large sums of surplus oil rents.

Path dependency and inertia soon set in, reinforced by an outward-facing cultural logic of developmentalist and postcolonial inferiority that only, perhaps paradoxically, increased with the nationalisation of oil in 1976. 'Some day soon […] we will look like you', said former president Carlos Andrés Pérez to one North American researcher in 1979 (quoted in Karl, 1999: 32). Development, in other words, entailed the transformation of Venezuela into a replica of the North.

Yet the amount of wealth generated by the oil industry in Venezuela is striking in every (positive and negative) sense. Venezuela was one of Latin America's fastest growing economies from 1920 until the general regional collapse
of the 1980s – at which point its decline was in many ways more pronounced
than that of its neighbours (Lander, 1996). After years of renegotiating con-
tracts with foreign oil companies, Venezuela nationalised the petroleum sector in 1976. Despite the fact that the new state enterprise, PDVSA, became
more of a 'state within a state' than a public institution subordinate to elected
political authorities (Mommer, 2003: 131), the immediate revenue benefits of
nationalisation and events in the Middle East were massive. Between 1972
and 1974 the price of a barrel of Venezuelan crude nearly quadrupled, raising
over $247 billion in export revenue by 1985. By comparison, notes Jonathan
DiJohn, during the same period exports from Brazil – with nearly ten times
the population of Venezuela – only amounted to $194 billion. At the peak of
the 1970s oil boom (1974–1978), the Venezuelan state brought in more in fiscal revenues than they had in the past 50 years combined (DiJohn, 2009: 22).
While some of these windfalls trickled down to the population at large, the
vast majority of it flowed away with the notorious corruption and inept planning of then-president Carlos Andrés Pérez, at that time in his first presidency
(1974–1979). In addition to failed development schemes (Coronil, 1997), Pérez
used the windfall to underwrite international loans – both for the government and for private sector businesses in his circle – effectively signing off
future oil profits as collateral (Mommer, 2003: 134). Even though Pérez ended
his term amid scandals concerning corruption, the poor performance of his
industrialisation schemes, and a recession visibly on the horizon, his prede-
cessor continued the practice. By the time of the collapse in oil prices and the
general regional economic crisis of the 1980s, Venezuela had gone from one
of Latin America's richest to one of its most indebted economies.

By the twenty-first century, the situation started to improve for the majority of the population. After the 'lost decade' of the 1990s – by 1997 the
percentage of the population living in poverty had peaked at 60.9 percent
and in extreme poverty at 29.5 percent (Weisbrot, Ray and Sandoval, 2009:
10) – the government of Hugo Chávez moved to democratise the distribution
of oil rents through a wide-range (and by late 2015, despite a Saudi-triggered
collapse in oil markets starting in the summer of 2014, still growing) of social
programmes. After initial clashes with the directorate of PDVSA that peaked
in a crippling lockout of the oil industry from December 2002 to February
2003, the government rolled out its *misiones bolivarianas* (Bolivarian missions),
a host of social welfare programmes that tackle, among other issues, housing,
food security, education, ecological conservation, cultural pride, cooperative
enterprises and even veterinary care. Between 2003 and 2007 'the poverty
rate was cut in half, from 54 percent of households to 27.5 percent. Extreme

poverty fell even more, by 70 percent – from 25.1 percent of households to 7.6 percent' (Weisbrot, 2008: 1). Inequality (measured by the Gini coefficient) fell from 47 in 1999 to 41 in 2008, significantly below the regional average of 50 (ECLAC, 2010: 173).

The petrostate thesis begins with the observation of these sorts of boom and bust cycles. Deficient institutions and embedded corruption in turn result in a 'paradox of plenty' in which a surfeit of oil money 'produce[s] poverty, inequality, and political crises' sowing the seeds for future, potentially more global, crises (Karl, 1999: 33). While recognising the effects described by such theories, analyses also need to recognise the structural effects of capitalism's uneven global development. Which is to say, Venezuela's oil industry did not emerge in a bubble. Nor was Venezuela somehow previously exterior to global markets. With oil, rather, Venezuela's status as a 'nature exporting societ[y]' (Coronil, 1997: 7) was reinforced, as it was integrated into an emerging global regime of energy extraction, distribution and exchange, intensifying and in some cases rerouting existing relations within Venezuela and between Venezuela and the world. More than the closed-border economism of the petrostate thesis, in other words, oil not only became a new medium through which Venezuela's status in the global economy as exporter was reinforced, as I argue in what follows it also became a new idiom through which the coloniality of power was both experienced and expressed.

Oil's place in the current Bolivarian moment exhibits the degree to which development and political economy are never simply matters of policy or economics. They are, rather, matters of the formation, placement and reproduction of individual and collective subjectivities. Since the early twentieth century this structural dynamic has been dominated by petroleum extraction, by the prerogative to progress along a civilisational path forged by European norms, experiences and narratives, and by an elite anxiety about oil's ostensible incompatibility with North Atlantic modernity. In the past, not only have all aspects of government policy been driven by the dynamics of petroleum production, so too has Venezuela's self-identification as a developing nation. To understand why this process of self-identification is more than just a reflection of material reality – as well as the mechanisms by which it becomes self-reinforcing and naturalised, and how one might hope to escape from a world structured by maldevelopment – we must now shift from political economy to epistemology. It is here that the coloniality of oil plays a vital role.

Oil and the Coloniality/Modernity Perspective

Coloniality – often articulated as coloniality/modernity to insist that one cannot decouple the 'emancipatory kernel' of Enlightenment philosophy from the ongoing experience of cultural, epistemological and physical geno-cide (Dussel, 1995b) – is an analytical field that spans academic disciplines and activist projects. Coloniality functions, according to Quijano, through ordering knowledge, identities and social position with the aim of controlling labour and securing capital through the production of raced, gendered and located bodies (Quijano, 2014: 289). While direct colonial rule in Latin America ended in the nineteenth century, coloniality persists as a logic of power, knowledge and subjectivity to the present. Critiques attuned to power's colonial functioning insist that Latin America is not merely some sort of residue of European conquest. The region has rather been a 'space where coloniality has been perpetrated and perpetuated as a function of capitalism […] an arena where multiple and conflictive struggles are being fought and where knowledge is not just appropriated and recycled but produced both in dominant and dominated languages and cultures' (Moraña, Dussel and Jáuregui, 2008: 16). The critique of coloniality, then, exposes fields of contestation once covered over by the common sense of developmentalist discourse. It contends that our profoundly uneven global economy adheres through erasing and deflecting ways of being, knowing, working and relating that are not in line with the (self-serving) of the North Atlantic. Coloniality is, in other words, a life world, the stuff of everyday habit and common sense (Ari, 2014).

Quijano contends that if explanations of colonialism emphasise how power operates most recognisably as an external relation of physical domi-nation, the violent extraction of value through slavery and *enconmienda*, and militarised control over territory, coloniality 'consists, in the first place, of a colonisation of the imagination of the dominated; that is, it acts in the interior of that imagination, in a sense, it is a part of it' (Quijano, 2007: 169). Elsewhere he observes that coloniality 'determine[s] the social geography of capitalism' (Quijano, 2003: 208); it underlies 'all forms of the control of subjectivity, culture, and especially of knowledge and the production of knowledge' (Quijano, 2003: 209). As a logic, then, coloniality naturalises asymme-tries and structures of domination and submission, forming and placing subjects through binaries and exclusions: modern/non-modern, devel-oped/developing, European/non-European – to list only a few examples. Within the topography established by these boundaries, Latin America has since the sixteenth century played the subaltern foil to Europe's dominant and developed role as the world's unique vector of 'linear, unidirectional, and continuous' historical progress (Quijano, 2014: 287).

In Dussel's words (1995a), more than 'discovering' or 'inventing' a new world, colonisation entailed the 'covering over' of existing ones. This oper-ation is repeated every time a modern value – democracy, individualism, scientific inquiry, rationalism – is posited without taking into consideration the foundational genocides against the indigenous peoples and African slaves on which modernity was founded. In this moral universe, what is more, superiority and culpability are inversely but non-causally related, rendering questions of development and underdevelopment circular, onto-logical, and genocidal (Dussel, 1995b). The third world is underdeveloped because it is underdeveloped, the rich are rich because they are rich.

Coloniality is a logic that traverses global and local power relations. It constitutes the epistemological ground of the North Atlantic's domi-nance over the Americas. It operates perhaps most importantly through the self-perceived gap between local rulers and their racialised others in places like Venezuela. In this sense Latin America becomes less a geographical designation and more a tragic attempt by elites transform themselves into Europeans (Mignolo, 2005: 58-60). As a divisive and ultimately self-defeating developmentalist logic, then, coloniality provides the intellectual architec-ture for a series of exclusions that predate and adapt to the formation of the Venezuelan petrostate.

For example, North Atlantic oil countries are defined as sites of consump-tion. Especially throughout the twentieth century they have been defined by petroleum at the end of its commodity chain, resulting in zones of protected convenience – of open roads, suburban sprawl and the middle classes of the mid-twentieth century. According to oil's colonial logic they remain so, despite (for example) the United States and Canada's increased twenty-first century dependence on extractive industries and financial speculation tied to tar sands and shale fracking (Mitchell, 2013: 259).

When citizens of the global North raise alarms over oil they are concerned that the convenience, freedom and wealth of oil-driven industrialisation has poisoned the planet and should thus not be repeated. Such concerns reinforce the modern/colonial hierarchy under the guise of eco-consciousness, divid-ing the world into good (or at least piously guilty) oil countries and bad (irre-sponsible, short sighted, polluting) ones. In this post-petroleum developmen-talism the North is the agent of Enlightenment; the South is an ill-disciplined pupil.

For producer states like Venezuela oil is considered a curse. Here the religious language insinuates a metaphysical explanation lurking behind modernity's inequalities. Oil's stain spreads, causing corruption and mal-forming productive and economic infrastructure like some sort of original sin. The petrostate in Venezuela has been described as particularly overpowering – 'magical', in Coronil's terms. As a rent-seeking and dis-tributing entity, it has transformed nature into the trappings of modernity at no direct cost to the people. According to Arturo Uslar Pietri, who among other things is something like the father of petro-scepticism in Venezuela, oil 'eroded the morals' of the population (Uslar Pietri, 1989: 112). Given the coterminous historical relationship of the oil economy and the modern nation-state, furthermore, Venezuela has never organically developed the sorts of institutions and subjects necessary for navigating such riches responsibly. To take just one characteristic comment on this dynamic, 'the issue is not the oil, but the political and economic system that predated it […] unlike the West's developed democracies, newer oil-states avoided going through the arduous process of extracting taxes from a reluctant population, granting rights in return' (Schubert, 2006: 65). Leaving aside for one moment the question of lateness – Norway only started exploiting North Sea deposits in the late 1960s and industrialised extraction in Canada's Athabasca Tar Sands is a largely twenty-first century phenomenon, whereas Venezuela has been exporting since the 1920s – analyses such as these are symptomatic of the coloniality of oil in a few strikingly important ways.

First, in response to elite anxieties around development, and then oil and development, Venezuela's twentieth-century dictators found justification in positivist theories of economy, culture and society that placed blame for underdevelopment on the population itself. According to these scientific discourses, the effective constitution of Venezuelans – determined by their racial and cultural makeup, the geography of the country and their colonial history – destined them to be forever backward and hence incapable of the responsible practice of democracy (Tinoco Guerra, 2010: 101; Urbaneja Bautista, 2013: 77). The best form of republican government was thus developmental dictatorship. No other, it was concluded, could maintain order and peace while transforming the population – via every measure from education to eugenics – into properly modern citizens (Herrera Salas, 2005: 75-76). A majority of the citizenry was correspondingly infantilised, ignored and violently repressed for stepping out of the roles proscribed by the state's architects of development (Cartay, 2005: 196).

The coloniality of oil results in a common sense conclusion on the political cultures of petrostates. While an attention to culture offers a healthy corrective to economism – the notion that political experience is subordinate to the economic mode of production – it also has the effect of individualising structural global inequalities and of blaming the underdeveloped for their underdevelopment. A further consequence of this dynamic is the reinforcement of the normative assumption, quite prominent among intellectuals trained in the North Atlantic, that the most desirable form of politics is the liberal social contract. The problem with petrostates is thus not a given industry, but rather that state-society interactions are not based on relations of exchange. As a result, subjects lack the autonomy necessary for effective individuality and citizenship. Finally, these sorts of pronouncements on the resource curse and the petrostate recognise that citizens must be formed over a potentially long and difficult period of time. While this final aspect importantly implies that citizens are made rather than found in some a contrived state of nature, it also harks back to the exclusionary positivisms of Venezuela's past: since citizens are produced rather than born, democracy need only apply to those who qualify for participation. Matters of political and economic importance are thus best left to the experts.

Long before the petrostate thesis, Venezuelan pundits have been preoccupied by the effects oil might have on the moral fibre and economic performance of the country. As early as 1936, Arturo Úslar Pietri warned of the need to *sembrar el petróleo* (sow the oil) lest Venezuela fall into the state of economic and moral degradation he saw as 'inevitable' for a society that was less a country than a 'parasite' feeding off a particular industry (Uslar Pietri, 1989: 113). As long as Venezuela is defined by oil, it cannot hope to define itself as modern.

However, the call to sow the oil has historically carried a deeper resonance among elites than the economic call to diversify the economy, as it has been articulated within a larger civilisational discourse of concern around Venezuela's identity as a developing nation. Perhaps the most telling expression of this discourse has been the policy – up to and during the dictatorship of Marcos Pérez Jiménez (1948–1958) – of importing skilled labour from Europe to modernise the oil industry. Venezuelans, it was supposed, lacked the technical competence and the work ethic to do so themselves. 'Foreigners assumed the characteristic role of modernisers, confronted by a backward labour force that had to be transformed' (Tinker Salas, 2009: 95). The habits of modernity, in other words, had to be *imported* to Venezuela from afar. Venezuelans could at best hope to learn by proximity and to one day pass for moderns themselves.

The political sequence taking place in Venezuela since the 1990s – first in resistance to neoliberalisation and then with the institutional changes that followed the election of Chávez in 1998 – breaks with this self-defeating subject and the coloniality of oil. Against the technocratic imposition of structural adjustment and the elitist obsession with catching up to the North Atlantic, the Bolivarian Revolution has unfolded in the course of a decolonising moment in Venezuela. The shift is all the more striking given the liberal triumphalism after the cold war and the subsequent lack of structural alternatives to a by now all but fully consolidated globalised capital. However, just as coloniality/modernity is an arena of struggles over meaning-making, subject production and the accumulation of wealth (Moraña, Dussel and Járegui, 2008: 16), so too have been attempts to move beyond these global structural logics of domination and subordination. The process, in other words, is now more open, tentative and contingent than ever.

Towards a Rebellion against Coloniality

On 12 October 2004, activists removed the iconic *Colón en el golfo triste* (Columbus in the Sad Gulf) statue from its pedestal at the middle of the Paseo de Colón in central Caracas. In Venezuela, Columbus Day had been celebrated as the *día de la Raza* (day of the race) – commemorating the encounter of the Genovese privateer with what would become the Américas as the foundation of the *mestizo* Latin American race – since 1921. The activists who removed the statue of Columbus effectively pressed an important symbolic decree made by the president two years earlier into a physical reconfiguration of the capital city's mythic and aesthetic make-up. In Decree 2028 of 10 October 2002, Chávez renamed 12 October the *día de la resistencia indígena* (day of indigenous resistance). The decree highlights the way in which previous governments 'celebrated' and 'exalted' colonisation and its racial legacies. 'The concept of race', it continues, has been noted as a 'basic category of the relations of domination within the colonial system established in the Américas since the arrival of Europeans'. It argues that changing the name of the national holiday is a necessary first step towards recognising the 'pluriethnic and pluricultural' identity of Venezuela and a means of overcoming 'colonial and Eurocentric prejudices that persist in the study and teaching of history and geography' (Presidencia de la República, 2002).

By 2009, the last of Caracas's statues of Columbus had been removed from the Parque Calvario. The park's name and its Christian connotations was renamed in honour of Ezequiel Zamora – the nineteenth-century general who rallied peasants under the slogans 'Tremble, Oligarchs!' and 'Everyone is Equal, down with the *Godos* [Spaniards/oligarchs], property for the commons, we are constructing a homeland for the Indians' (quoted in Müller, 2001: 39). In 2015, President Nicolás Maduro presided over the erection of Columbus's replacement at the *Paseo de Colón*: a muscular and combative rendering of the cacique Guaicaipuro – a chief famous for leading the anti-Spanish resistance at the time of colonisation, who is central to popular spiritualist movements and who has figured prominently in the iconography of the Bolivarian Revolution.

Acts such as the toppling of the Columbus statue, and the resignifying of spaces and public holidays are symptoms, not drivers, of a longer-term process in which the racialised inequalities always lurking beneath the established façade of a harmonious 'racial democracy' are exposed (Herrera Salas, 2005: 86; Quintero, 2012: 163). In the place of entrenched modern/colonial discourses that linked development to the transcendence of both Venezuela's racial and cultural composition as well as its petrostate status through European immigration, the bettering of the race and the inculcation of a protestant work ethic (Herrera Salas, 2005; Quintero, 2012), contemporary movements distance themselves from entrenched hierarchies and lingering Creole racisms. The result is a complex of direct actions, cultural formations and affirmations, and an inclusive experimentation with new forms of social organisation and participation. Veteran Afro-Venezuelan activist and theorist Jesús 'Chucho' García has described this in terms of a need to construct a situated 'alternative to development' from a base in Afro-Indigeneity. Failure to orient the trajectory of the revolution by the 'shared but differential responsibilities' to reverse the genocidal and ecocidal effects of the modern/colonial world, he warns, will only reproduce the disasters of previous generations (García and Quintero, 2002; García, 2015a, b). In short, what is necessary is not only to merely 'sow the oil' and develop, but rather to dismantle the colonial architecture of developmentalism as experienced both in Venezuela's position in the capitalist world system and in the reproduction of social hierarchies at the level of the subject.

The pressing need to construct alternatives *to* development has been recognised on an appreciable scale since the crises of neoliberalisation in the 1980s and 1990s. In spite of itself, structural adjustment and neoliberalisation also opened up space for the contestation and dismantling of aspects of Venezuelan developmentalism and racial democracy. In the ensuing social upheavals, newly mobilised political subjectivities stepped away from the failed dialectic of the coloniality of oil. The decolonising moment that distinguishes much of the present from recent memory, in other words, begins with the experiments in *autogestión* and other grassroots rebellions against austerity and neoliberal globalisation that preceded, triggered and animate the most progressive aspects of the Bolivarian Revolution.

Autogestión refers to self-organisation in political, economic and social relations. It also suggests the formation of alternative modes of engagement: a politics beyond the citizen-state relation, modes of production based in collective and democratised workplaces, and urban networks of mutual aid that aim to supplant traditional (and often corrupt) authorities. When most successful, the operations of *autogestión* force existing institutions to adapt to the organisational power of the new bodies – from self-management to *cogestión* (co-management), in other words. In twenty-first-century Venezuela, these modes of postliberal sociality are perhaps best seen in the 'protagonistic citizenship' of occupied factories and socialist production centres (Azzellini, 2015), and calls to construct a 'communal state' from the aftermaths of representative democracy (Ciccariello-Maher, 2014).

As the neoliberalising state withdrew from its welfare functions, autonomous social movements – especially strong in the urban periphery – reshaped the definition and practices associated with urban and civic space. For example, Sujatha Fernandes (2007) notes that with austerity and the discrediting of traditional power brokers like electoral parties and trade unions, women formed new political spaces and created new roles for themselves. In the face of a traditionally hierarchical, clientelist and *machista* political culture – technologies by which modern/colonial and capitalist social relations are reproduced in the most intimate and quotidian of experiences (Quijano, 2000: 76) – women formed and politicised already existing gendered spaces. From these autonomous spaces – such as soup kitchens and the *círculos femininos* (women's circles, that often emerged as schisms or offshoots from movements and neighbourhood associations otherwise dominated by men) – poor and predominantly non-white women became powerful brokers for their communities in negotiations with state and non-state institutions. In other words, as previous regimes of political legitimacy and behaviour collapsed, women challenged the place and status of the domestic sphere and the reproduction of life itself, insisting these be considered public, political and collective (Ciccariello-Maher, 2013; Motta, 2013).

During the 1990s, new leaders of the political left, such as Aristóbulo Istúriz in Caracas, attempted to support and institutionalise autonomous bodies such as the *círculos* (neighbourhood assemblies), *mesas técnicas* (working groups), and social businesses as recognised players in the increasingly *de facto* if not *de jure* directly democratic governing of the city (López Maya, 2011: 14). For example, the *mesas técnicas de agua* (MTA, water working groups) were formed during the Istúriz administration and were active from 1993 to 1996. These bodies (dismantled shortly after Istúriz was replaced as mayor of Libertador, the largest municipality in the capital, by Antonio Ledezma in 1995) were coordinated between community assemblies, government officials and the city-owned water provider, Hidrocapital, to plan and provide potable water to the neediest parts of Caracas. The memory of the MTAs as a project in building *cogestión* (co-management) from emergency *autogestión* would eventually be resurrected in 2001. They have since spread throughout the country as the preferred model for the management and development for water infrastructure. By 2007 there were over 2700 MTAs across Venezuela (López Maya, 2011: 29).

It bears emphasising that social organisation based on *autogestión* in Venezuela emerged not from ideological preference but rather out of necessity. Put differently, autonomous self-organisation is a way to negotiate a difficult existence for those pushed to the margins of capitalist economies and societies; it is first and foremost a fact, not a political programme. Where Venezuela differs by the 1990s and into the twenty-first century, however, is that these facts have moved to the centre of political life and increasingly shaped the collective imaginary of what by 1998 was called the Bolivarian Revolution. The emphasis on new political subjects is thus not to suggest that the daily practices carried out to negotiate the raced, gendered, and geographical exclusions of twentieth-century Venezuela were not always-already political or politicised (Duno-Gottberg, 2013). It is rather to recognise the novelty of a political sequence that follows the lead of bodies once excluded from the modern/colonial-capitalist world system.

More recently, the state has attempted to incorporate and normalise *cogestión* into the political infrastructure of Venezuela in the form of the *consejos comunales* (CCs, communal councils). Among their many functions, the CCs act to facilitate participatory budgeting and a means to circumvent the clientelist machines still very much in effect in much of the country – especially in the poorest areas of the rural and urban peripheries. CCs receive funds directly from the central state in order to avoid interference from entrenched and corrupt local officials. Importantly, however, the 2005 law by which the councils were created 'does not give any entity the authority to accept or reject proposals presented by the councils' (Azzellini, 2013: 27). In other words, while funds come from the state, no strings are attached, thus avoiding the traditional concern among analysts surrounding vote-buying (for this latter reading from a North Atlantic and Liberal perspective, see Hawkins and Hansen, 2006; Corrales and Penfold, 2011).

An emphasis on collective and horizontal forms of economic production and management also distances the Bolivarian moment from key aspects of the petrostate and the coloniality of oil. For example, the 1999 Constitution, which mandates that the government recognise, promote and protect worker self- and co-management, and *Misión Vuelvan Caras* (Mission About Face – now renamed Mission Che Guevara), that aids in coordinating, training, and funding communal and collective businesses. By September 2006, already roughly 12 percent of the national workforce was employed in the social economy (Harnecker, 2007: 28-29). By contrast, the oil industry has never directly employed a significant portion of the population. Salas notes: 'in 1941 the number of people on the payrolls of all the major oil companies accounted for 1.9 percent of the labour force, and by 1948 it had peaked at 4.5 percent […] in the 1970s improvements in technology diminished the need for workers in the industry, except those with superior skills' (Tinker Salas, 2009: 172). In the 2013–2019 National Plan for Social and Economic Development collectives, communes and mixed companies are posed as primary tools for construction of a systemic alternative to 'destructive and savage capitalism' that can guarantee social stability and 'the greatest degree of happiness' for the population (Gaceta Oficial de la República Bolivariana de Venezuela, 2013: 11). The key here is not just that the Venezuelan state supports alternative economics, or that Bolivarian economic policy has taken a more explicitly socialist approach to familiar goals of state planners to internally diversify an economy over reliant on oil exports, but that it is has been driven to do so by a citizenry that organises itself in opposition to the modern/colonial logics of development in Venezuela.

The extent to which the state's attempts to translate political and economic *autogestión* into *cogestión* can capture and extend the advances of a larger decolonising moment remains unclear; it is a work in progress. And this would always be the case, regardless of the electoral and institutional make-up of the government. This is because decolonisation neither begins nor ends as a project of the modern state, Venezuelan, Bolivarian or otherwise. At best, the state can operate as a powerful ally in the search for an alternative to development and the dismantling of the modern/colonial world system. At worst, even the best-intentioned regimes risk reproducing the tragic dialectic of development and coloniality so rooted in the identity of 'nature exporting socieities' (Coronil, 1997: 7). As the Bolivarian Revolution moves into an increasingly uncertain and hostile national, regional and global conjuncture, it will do well to recognise the strengths of its origins. From this perspective, a future political economy will have less to do with the extraction and circulation of commodities and more to do with the production of social relations capable of pressing the current decolonial moment to its most radical conclusions.

Like most of the region, the Venezuelan economy in the twenty-first century became superheated due to a boom in primary product exports and the industrialisation of China. The boom in oil prices facilitated a wave of social spending that was unprecedented even in Venezuela, where schemes to spend the country's way into modernity have a long and storied record. Fifteen years on, this expansionary cycle has ended (ECLAC, 2015). By December 2015, these economic woes and the uninspiring performance of the Maduro administration after two years in government led to the massive defeat of the ruling United Socialist Party of Venezuela in legislative elections.

In the weeks following the elections, the parade of triumphant post mortems for the Bolivarian Revolution issuing from the mouthpieces of the North Atlantic have been as predictable as they have been overstated. According to this line of reasoning, the Bolivarian Revolution can be reduced to the figure of the former president, Hugo Chávez, and the stated goal of constructing a 'socialism for the twenty-first century' was little more than the latest familiar and sad iteration of a failed populism in Latin America. As Mexican neoliberal strategist Jorge Castañeda concluded a decade ago, 'Chávez is not Castro; he is Perón with oil' (Castañeda, 2006: 38). Echoes of Castañeda have animated much discussion of the Bolivarian process ever since: experiments in the democratisation of consumption and the president's attempts to stake out an independent path in international relations were deemed irrational and dangerous. The sentiment, as well as uglier and more red- and race-baiting barbs, has been the sermon of the domestic opposition in Venezuela since Chávez's election in 1998.

These analyses miss what is distinctive about the Bolivarian process in large part because they are reflective of what I have described in this chapter as the coloniality of oil. From this perspective, any attempt to forge alternatives to development, or to build a politics that displaces the authority of experts and politicians trained in the North Atlantic is doomed to failure at best, but is usually also seen as dangerous and destabilising. Put in the theoretical language of the modern/colonial reproduction of political subjectivity in places like Venezuela, the biggest threat to the tragic dialectic of developmentalism in not to counter thesis with antithesis. It is, rather, to reject the failed dialectic in its entirety.

The Bolivarian project is distinct from its predecessors in the degree to which it has been animated not only by alternative development schemes – regional integration, multidirectional and multipolar trade and foreign policy, south-south development – but the degree to which these moves have also embodied attempted alternatives to the patterns of maldevelopment rendered as common sense by the coloniality of power. This is why concerns over the ostensible new dependency of Venezuela and Latin America on China, or of the end of historically high oil prices, or even the electoral reversals suffered by the Maduro government miss the mark. The importance of the Bolivarian experiment in Venezuela lies not in the investment of oil money in public infrastructure, an approach that defined the dictatorships and pacted democracy of the twentieth century as much as it has the protagonism of the twenty-first. What is key is, rather, the degree to which these projects have been driven from below, by the excluded, who cannot and will not be easily pushed back into previously dominant modes of obedience, passivity and silence.

In other words, rather than worrying over its status as an oil country, or answering the impossible riddle of how best to catch up with Europe, social change in Venezuela is driven by an insistence that its identity is based in the expression and generation of political subjectivities – the non-white, the purposefully non-modern, the informal, the poor the multitude – covered over and excluded throughout the twentieth century. And in so doing, it recognises that the question and pursuit of modernisation has always been a trap. In so doing it breaks from the coloniality of oil.

Acknowledgements

Many thanks are in order to V. Rivas, S. Antebi, J. Price, L. Schwartzmann, G. Cederlöf, C. Hebdon, T. Enright and A. Hirsch for their helpful comments and suggestions.

References

Ari, W. (2014) *Earth Politics: Religion, Decolonization, and Bolivia's Indigenous Intellectuals*. Duke University Press: Durham.

Azzellini, D. (2013) 'The Communal State: Communal Councils, Communes, and Workplace Democracy'. *NACLA Report on the Americas* **46**(2): 25–30.

Azzellini, D. (2015) *La constucción de dos lados: poder constituido y poder constituyente en Venezuela*. El Perro y la Rana: Caracas.

Bautista Urbaneja, D. (2013) *La renta y el reclamo: ensayo sobre petróleo y economía política en Venezuela*. Editorial Alfa: Caracas.

Cartay, R. (2005) *Fábrica de ciudadanos: la constucción de la sensibilidad urbana (Caracas 1870–1980)*. Fundación Bigott: Caracas.

Castañeda, J. (2006) 'Latin America's Left Turn'. *Foreign Affairs* **85**(3): 28–43.

Castro-Gómez, S. (2008) '(Post)Coloniality for Dummies: Latin American Perspectives on Modernity, Coloniality, and the Geopolitics of Knowledge' in M. Moraña, E. Dussel and C. Jáuregui (eds.) *Coloniality at Large: Latin America and the Postcolonial Debate*. Duke University Press: Durham, 259–285.

Ciccariello-Maher, G. (2013) *We Created Chávez: A People's History of the Venezuelan Revolution*. Duke University Press: Durham.

Ciccariello-Maher, G. (2014) 'Building the Commune: Insurgent Government, Communal State'. *South Atlantic Quarterly* **113**(4): 791–806.

Coronil, F. (1997) *The Magical State: Nature, Money, and Modernity in Venezuela*. University of Chicago Press: Chicago.

Corrales, J. and Penfold, M. (2011) *Dragon in the Tropics: Hugo Chávez and the Political Economy of Revolution in Venezuela*. Brookings Institution Press: Washington, D.C.

DiJohn, J. (2009) *From Windfall to Curse?: Oil and Industrialization in Venezuela, 1920 to the Present*. Pennsylvania State University Press: University Park.

Duno-Gottberg, L. (2013) 'Mala conductas: nuevos sujetos de la política popular venezolana'. *Espacio Abierto* **22**(2): 265–275.

Dussel, E. (1995a) *The Invention of the Americas: Eclipse of the 'Other' and the Myth of Modernity*. Continuum Press: New York.

Dussel, E. (1995b) 'Eurocentrism and Modernity (Introduction to the Frankfurt Lectures)' in J. Beverly, J. Oviedo and M. Aronna (eds) *The Postmodernism Debate in Latin America*. Duke University Press: Durham, 65–76.

Dussel, E. (2000) 'Europe, Modernity, and Eurocentrism'. *Nepantla: Views from the South* **1**(3): 465–478.

Economic Commission for Latin America and the Caribbean (2010) *Time for Equality: Closing Gaps, Opening Trails*. [WWW document]. URL http://www.cepal .org/publicaciones/xml/1/39711/100604_2010-115-SES-33-3-Time_for_ equality_doc_completo.pdf [accessed 20 August 2014].

Economic Commission for Latin America and the Caribbean (2015) *Latin America and the Caribbean in the World Economy*. United Nations: Santiago.

Fernandes, S. (2007) 'Barrio Women and Popular Politics in Chávez's Venezuela'. *Latin American Politics and Society* **49**(3): 97–127.

Gaceta Oficial de la República Bolivariana de Venezuela (2013) Ley del Plan de la Patria: Segundo Plan Socialista de Desarrollo Económico y Social de la Nación, 2013–2019. [WWW document] URLhttp://gobiernoenlinea.gob.ve/ home/archivos/PLAN-DE-LA-PATRIA-2013-2019.pdf [accessed 21 August, 2014].

García, J. (2015a) *1492: Cambio climáctico y afroindianidad*. [WWW document]. URLhttp://www.aporrea.org/actualidad/a215659.html [accessed 1 November, 2015].

García, J. (2015b) *¿Qué está pasando con las empresas socialistas en Barlovento?* [WWW document]. URL http://www.aporrea.org/actualidad/a213507.html [accessed 1 November, 2015].

García, J. and Quintero, C. (1999) *Afroindianidad: desarrollo sustentable*. Ediciones los Heraldos Negros: Caracas.

Harnecker, C. (2007) 'Workplace Democracy and Collective Consciousness: An Empirical Study of Venezuelan Cooperatives'. *Monthly Review* **59**(6): 27–40.

Hawkins, K. and Hansen, D. (2006) 'Dependent Civil Society: The Círculos Bolivarianos in Venezuela'. *Latin American Research Review* **41**(1): 102–132.

Herrera Salas, J. (2005) 'Ethnicity and Racism: The Political Economy of Racism in Venezuela'. *Latin American Perspectives* **32**(2): 72–91.

Karl, T. (1997) *The Paradox of Plenty: Oil-Booms and Petro-States*. University of California Press: Berkeley.

Karl, T. (1999) 'The Perils of the Petrostate: Reflections on the Paradox of Plenty'. *Journal of International Affairs* **53**(1): 31–48.

Lander, E. (1996) 'The Impact of Neoliberal Adjustment in Venezuela, 1989–1993'. *Latin American Perspectives* **90**(23): 50–73.

Mignolo, W. (2005) *The Idea of Latin America*. Blackwell: Malden.

Mitchell, T. (2013) *Carbon Democracy: Political Power in the Age of Oil*. Verso: New York.

Mommer, B. (2003) 'Subversive Oil' in S. Ellner and D. Hellinger (eds) *Venezuelan Politics in the Chávez Era: Class, Polarization, and Conflict*. Lynne Rienner: Boulder, 131–146.

Moraña, M., Dussel, E. and Jáuregui, C. (eds.) (2008) *Coloniality at Large: Latin America and the Postcolonial Debate*. Duke University Press: Durham.

Motta, S. (2013) 'We Are the Ones We Have Been Waiting For: The Feminization of Resistance in Venezuela'. *Latin American Perspectives* **40**(4): 35–54.

Müller, L. (2001) *La guerra federal en Barinas (1859–1863)*. Ediciones de la Universidad Ezequiel Zamora: Barinas.

Naím, M. (2009) 'The Devil's Excrement'. *Foreign Policy* **174**: 160–159.

Pérez Alfonzo, J. P. (2011) *Hundiéndonos en el excremento del diablo*. Banco Central de Venezuela: Caracas.

Quijano, A. (2000) 'El fantasma de desarrollo en América Latina'. *Revista venezolano de economia y ciencias sociales* **6**(2): 73–90.

Quijano, A. (2003) 'Colonialidad del poder, eurocentrismo, y América Latina' in E. Lander (ed.) *La colonialidad del saber: eurocentrismo y ciencias sociales*. CLACSO: Buenos Aires, 201–246.

Quijano, A. (2007) 'Coloniality and Modernity/Rationality'. *Cultural Studies* **21**(2-3): 168–178.

Quijano, A. (2014) 'Colonialidad del poder y clasificación social' in D. A. Clímaco (ed.) *Cuestiones y horizontes: antología esencial*. CLASCO: Buenos Aires.

Quintero, P. (2012) 'La invención de la democracía racial en Venezuela'. *Tabula Rasa* 16: 161–185.

Sanoja Obediente, M. (2011) *Historia sociocultural de la economía venezolana*. Banco Central de Venezuela: Caracas.

Schubert, S. (2006) 'Revisiting the Oil Curse'. *Development* **49**(3): 64–70.

Tinker Salas, M. (2009) *The Enduring Legacy: Oil Culture, and Society in Venezuela*. Duke University Press: Durham.

Tinoco Guerra, A. (2010) 'Arturo Uslar Prieti y el antipositivismo en Venezuela'. *Utopía y Praxis Latinoamericana* **15**(48): 97–105.

Uslar Pietri, A. (1989) '¿En qué medida se ha cumplido el vaticinio de Uslar Pietri ("Ahora", 1936) sobre el parasitismo rentista en la Venezuela petrolera?' in F. Mieres (ed.) *Hacia la Venezuela post-petrolera*. Academia Nacional de Ciencias Económicas: Caracas, 105–121.

Watts, M. (2004) 'Resource Curse?: Governmentality, Oil, and Power in The Niger Delta, Nigeria'. *Geopolitics* **9**(1): 50–80.

Weisbrot, M. (2008) 'Poverty Reduction in Venezuela: A Reality-Based View'. *ReVista Harvard Review of Latin America* Fall 2008. [WWW document]. URLhttp://www.cepr.net/documents/publications/weisbrot_revista_fall_2008.pdf [accessed 20 August 2014].

Weisbrot, M., Ray, R. and Sandoval, L. (2009) 'The Chávez Administration at 10 Years: The Economy and Social Indicators' [WWW document]. URL http://www.cepr.net/documents/publications/venezuela-2009-02.pdf [accessed 20 August 2014].

5

Somatic Power in the Bolivarian Revolution: Biopolitics and Sacrifice in the Case of Franklin Brito

PAULA VÁSQUEZ LEZAMA

French National Centre for Scientific Research

Franklin Brito died in August 2010 in a storeroom at the Caracas Military Hospital. On 12 December 2009, a criminal court had issued an order to transfer him to said establishment. A joint police and military unit cleared out the encampment where he had carried out his sixth hunger strike – a mat, a chair and a few belongings– which had been set up on the pavement in front of the doors of the Caracas offices of the Organisation of American States (OAS). Brito was 1.90 metres tall and weighed 60 kilograms when he was arrested after a three-month hunger strike. He could barely walk. The unit that removed him and shoved him into an armoured transport was made up of 60 police officers and some members of the National Guard. Farmer Franklin Brito had undertaken six hunger strikes between October and December 2009; on one of these strikes he mutilated the little finger of his left hand in protest against the confiscation of his farmland and his tractor. During fieldwork in Caracas in 2011, I met Franklin Brito's daughter and wife in order to write the history of his hunger strikes.

In this chapter I will examine the various aspects of the political discursive and symbolic struggle that led Brito to his death, and the existential dimension of the political sense of his ordeal. The analysis of Brito's extreme corporeal action that I present proceeds along three lines. The first addresses what the Brito case tells us about the social conflicts that affect Venezuelan society, in particular access to land, since the conflict that motivated Brito's strike was a land tenancy problem derived from the attempts at agrarian reform during the Bolivarian Revolution led by Hugo Chávez. Initially, Brito was not allied with any political cause; his arrival on the public stage did not result from a collective claim but rather a personal demand for justice.

The second line of inquiry addresses the place Brito occupies in the political sphere, showing the vicissitudes of his trajectory towards being recognised as a legitimate plaintiff. I shall attempt to discern the often

Translated by Luis Carpio and Jacinto Fombona.

invisible and non-explicit mechanisms through which power is exercised progressively to undermine the striker's human condition, ending with his total non-recognition as an individual with rights. The third analytical element developed here relates to the connections between embodiment and biopolitics, in the sense proposed by Michel Foucault at the end of the first volume of his *History of Sexuality* (1978). This chapter draws on my research on Venezuela, which has demonstrated a transformation of the physical body into a political body. My previous publications (Vasquez Lezama, 2010, 2014) shed light on the configuration of various biopolitics implemented by the Chávez regime, the most significant of which was the displacement of the population and the confinement of the victims of the tragic mudslides of 1999 in Vargas State that affected the Venezuelan coast in 1999.

By contrast, in Brito's case his physical body, as well as his voice, are the place and the means of protest. He was reduced to a condition in which he had no voice as a political subject or even as a citizen. Hence, his annihilation as a subject and reduction to a physical body show how he became an individual 'subject to' rather than 'subject of', following the difference that Foucault drew between subjection and subjectivation (1994: 556). Tragically, in the self-inflicted ordeal of his hunger strike, Franklin Brito's physical body became a site where the diverse social and political conflicts that characterise the Bolivarian Revolution converged.

The Brito Case

In 1998, on his rise to power through democratic means, Lieutenant Colonel Hugo Chávez convened a Constituent Assembly which one year later drafted and approved a new Constitution. On 30 July 2000 the newly denominated Bolivarian Republic of Venezuela held general elections through which the president was re-elected, and a new National Assembly elected, given that the old Congress and Supreme Court had been dissolved to make way for the new institutions. The government gained the majority of the governorships and seats in the National Assembly. Even though the conditions for Chávez to exercise power could not have been better, in 2001 the National Assembly authorised him to govern by decree for a year. Forty-nine decree-laws were enacted in the framework of the powers granted by the Enabling Law, which affected the distribution and tenancy of land, banking operations, freedom of the press, private property and the regime of oil exploitation. With the Land Law, which was never subjected to parliamentary or public debate, came the first moves in an attempt at agrarian reform which prioritised collective property and gave the National Lands Institute great scope for discretion. In 2006, the Bolivarian project set the goal of achieving what was termed 'Twenty-First-Century Socialism' by means of the Communal State. The Revolution's official discourse held that this state is founded upon participation but, in reality, a profoundly vertical political practice prevails, whereby all power is concentrated in the executive branch. On live television during his visits to every corner of the country, Chávez ordered the expropriation of lands, banks, businesses and hotels. He consolidated a mode of governance without institutional mediation.

In 1999, with the intention of developing more resistant strains of *ñame* (yam or *Discorea*), a greatly prized tuber in the Caribbean, Franklin Brito, a farmer, agricultural producer and biologist, acquired 290 hectares from the state under the legal formula of 'definitive onerous title' in the Sucre Munici-pality of Bolívar State, 800 kilometres south of Caracas, in the Guayana region. Brito had some training in agronomy and, although he had not completed his Bachelor's degree, he had studied biology and agronomy at the Univer-sidad Central de Venezuela. He combined work at the farm, which he called 'Iguaraya' in honour of his wife's surname, with his job as a biology teacher at the town's secondary school. His wife, Helena, was a primary school teacher. They lived with their three children in a modest house at the farm and had a lorry to transport the produce which they marketed through small distribu-tion networks.

For approximately three years Iguaraya was quite productive in water-melon, papaya and yam. The latter thrives best in the forestry reserve zone, where it is very complicated to combat fungus with pesticides. According to Ángela Brito, Franklin's eldest daughter, her father had found out that in Costa Rica they had combated a similar plague to that which attacks yam by planting more resistant seeds. And that is what he proposed: to bring in fungus-resistant seeds. Brito presented a report showing those findings to the Corporación Venezolana de Guayana (CVG), an organisation that fosters the development of this southern region of the country and draws financing from funds generated by the mining and the steel industries. During the era of 'Great Venezuela' in the 1970s oil boom, the CVG was a very powerful cor-poration that financed large-scale development projects. What Brito did not know then was that the mayor's office planned to solve the problem of disease in the plantations with the use of agrochemicals and had already requested financing from the CVG.

According to Ángela, her father's report went through the National Assem-bly and was evaluated by the Instituto Nacional de Investigaciones Agrícolas (INIA, National Institute for Agricultural Research), the latter having recom-mended her father's project. Given this judgment, the CVG declined to finance the mayoralty's project. In the video recorded by Franklin Brito in 2009, on the 93rd day of his hunger strike, he explains what happened in a coherent and structured manner:

They intended to solve the problem of a disease in the yam fields using agrochemicals and I recommended using a resistant variety. Because of this intervention, the mayor's project was not financed by the CVG and thus began the harassment against me and my family. (Brito, 5 October 2009)

As a result of the report on yam, Brito was dismissed from the state secondary school. Ángela later told me that her father began the hunger strike because he was unjustifiably fired from the school, probably because the headmistress was the mayor's cousin. One day the doorman shut the door in his face and he was never allowed in again. Brito gathered signatures from all the students, but it was all in vain. A few days later the Britos' farm was invaded. Alleged farmers occupied the lands through the small road that joins the property to the main highway passes. They were left isolated. Helena remembers the befuddlement at the stripping of their lands:

Everything depends on the mayoralty and agriculture. We depended on the aid of relatives, of my father and my sister-in-law. We made lodged formal complaints, but no one listened to us. We were like that for two years and Franklin was very depressed.

Ángela elaborates on the methods used by the 'neighbour', the occupier of the land, to impede access to Brito's property:

At first they made a fence and then a ditch so we could not pass through the only access. My father would knock down the fence and go through it. Later, the neighbour made a bigger ditch and placed an armed guard there. Another time they hired someone who beat my father in the street. He threatened him and told him that if he crossed again they would kill him. (Interview, Ángela Brito)

The enabling laws enacted by Chávez at the start of his mandate created *cartas agrarias* (agrarian letters, which provide provisional titles of land property to occupiers) and with them the legal basis, termed by government itself as provisional, that authorises 'peasant families' to occupy state-owned lands administered by the National Lands Institute (INTI). Therefore, if the invaders of Iguaraya farm were in possession of agrarian letters, they were acting with the blessing of the local, and even national, governments.

Brito and his family left their land, abandoning their house and crops. Helena remembers that, determined to 'take extreme measures to see if anyone listened', they embarked on a long road of seeking justice, which first involved 48-hour vigils outside the gates of the Miraflores Presidential Palace

(Interview, Elena Brito). From there, they went on to the Vice-Presidency, where the entire family stood guard for eight days. On the ninth day they were driven away.

On 10 November 2005, Brito used gardening shears to cut off the phalanges from the little finger of his left hand in front of the Supreme Court in Caracas. He did this after calling some journalists and announcing a peaceful protest. The mutilation was filmed and transmitted on the afternoon newscast. From that point on, President Chávez intervened in the matter, designating a commission that would travel with Brito to the farm. Brito came into disagreement with the commission en route, when he realised that its purpose was not to revoke the invaders' agrarian letters but to negotiate with them: 'They wanted to return my land physically but not legally and I want them to acknowledge what they did to me' (Brito, 5 October 2009). The reconciliation that Chávez proposed was informal; an arrangement beyond the law and institutions, which was not a matter of justice but of personal will.

Brito's case shines a light on the question of lands and the conflicts that arose when the agrarian reform implemented by the Bolivarian Revolution was set in motion. At first, the policy of land distribution was welcomed with some enthusiasm by Venezuelan society. Many projects were prepared and the government favoured initiatives such as co-operatives and credits. The alarm bells quickly sounded as corruption, diverting of funds and government inefficiency tarnished the possibilities of success of Chávez's policies. But the euphoria generated by Chavismo in Venezuelan society left no room for a critical examination of the 'revolutionary' process.

Confinement and Biopower

Embodiment is a social experience. The concept of 'embodiment' proposed by Marcel Mauss (1999) on the social meaning of the human body in daily life is expounded in his essay on the 'techniques of the body' in the early 1930s. Grounded in a study of the body's use and its heterogeneous modes of action in different societies, Mauss considers the body to be the locus of magic, symbolism and tradition. The body, the self-inflicted ordeal and Franklin Brito's bodily control lend themselves to casuistic analysis, since the Brito case crystallises a series of unresolved conflicts in Venezuelan society. Brito's death throes at the Military Hospital in Caracas lasted several months but little was known about the conditions of his forced hospitalisation in a storage room that also housed the machinery for the building's air-conditioning. During that time there were many restrictions on his receiving visitors and only a photographer from the Venezuelan newspaper *Tal Cual* was able to gain access and take photographs which were published weeks before his death.

Brito's family and lawyer Adriana Vigilanza, obtained court authorisation for a Red Cross doctor to visit him but hospital authorities denied him access. Brito then began a six-day thirst strike until the officials responsible finally allowed the Red Cross doctor access. By this time, Brito weighed 43 kilograms. The Red Cross confirmed the precarious state of his health and recommended specialised treatment but did not comment on the conflict that had pitted Brito against the authorities. The Venezuelan government classified Brito as 'suicidal' and 'mentally unbalanced'. On 14 December 2010, five months after the striker's death, the national ombudsman Gabriela Ramírez declared that she would be accusing the Brito family of 'incitement to suicide' (Rodríguez, 2013). Similarly, she assured the press that the farmer 'did not possess the mental conditions to bear out his demands'. These assertions are congruent with those made by Caracas Psychiatric Hospital Director Ángel Arriera, a pro-government political militant and activist, who stated that Brito suffered from 'delusional disorder' and a paranoid personality (Rodríguez, 2013). For public opinion manufactured by the government, Brito went from being a hunger striker to a dangerous psychiatric patient manipulated by groups that opposed Chávez's government. This diagnosis was strongly refuted by other psychiatrists who followed the case, and the Venezuelan Association of Psychiatry published several communiqués that stated that accusing non-conformists of mental illness was tantamount to discrediting protest in the country (Rodríguez, 2013). After the farmer's death his family had to seek legal help in order to defend themselves from the charges of incitement to suicide.

During his hunger strikes Brito used a notebook to keep rigorous records of the quantity of water he ingested and of urine he passed in order to balance his hydration. When he was locked up in the storeroom, the medical personnel took away his notebook, and without that control he inevitably lost more weight and suffered physical decompensation. Once he lost consciousness and was at the mercy of the hostile medical staff; when he awoke for a few hours he was force fed. According to the medical report, he died of respiratory failure caused by septic shock, but his daughter claims that the shock was caused by abrupt and excessive rehydration. There is no doubt that Brito had already suffered from the irreparable consequences of successive and prolonged hunger strikes. However, the equilibrium between hydration and physiological decompensation that Brito managed to create by controlling his body is worthy of note, since it was a very sophisticated and efficient technique for hunger strikes. Brito's wife explains:

> The doctors could be there and know how much serum they were administering, but Franklin knew how many electrolytes that serum contained and if his body really needed that amount of electrolytes,

because he had been managing hunger strikes for many years back and there was never any decompensation. So, when Franklin's condition got worse, he told them, yelled at them: 'You are murderers, you want to kill me! You're filling me with liquids, you're filling me with sodium!' (Interview, Helena Brito)

Returning to the set of circumstances that led the Brito family to this situation in 2005, at the time of the negotiations the family was in an extremely precarious economic situation, so Brito accepted the government proposal of financial compensation in (old) bolivars equivalent to US$370,000 to make up for the unjustifiable dismissal from the school, the loss of property and damage to the crops. He also received a new tractor. Helena explained to me that they accepted that money in order to pay for the one-room lodgings the family had been residing in for several years and to pay for food.

However, the sum is not really as generous as it may seem; amongst other things, it encompassed the exoneration of a credit. In a 2009 testimony Brito clarified that this was '800 million (old) bolivars, since they were received in 2005' (Brito, 5 October 2009). According to the exchange rate in place in 2005 (when US$1 was worth 2150 bolivars), the sum was US$372,093,00. However, the amount has been the object of much speculation and is a sensitive issue for the family. Press reports that revisit the case are confusing, as they were produced after the change in currency from the bolívar to the Bolívar Fuerte (VEF) in January 2008, when the currency lost three zeroes, making 1000 bolivars equivalent to one VEF. The compensation was awarded before this change took place, thus reducing the sum in real terms.

The government handed over the money in a highly unorthodox manner; Ángela Brito recalls that cash was sent in an envelope from the Ministry for the Interior and Justice to the hospital where Brito lay recovering from one of his hunger strikes and brought by a motorcycle deliveryman and a bodyguard of the Minister for the Interior and Justice, Jesse Chacón. Brito was asked to sign an affidavit stipulating that the payment was non-binding in a court of law and later the family learned that the minister had justified the payment by claiming that Brito had sold him a house. Before returning the farm, they also asked that he sign an affidavit stating that the invasion had never taken place and that the National Lands Institute had never issued the agrarian letters pertaining to his farm. Brito refused to sign this falsehood but, once he had received the money, the government's image was saved and the case closed. At no time was there legal acknowledgement of damages nor were the agrarian letters revoked. Iguaraya's invaders withdrew from the occupied lands when they failed to receive subsidies promised to work the land. Once the most productive in the area, the property in litigation was left in utter abandonment.

President Chávez addressed the problem again in 2007 after Brito, with the help of Adriana Vigilanza, a lawyer that he found through Comité de familiares y victimas (COFAVIC, Committee for Families and Victims), took the case before the Inter-American Court of Human Rights. Brito justified the decision to amputate his finger through his belief that it was the only way for Chávez to intercede in his case. Feeling that he was neither heard nor taken into account, he believed the institutional path to be futile. His struggle was for a formality that made no sense within the networks of informal mechanisms of power and of the personal arrangements that he had to establish with those who detained him. Brito's demands were, in a sense, nonsense to the institutional logic of Venezuela's Bolivarian Revolution. In Brito's own words:

> And so, on 10 November 2005, I amputated my first finger and on 13 November 2005 the President publicly commanded the then Minister for Internal Affairs and Justice, Jesse Chacón, to solve my problem in his name. And Minister Chacón committed himself to pay me for the damage to my crops, to pay me and my wife what was owed by the Ministry of Education for three years, to return my farm and to support us through some credits to allow us to begin production anew. Minister Jesse Chacón only fulfilled the promise of paying us for the Ministry of Education's debt and the damage to the crops. The people he tasked with returning the farm said that the only way that they would return the farm was for me to sign an affidavit, with the invader beside me, in front of the invader, saying that this person had never invaded and that the INTI never granted agrarian letters encompassing my farm and because I would not agree to do that, because it had not been so, they did not return my farm. (Interview, Brito, 5 October 2009)

It was after the amputation that Chávez turned his gaze towards Brito and intervened in the matter. As Brito points out, the president designated a commission, but the purpose of the commission was not to revoke the invaders' agrarian letters but to negotiate with them. Why were agrarian letters issued to occupy lands that were not idle? It was a blatant reprisal by the local authorities against Brito for a technical report showing that it was not necessary to purchase pesticides to combat fungus. This notwithstanding, Brito was not considered a victim, as he demanded, but as a party who had to reach an amicable agreement. The problem was that he was unwilling to negotiate; he considered himself a victim and not a party who had to reach an agreement. This way of posing the matter makes it difficult for other actors to take sides in the conflict, since this discourse is not based on the demands of a group but on the denouncement of an outrage.

Compassionate Militarism

In Chávez's carefully crafted rhetoric, since his failed 1992 coup d'état, the figure of Simón Bolívar has been of paramount importance, mainly because he stands as the symbol of national unity based on the harmonious identification of the armed forces with *el pueblo* (the people). Chavismo – the political movement created by Hugo Chávez in the 1990s – merges with a specific political and cultural tradition in which the armed forces are seen as the only institution with the historical responsibility of organising the nation-state. Furthermore, in his often highly theatrical discourse, Chávez justified the need for the military forces, especially the army, as an institution with an essential role to play in social welfare. A good example of this conception of the armed forces as a 'militia for social assistance' that transpired is Chávez's insistence that the soldiers leave the barracks and get engaged in *the* most important battle to be waged: the battle against poverty.

The issue that I want to tease out is the militaristic ethos of Bolivarianism (Carrera Damas, 1989) as a purported national ideology. In other words, the entrenched idea that the armed forces, especially the army, is the *only* institution historically capable of establishing, regulating and maintaining the Republican order, as demonstrated after the turbulent nineteenth century, when Venezuela's political fate was all but subject to the capricious authoritarianism of regional caudillos. In the case of Venezuela's greatest hero, the retelling of his 'victorious' deed, with quasi-mythological undertones, laid the foundations of what has been called a 'Bolivarian theology' (Castro Leiva, 1984) – a conception of Bolívar as a tragic hero whose selfless sacrifice constitutes the principle of both the motherland's redemption from centuries of colonialism and the people's hope of liberation – a secular yet quasi Christian narrative according to which the armed forces are 'providentially' appointed with the mission of bringing about national emancipation. The political project spearheaded by Chávez is a direct descendant of this tradition.

The political use of the Bolivarian myth – its instrumentalisation through ceaseless invocations and ever-present images – follows a strategy of hope renewal and the mobilisation of strong nationalist sentiments. Chávez's political discourse stood always in stark opposition to traditional political parties. It typified a nationalist version of the civil cult to Bolívar, in which the hero's figure became an ideological buoy to keep his strongly anti-partisan political movement afloat. In fact, it could be argued that as a political faction, Chavismo was founded on a civic-military alliance that was substantially more nationalist than revolutionary. At the beginning of 1990s, when the first *Bolivarianos* made their entry onto the political scene, their ideology did not match *at all* that of a progressive discourse or a movement of social transformation.

Quite the opposite: when they first arrived on the political scene, the Bolivarian commanders displayed an unwavering militaristic political identity: a quasi-mystical identity connected to Catholic iconography and also to popular religious imagery, which was intended to invest the Bolivarian leaders (one could say, somewhat successfully) with a quasi divine character, through the deployment of images and symbols regarded as sacred in the political arena.

The strategic merger of the civil cult of Bolívar with a radical rhetoric of social transformation was effective in bringing about the consolidation of a political consciousness governed by redemptive images, which ultimately helped legitimate the Bolivarian Revolution from 1998 until the death of its leader in 2013. As Michael Taussig has shown, by 1992 Hugo Chávez had already begun to incarnate for the popular imagination a new sacralised version of the Bolivarian cult, by presenting himself as the emissary of Simón Bolívar's spirit (Taussig, 1997: 108). His failed coup d'état was a message addressed to the people from Bolívar himself, of the beginning of a new and radically powerful chapter in the Gospel of Bolívar, according to Hugo Chávez.

The political model implanted when Chávez triumphed in 1998 was founded on an outright rejection of Puntofijismo, the previous political model, considered corrupt and inefficient in many respects as well as unable to guarantee the full exercise of social and political rights, especially for the least-favoured social classes (Rey, 1991). President Chávez's political project was also founded on a rejection of formal, liberal, 'representative democracy', but the creation of a 'participatory democracy' failed; it has never managed to become pluralist in practice (Gómez Calcano and Arenas, 2012). The vertical construction of this new bureaucracy through the subsequent creation of an official party, the United Socialist Party of Venezuela (PSUV), comes into direct conflict with the pluralist principles of the 1999 Constitution. These structural changes in the institutions gradually resulted in the almost total concentration of power in the executive.

The Brito case condenses a political logic and a way of governing that I have labelled 'compassionate militarism' (Vásquez Lezama, 2014). An authority, often military, is the one that decides who suffers and who does not, who deserves the attention of the government and who is legitimised to present demands. The power that officials bring to bear upon people's daily lives in the political system created by Chavismo is immense. The decisions that those in power make, be they due to corruption or clientelism, are justified through emotions. Brito's refusal to validate the solution proposed by Chávez demonstrates the limits of the revolutionary narrative, of the history that Venezuelan officialdom wanted to write and which, in this particular case, was unable to. In this official discourse, it was Chávez who decided what was fair and what was not. He, and only he, could solve, could resolve and dilute conflict. But Brito wanted legal recognition and rejected any compensation stemming from an amicable arrangement. In this regard, the farmer challenged the entire political edifice that characterises Chavismo: a political system where the military authority decides which social group is suffering and which not; which group, or rather, which discursive construct of a social group devised by Chávez – the 'victims' or the *pueblo soberano* (sovereign people) – will be considered as legitimate plaintiff. This operation is performed not from a legal point of view but from an emotional and affective one, rooted in the relationship that the leader establishes with his followers.

Somatic Culture

Franklin Brito's suffering physical body provokes particular emotions in a given cultural context. This context is part of what has been named 'somatic culture' (Detrez, 2002), that is, everything related to the body and translated into the common sphere of social life in a coherent manner. Brito's protest, in fact, was a somatic process, which deployed a particular corporeal practice of extreme degradation of the body, a practice that Venezuelan society rejects on the basis of its cultural principles. The media presence of images of Brito's extremely thin frame, his gaunt visage, his seated, waiting posture, shirtless and prostrate, is deeply troubling in symbolic terms. Brito was neither disenfranchised nor mad. In full knowledge of the facts, Brito placed himself in an unacceptable physical state, violating his body's integrity in order to denounce his accusers. The manner in which a culturally repugnant act is transformed into an act of protest is, above all, a political phenomenon.

Franklin Brito carried out a total of six hunger strikes, including one with lips sewn shut and the amputation of a phalanx. Reconstructing the Brito case can make it intelligible in a context and political process marked by violence. The Brito case is, in effect, a unique case, which generates problems and raises questions. The singularity of the incarnation of a conflict and the fact that Franklin Brito's was the first death by hunger strike in Venezuelan history, turn him into a sort of disruptive body that appears dramatically in the political sphere without the meaning of his action being fully understood.

Violence against oneself and self-inflicted torture are no novelty in Venezuela. However, such manifestations were restricted to closed, confined spaces, situated at the margins of society, particularly in prisons and juvenile detention centres. Franklin Brito's hunger strikes and self-mutilations, carried out in the public space and before the media, mark a before and after in the history of protest in Venezuela. It was towards the end of the 1990s that the Venezuelan press began to mention the 'blood strikes' or 'cutting' of the arms by prisoners with razor blades in order to provoke bloodletting, notably among the prisoners at El Dorado jail, an establishment situated in an isolated zone of the Venezuelan Amazon jungle in the south of the country known for having violent, subhuman conditions of detention (López Maya, 2003). Over the past 30 years conditions in Venezuelan jails have worsened; since 2004, the percentage of prisoners awaiting sentencing has oscillated between 50 and 70 percent and Venezuelan jails have been classified as the most violent in the continent with 498 dead per year in 2008 out of a population of 22,000 inmates (Clarembeaux, 2009). Blood strikes have also been reported in juvenile detention centres (Márquez, 1999: 207-208). For those social groups marginalised and subjected to violent institutional treatment, the physical body was a resource that allowed them to be seen and heard, through spectacular and extreme gestures such as self-mutilation.

President Chávez's discourse positioned him permanently as a victim: victim of his illness, victim of conspiracies and victim of the repression of his failed coup d'état through his identification with the fallen soldiers of February 1992. Following Girard (1972), sacrifice works to the degree that it is founded upon a mechanism of victimisation: the scapegoat phenomenon makes sense. With these elements to hand, let us see how the logic of sacrifice functions in Bolivarian Venezuela. The fighting between loyalist troops and coup plotters on 4 February 1992 left around 200 dead. The official count, however, is seventeen. Since the coup failed and its leaders surrendered, it was inevitable that the soldiers' deaths should have been perceived as useless. At the time of the surrender they were an unnecessary sacrifice, blood spilt in vain. The political appropriation of these deaths and their reconfiguration as images of sacrifice for the fatherland through commemoration rituals conceived and orchestrated by the Bolivarian government, would not take place until much later, once Hugo Chávez came to power in December 1998. The depictions of 4 February 1992, presented during official rituals held during Chávez's two administrations, functioned as a very efficient recovery of the language of sacrifice. The transmutation of Bolivarian soldiers into martyrs has been a difficult task for the ideologues of the Bolivarian Revolution and it is worth asking if they have really been efficient at it.

But reducing Brito to the figure of martyr is risky, as that invokes the idea of necessary sacrifice and I believe that, in the case of Franklin Brito, we see the configuration of a useless sacrifice to the extent that neither the hate nor rancour dominating the social group were removed, which would be the primordial function of any sacrificial action, following Girard. During this research I also interviewed Vilcar Fernández, a student at Universidad de los Andes in Mérida, who carried out three hunger strikes and stitched his lips shut during the student protests of 2010. The Mérida students met with José Miguel Insulza, Secretary General of the OAS in March 2011. In official media channels such as TELESUR, the students were described as a 'conservative movement'. It could be said that they were able to raise their case via the mass media more efficiently than Brito, since they managed to get the government to sit down repeatedly after holding several hunger strikes between 2009 and 2011. At the time of our interview, Vílcar Fernández believed that he had walked away victorious from his struggle against the government, having reached some agreements, and the hunger strikes had ceased.

By contrast, and in spite of COFAVIC's mobilisation before the Inter-American Court of Human Rights, there were no crowds at the doors of the hospital and no mobilisations after Brito's death. His funeral was held at Río Caribe church, very close to Irapa, Sucre State, in the east of the country, the town where he was born in September 1960. Helena Brito's reference to the shame they felt as people and as a family in the face of the profound degradation to which Brito submitted his body is significant and is part of the question of the relationship between culture and emotions. In a society in which the beauty of the body is the mirror of social priorities and aspirations (Gackstetter Nichols, 2013), Brito's actions were in fact denigrating:

> The press did not give great coverage nor was there total support. The few journalists that really approached us and did their job properly did it in the knowledge that Franklin deserved full respect and support. In the beginning it was difficult because it was a lonely struggle, a shameful struggle. We felt lonely, though our protests were public and our protest was done in the name of the rights of all Venezuelans and not in the name of the Brito family, and they dared not stand up to the government. (Interview, Helena Brito)

The dominant models of beauty and of bodily care in Venezuela are entrenched in the media space where Brito was exposed. This explains the feelings of shame and loneliness experienced by his family: the image of a man so physically degraded affords few opportunities for generating reactions other than disgust or repugnance. For Brito to be recognised as someone worthy of at least being heard required immense discursive work, because his image broke, on an aesthetic level, with very strong cultural canons and norms related to the inviolability of the body.

Conclusion

It is a principle of modernity to keep consciousness of the physical body at arm's length. But if there is a place where power manifests itself, it is precisely in the flesh of the individual, to the point that it would not be an exaggeration to speak of the incorporation of power, as shown by Ernst

Kantorowicz (1989) in a political theology essay on medieval royalty. Power becomes incarnate, but not just on the side of the powerful, the sovereign, but also on the side of those subjected to his rules. In this regard, Franklin Brito is an example of the way in which the body comes into view: his body is the only truth he had in order to be considered worthy in a given moment of his story.

Brito challenged Chavismo's political edifice insofar as it constitutes a military authority that decides which social group is suffering and which not, and which will be considered legitimate plaintiffs. Did the concrete systematic elements of the discourse of confrontation that characterised Chávez (Langue, 2014: 122) preclude the resolution of this case? Why was there nothing in Venezuelan public space to transcend and overcome the deep senses of resentment, anger and rancour of Brito's family and all the people that supported him in his struggle? In any event, this case demonstrates the limits of the revolutionary narrative, since Brito sought legal recognition and rejected any compensation stemming from an 'amicable' arrangement.

In Venezuela, the physical body has become the site for speech by those whose voices no longer correspond to the norms imposed by the state. This form of communication draws on a process of recognition of radical physical alterations as well as the Christian ethos that characterises Latin American societies. Together, these forces of recognition make the body a privileged medium for the expression of individuals' voices. The physical body is at once the place and the instrument of the protest action. Hence, Brito's case is paradigmatic and unique, since it took protest to an extreme never seen before in the country. Even though Brito's struggle was not absorbed by the fight for a collective political cause, it had universal transcendence because it condensed a series of institutional ills and incarnated them – literally – in public space. His individual action challenged the institutional system, the political regime, as well as the specific manner in which Chávez's Bolivarian Revolution conceived the power of the state.

References

Carrera Damas, G. (1989) *El culto a Bolívar*. Grijalbo: Caracas.

Castro Leiva, L. (1984) *De la patria boba a la teología Bolivariana*. Monte Ávila Editores: Caracas.

Clarembaux, P. (2009) '*A ese infierno no vuelvo*'. *Un viaje a las entrañas de las cárceles venezolanas*. Ediciones Puntocero: Caracas.

Csordas, T. (1990) 'Embodiment as a Paradigm for Anthropology'. *Ethos* **18**(1): 5–47.

Detrez, C. (2002) *La construction sociale du corps*. Seuil: Paris.

Foucault, M. (1978) *History of Sexuality, Vol. 1*. Pantheon Books: New York.

Foucault, M. (1994) *Dits et écrits IV*. Gallimard: Paris.

Gackstetter Nichols, E. (2013) 'Decent Girls with Good Hair: Beauty, Morality and Race in Venezuela'. *Feminist Theory* 14(2): 171–185.

Girard, R. (1972) *La violence et le sacré*. Hachette Littératures: Paris.

Gómez Calcano, L. and Arenas, N. (2012) 'Le populisme chaviste: autoritarisme électoral pour amis et ennemis'. *Problèmes d'Amérique latine* 4(86):13–30.

Honneth, A. (2008) *La société du mépris. Vers une nouvelle théorie critique*. La Découverte: Paris.

Kantorowicz, E. (1989) *Les deux corps du roi. Essai sur la théologie politique au moyen âge*. Gallimard: París.

Langue, F. (2014) 'Ressentiment et messianisme du temps présent vénézuélien' in L. Capdevilla and F. Langue (eds.) *Le passé des émotions. D'une histoire à vif Amérique latine et Espagne*. PUR: Rennes, 122–142.

López Maya, M. (2003) 'La protesta popular venezolana entonces y ahora: ¿cambios en la política de la calle?' *Politeia* 26: 86–99.

Márquez, P. (1999) *The Street is my Home: Youth and Violence in Caracas*. Stanford University Press: Palo Alto.

Mauss, M. (1999) *Sociologie et anthropologie*. Presses Universitaires de France: Paris.

Rey, J. (1991) 'La democracia venezolana y la crisis del sistema populista de conciliación'. *Revista de estudios políticos (nueva época)* 74: 533–578.

Rodríguez, P. E. (2013) 'Franklin Brito, a tres años de su muerte'. *Prodavinci*, 8 August 2013. [WWW document]. URL http://prodavinci.com/2013/08/30/actualidad/el-caso-de-franklin-brito-a-tres-anos-de-su-muerte-por-pedro-enrique-rodriguez/ [accessed 16 November 2017].

Taussig, M. (1997) *The Magic of the State*. Routledge: New York and London.

Vásquez Lezama, P. (2010) 'Compassionate Militarization: The Management of a Natural Disaster in Venezuela' in D. Fassin and M. Pandolfi (eds.) *Contemporary States of Emergency. The Politics of Military and Humanitarian Interventions*. Zone Books: New York, 135–149.

Vásquez Lezama, P. (2014) *Le chavisme, un militarisme compassionnel*. Editions de la Maison des Sciences de l'homme: Paris.

Interviews

Brito, Helena (2010) Wife of Franklin Brito, October, Caracas.

Iguaraya de Brito, Ángela (2010) Daughter of Franklin Brito, October, Caracas.

Fernández, Vilcar (2010) Student hunger striker from Universidad de los Andes, October, Caracas.

6

Community, Heritage and the State: Rebuilding Armando Reverón's El Castillete

DESIREE DOMEC

Independent scholar

The devastating landslides that occurred in Venezuela in 1999 also swept away El Castillete: the dwelling place and studio of Venezuelan artist Armando Reverón (1889–1954). El Castillete was one of Reverón's most intriguing artistic achievements, offering important insight into his creative process. A pleasant, medium-sized construction made from local materials, like stones, tree trunks and bamboo, with adobe walls and a palm leaf roof, El Castillete was built by the artist himself in 1921 in Macuto, a small town on the Venezuelan coast. It was spontaneously conceived to provide a suitable habitat for his imagination and need for isolation. There, Reverón captured the blinding light of the tropics and converted it into painting. Known as el *'el mago de la luz'* ('the magician of light'), Armando Reverón's immense contribution to modern art has now achieved international recognition, not least in the retrospective exhibition of the artist's work held at the Museum of Modern Art in New York in 2007 (Fig. 1).

After Reverón's death El Castillete was declared a museum, national cultural heritage, and a centrepiece in the cultural memory of the local community. Its loss occurred at a time when Venezuela's cultural institutions and policies were undergoing a period of transition and reformulation. This chapter examines how El Castillete became a contested space that elucidates tensions between the community of Macuto, invested in its recovery using grassroots tools of social empowerment to engage with public cultural institutions, and the state institutions responsible for overseeing the management of the nation's heritage. The discussion below draws on extensive ethnographic material that reveals the intimate bonds the local community established with 'Armando', as neighbours affectionately recall this member of the seaside community on the margins of the nation's art scene. It examines these emotional bonds against recent state policies devised to uproot and monumentalise Reverón's legacy that give short shrift to community involvement in what policies are developed and how they are implemented

Figure 1.   Front View of *El Caney* and Side of the Bedroom. Victoriano de Los Ríos, *Untitled*, Circa 1950, Gelatin Silver Print.

Source: Galería de Arte Nacional (GAN) Collection – Fundación de Museos Nacionales (FMN). Ministerio del Poder Popular para la Cultura.

in practice. In this sense, the article seeks to explore the importance of social participation as guarantor of the sustainability of cultural projects and the associated implementation of cultural policies.

The Artist's Studio

In his early 30s Armando Reverón withdrew from the distractions of the city in order to dedicate himself purely to painting, accompanied by Juanita, his

Figure 2. Armando Reverón, *Luz trás Mi Enramada (Light Behind My Arbour)* 1926, Oil on Canvas, 48 x 64, 7 cm.

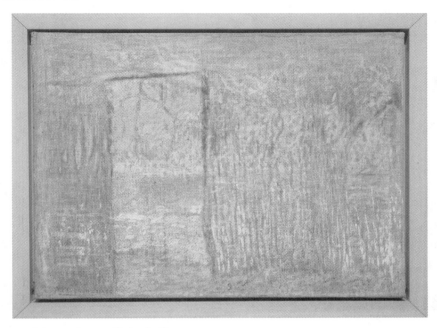

Source: Colección Patricia Phelps de Cisneros.

dedicated companion and model. In El Castillete, the artist created a unique environment, an imaginary world surrounded by dolls made using waste materials, everyday musical instruments made from cardboard and wood, and animals, especially monkeys (Peréz Oramas, 2001: 23). El Castillete began as a single hut (*caney*) known as the simplest form of tropical housing, but over the following 35 years it was in permanent transformation as the artist sought to fulfil his creative needs and desire for isolation. The site slowly expanded and successive rooms surrounded the *caney* to serve as the artist's studio. All the modules were built with half stonewalls, in part to separate the indoor spaces from the dense vegetation outdoors. Light curtains, made from cloth or reeds, served to complete the enclosures, thus allowing light to filter through into the interior spaces (Fig. 2).

Despite the singularity of El Castillete, and the fact that it was built in traditional materials and using the knowhow of the local community (Brunskill, 1971), the site was not considered a precedent in Venezuelan architecture, nor an example of vernacular architecture. This was because El Castillete was a combination of autochthonous construction techniques, which could not be

Figure 3.   View of a Patio (Courtyard) of a Colonial House. All Living Spaces are Enclosed and Surrounding the Courtyard. Casa de Estudio de la Historia de Venezuela 'Lorenzo Mendoza', Caracas.

Source: Desiree Domec.

classified under a specific housing type or geographical region (Interview with Gasparini, 2008). Indeed, its architectural features were markedly different from the typology of the traditional colonial house, which was built surrounding an internal garden (Fig. 3). In El Castillete the exact opposite occurred: the garden was not enclosed by the construction but embraced all the living spaces.

Even though the site bore a strong similarity to the typical indigenous construction known as *churuata*, which is also characterised by the use of a palm leaf roof with enclosures in braided leaves, reed or adobe (Fig. 4), El Castillete did not faithfully represent a traditional type of construction or follow an architectural plan.

Rather, Reverón chose to use organic materials randomly, in accordance with his needs and, most likely, with what was on hand. Even amid the boom in modernist architecture in 1950s Venezuela, El Castillete captured the attention of Italian architect, Gio Ponti, who, a few months after Armando Reverón died on 18 September 1954, published an article in *Domus* magazine that included a drawing by the architect made during a visit to El Castillete. Ponti's sketch became the only floor plan evidencing the distribution of the space made during Reverón's lifetime,

Figure 4. *Churuata*, Typical Indigenous Construction.

Source: Susana Arwas.

also serving to underscore the significance of the place in architectural terms (Fig. 5).

El Castillete as Museum

The first efforts to declare El Castillete a museum date back to 1964, amid measures to prevent the artist's remaining artworks falling into the unscrupulous hands of those who might take advantage of Juanita's innocence and needs (Interview with Calzadilla, 2013). On 8 October 1964, a public decree declared El Castillete a museum and set out the formalities for the acquisition of an adjacent plot of land to expand it. However, the situation did not advance so rapidly. Two years later, the poet Guillermo Meneses stated that 'the place where Reverón lived has undergone several changes and will need, if we are aiming at a real museum for Reverón, to follow the few photographic documents existing in order to achieve a proper reconstruction' (Meneses, 1966). Meneses was referring to the changes that Juanita had made to incorporate into El Castillete a couple of rooms to rent, and recommends photographs by Alfredo Boulton, Victoriano de los Ríos, as well as documentaries by Margot Benacerraf, Alfredo Anzola and Roberto J. Lucca, as references that would

Figure 5.   Drawing of El Castillete by Gio Ponti, Identifying the Use of Each Space. *Untitled*, 1954, Architect Gio Ponti, Ink on Paper.

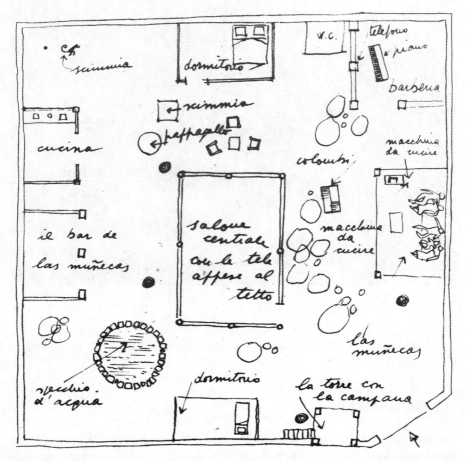

Source: Galería de Arte Nacional (GAN) Collection – Fundación de Museos Nacionales (FMN). Ministerio del Poder Popular para la Cultura.

enable the Instituto Nacional de Cultura y Bellas Artes (National Institute of Culture and Fine Arts, INCIBA) to ensure the reconstruction of the site was faithful to its original design.

In 1967, staff at the Museo de Ciencia (Science Museum) discovered boxes containing Reverón's objects and dolls (Lancini, 1967). The main theory was that they were removed with the intention of preserving them in better conditions than those to which they were exposed in El Castillete. However, they were returned there for another period and eventually made their way for good to the Museo de Bellas Artes, Caracas (Fine Arts Museum) in 1976.

Figure 6. Documents Recovered from El Castillete, Undated. Galería de Arte Nacional (GAN) Collection – Fundación de Museos Nacionales (FMN). Ministerio del Poder Popular Para la Cultura.

Source: Desiree Domec.

Meanwhile, Macuto was becoming a highly urbanised area and in 1970 the government received a request to declare a protection area around El Castillete to ensure a vegetation buffer would shield it. The Consejo del Distrito Federal (Federal District Council) declared an environmental protection area of a 60-metre perimeter around El Castillete, but unfortunately this was never applied.

In 1972, the year that Reverón's companion Juanita died, Rafael Pineda was appointed director of the INCIBA, which was in charge of overseeing the El Castillete museum project. Pineda was responsible for recovering invaluable archives that were still located at El Castillete when a fire broke out there in 1966. Some of the archives appear to be a personal collection of photographs belonging to the artist and the collection was left unaccounted for at the Galería de Arte Nacional (National Gallery of Art, GAN) until 2013, when I was presented with a box of paper items never inventoried because they were not considered of artistic interest. Today, these objects, including drawings by Juanita, photographs, and other items, are on permanent display as part of GAN's collection (Fig. 6).

From 1973, the INCIBA and other intellectuals led the project to turn the site into a museum, endowed with a small investment from INCIBA to restore the *caney*, which had been Reverón's studio, and other areas of El Castillete in need of restoration. With the aim of giving El Castillete a museological character and creating suitable areas for display, the team led further interventions into the space to adapt it to its new function. The museum was finally inaugurated on 16 June 1974 with an opening exhibition, entitled *Objetos y Obras de la Colección* (Objects and Works from the Collection), which displayed a selection of Reverón's paintings that belonged to the Fine Arts Museum, where most of the artist's works are held. The museum also featured Alfredo Anzola and Margot Benacerraf's documentaries and a video produced with photographs by Luis Brito and Sebastián Garrido. After the opening, a news article in *El Nacional* clarified the project further, stating that the Museo Armando Reverón (Armando Reverón Museum) would be a landmark 'museographic' centre (Garrido, 1978). INCIBA aimed to make the space a pioneering biographical museum, centred around Reverón, his belongings, and day-to-day life as an artist in his studio, alongside corridors and spaces annexed for temporary exhibitions of national and international artists (Hernández, 1974).

This project, however, was not to last and the museum was closed for periods between 1974 and 1981 due to budget shortages. In 1977 an Advisory Board for the Armando Reverón Museum was created to promote the museum, study a possible restoration project, and press for the acquisition of the plot of land adjacent to the museum for a purpose-built construction. After four years as a museum, El Castillete could not take further interventions; the place was starting to show signs of serious deterioration. At this point, the main objective was to restore El Castillete and prevent the total collapse of its structures, and Garrido made the following declaration to the press to this effect:

> It does not satisfy the necessary conditions. This place ought to be restored as the dwelling place of Armando Reverón, giving it its original appearance, which had been distorted with additions and modifications due to the idea of creating a museum within the original Castillete. This should be in a different place, and should fulfil the necessary conditions 'for a proper museum'. We believe that this museum could be a converted house next to El Castillete, whose owners could put it on sale. (Garrido, 1978)

The statement made clear the intention to preserve El Castillete with its original features and physically restore it. Yet from between the lines it is possible to deduce a further aim: to evoke the 'soul' of El Castillete, which was conceived as a 'proper' artist's studio museum, rather than gallery space.

As a result of the lobby, in 1979 the Instituto Nacional de Hipódromos (National Hippodrome Institute) donated 190,000 Venezuelan bolivars to purchase the house next door to El Castillete, where the children's workshop would then be located. In 1988, the museum reopened under a new legal framework, this time as a cultural foundation annexed to the National Gallery of Art and known as the Fundación Museo Armando Reverón (Armando Reverón Museum Foundation). The foundation raised sufficient funds for the purpose-built museum and the design was finally commissioned. In 1988, the Consejo Nacional para la Cultura (National Board of Culture, CONAC) and the Armando Reverón Museum Foundation requested that architect María Carlota Ibañez, head of CONAC's heritage department, undertake a full restoration of El Castillete as its decay had become a peril for visitors. This intervention was the first ethical and methodological restoration of El Castillete, producing preliminary drawings, description of materials, and careful measurements that are to this date a unique document of the exact location of each element of El Castillete. The new museum was completed by 1992 and El Castillete was dedicated exclusively to the depiction of the life of the artist (Fig. 7).

El Castillete was indeed a cultural space with endless tangible and intangible attributes that attested to the life of an extraordinarily creative man. By losing El Castillete to the landslides in 1999, the people of Macuto saw two major landmarks of their community, two elements of their cultural memory vanish, both of which, despite their different natures, offered opportunities to engage with art and heritage. One was the museum, the site of creation of an artist of international recognition and a place for creative development; the other was Reverón's dwelling place, a reference of overwhelming importance to the life of a founding member of the local community which recalls the recent history of Macuto.

Cultural Heritage Policies

It is important to situate the struggle to preserve El Castillete within the development of heritage legislation and changing concepts of heritage. In Venezuela, the discussion regarding the definition of cultural heritage was not based, as it was internationally, around concepts like natural heritage and, later on, intangible heritage. Instead, it was centred on periodical definitions; that is to say, until 1974 the official recognition of heritage in Venezuela was limited to colonial 'antiquities': artistic and historical heritage dated prior to 1830, as stated in the 'Ley de Protección y Conservación de Antiguedades y Obras Artísticas de la Nación' (1945) (Protection and Conservation Act for the National Antiquities and Works of Arts). This definition is echoed

Figure 7.   El Castillete as Museum, Undated.

Source: Galería de Arte Nacional (GAN) Collection – Fundación de Museos Nacionales (FMN).
Ministerio del Poder Popular para la Cultura.

in the 1961 Constitution, since it inherited the categorisation specified in the 1945 legislation on heritage and attributed the management of those assets to local authorities. In short, even well into the second half of the twentieth century, cultural policy-makers in Venezuela were not attempting to broaden the notion of heritage.

The legislation had two implications. First, the fact that the notion of cultural heritage was mainly associated with architectural assets and, more-over, with a very specific period prior to 1830, jeopardised almost 100 years of cultural production. Second, the delegation of responsibility for the care of cultural heritage to local authorities meant that local officials with per-haps little understanding of the assets at stake were in charge of delicate decision-making. Thus, from the mid-twentieth century onwards, when ideas of architectural modernism prevailed as a result of successive oil booms, his-torical heritage was seriously jeopardised both physically and ideologically.

In Caracas, neighbourhoods in the historical centre, such as El Conde, San Agustín del Sur, La Candelaria, Catedral and La Pastora, to name just a few, underwent radical urban transformation, and, in some cases, total destruction, owing to the appearance of mass-housing apartment buildings or modernist urban complexes, such as Centro Simón Bolívar and Parque Central, built in the 1950s and 1960s, respectively. The 1945 heritage law included the creation of a Junta Protectora y Conservadora del Patrimonio Histórico y Artístico de la Nación (National Board for the Protection and Conservation of National Historical and Artistic Heritage), but it was only in the 1970s, when architect Graziano Gasparini took over, that the first conservation projects to safeguard the remaining colonial architecture were carried out, thanks to his interest in colonial architecture (Burelli, 2009).

The twentieth century and the rush for modernisation also had implications for the vindication of indigenous legacies, since it deliberately made invisible indigenous groups and their heritage, highlighting other cultural values associated with the avant garde movements of the times (Sanoja, 1978: 4). By the late 1970s and beginning of the 1980s, the tensions in the anthropological field were very palpable, since the governing elites were doing very little to create awareness regarding indigenous legacy. This changed, however, with the advent of Hugo Chávez's socialist government, which accentuated the issue by creating a series of laws that returned land rights and even intellectual property over ancient knowledge and medicinal practices to indigenous communities (Asamblea de la República de Venezuela, 1999). From then on, the recognition of the legacy of minority groups was associated with the notion of cultural resistance, and policies were put in place to identify and foster elements of popular culture. As political discourse became increasingly radical over the ensuing years, the gap between what was considered 'elite art' and 'popular art' widened, with the latter gaining favour with cultural policies and institutions.

It was in this limbo regarding heritage legislation and cultural policy that El Castillete was located. At first, the impossibility of classifying the site in a particular architectural style led to the long negligence it suffered during the years of struggle to convert it into a museum. More recently, its timeless features did not fit into the mould of discourses of 'cultural resistance', since the Bolivarian Revolution did not see in El Castillete a representation of popular culture. It was only recently, when cultural legislation passed in 2013 emphasised the notion of *venezolanidad* (Venezuelan identity) as part of the collective imaginary, that the government labelled Armando Reverón's legacy as national cultural heritage. After fifteen years of oblivion, El Castillete was thrust into the centre of the cultural policy agenda.

Yet the history of El Castillete shows that this declaration itself was a moot point, since the site had already been declared 'immovable heritage' by the Instituto de Patrimonio Cultural (IPC) (Institute of Cultural Heritage) in 2004 during the aftermath of the landslides of 1999 (IPC, 2004: 39). Moreover, since Reverón's collection, including his handmade objects and dolls, had been under the custody of the National Art Gallery since the 1980s, they were already considered cultural assets of the nation that were thus automatically designated as cultural heritage. In short, given this uneven history, if a project for the recovery of El Castillete were finally accomplished, it would not be thanks to state institutions and heritage legislation, but rather to the active lobby by the community of Macuto, as will be shown below.

Macuto and Cultural Memory

Despite the great number of casualties during the tragic landslides of 1999, it is clear that the stories revolving around Reverón's life in Macuto have passed from generation to generation. In November 2012, during the fieldwork towards the production of a proposal for a recovery project of the site of El Castillete as part of my doctoral thesis, I interviewed Mrs Elba García, an 82-year-old lady who besides being one of the two living members of the community who had met Armando Reverón, was also his next-door neighbour. Her family's story was the story of Macuto. Sometime well into the conversation, the topic turned to the arrival of 'Armando' in Macuto. The familiar tone and use of his first name was indicative of a close relationship and friendship.

Mrs Elba recalled the fact that her father and her uncle Pepe had assisted Reverón with the construction of El Castillete, particularly the roof, which appears in Edgar Anzola's 1934 documentary about the artist. By 1951, when Elba was 21 years old, floods affected Macuto. She remembered clearly taking refuge with her family, 'Armando', Juanita and other neighbours, in a nearby building still under construction:

> It was around Christmas time when we heard the sounds of stones rolling down the mountain, we all ran to a nearby construction site. It was the first tall building and we took refuge on a second floor. Back in those days we did not struggle to find food as everyone had a small plot of land and all managed to save some of the harvest. We stayed there for a few days but we didn't get bored for one minute as Armando entertained us all day long with his stories and tales. It was a memorable time. (Interview with García, 2012)

In her testimony, Mrs García also recalls the celebrations of Corpus Christi, when Reverón was in charge of decorating the cross and organising open celebrations in the yard of El Castillete, as well as making costumes for carnival.

The younger generation also shows how deeply Reverón is lodged in local cultural memory. Elba's daughter, Dinohra, was trained at the Armando Reverón Museum's education department. Since then she has been an active member of the community and a custodian of a great deal of oral history from members of the community, since deceased. According to Dinohra's testimony, the other living person from Macuto who met the artist is called Alicia, who, although unidentified in Reverón's paintings, dressed up and posed for the artist as a young girl. When she married, her husband prohibited her from giving interviews since he considered it immoral to have posed for Reverón. Although Alicia's invaluable testimony has been censored, Dinohra insisted that Reverón used to dress his models in a flesh-coloured full-body legging to cover them up respectfully. Later, as the artist's need for isolation increased, live models were replaced by his handmade dolls.

What is interesting in Macuto is the local community's appropriation of a cultural icon such as El Castillete in order to redirect common energy towards rebuilding their community. In a sense, El Castillete stood as an emblem of the collective memory of how the community gathered together, of its own moral recovery in response to rupture and loss, followed by the need to commemorate things past and gone. In this context, it is worth noting the contributions of Jan Assmann's (1995) theory of 'cultural memory', which has expanded on Maurice Halbwach's theory of 'collective memory' and gained greater acceptance, particularly in the field of cultural studies. Collective memory 'is usually measured by the yardstick of the Nation, and is said to be collective because it is national' (Lavabre, n.d), whereas cultural memory is based on socially shared representations of the past, which are effects of the present identities that they nourish in part (Lavabre, 2010). Assmann (1995: 128) advocates the sub-divisions of collective memory into 'communicative' and 'cultural' memories, since communicative memory represents the 'person-to-person narration of recent events' and cultural memories represent ideas and beliefs that a group has carried beyond the temporal limits of personal memories. They are sometimes mythical or religious beliefs that the group has institutionalised without there being any personal memories. Memory is often regarded as a set of past events that are already settled and cannot be changed, but if we look at it in the light of cultural memory, memory is an activity occurring in the present, in which the past is continuously modified and re-described as it continues to shape the future (Bal, 1999: vii).

Cultural memory, as can be seen in the case of El Castillete, provides an ongoing relationship between past and present, promoting the renewal of local identity and values for a community stemming from a common inherited experience, thus compensating for the feeling of loss and tragedy. The fact that Macuto's community has achieved a level of engagement to the point of becoming guarantors of the preservation of the memory of El Castillete and the legacy of Armando Reverón, as a member of the community, stems from the close connection that people have established to the man behind the public persona. As Juan Calzadilla (1990) has written:

Many visited Reverón in Macuto as tourists with the intention to get hold of one of his paintings in exchange for some applause – while holding in its intimacy as a sad performance – his lucid and incomparable humour [...] this scenario only resulted in isolating the profound character of Reverón. This gave way to the thesis of his dual personality: one which was periodically assaulted by madness, while the other one held the strings of sanity allowing the artist to give himself to the creation of the artworks. This was the Reverón for the rich people, the other one for the poor.

Calzadilla's statement confirms the myth of duality behind Reverón's personality. He was both a reclusive man who used his histrionic faculties to satisfy curious visitors from the capital, and a man living a very simple life in his own particular environment (Fig. 8). It can be said that the choice Reverón made to live without commodities became a connecting factor that, through collective memory, allowed the members of the community across generations to identify themselves with Reverón the neighbour and thus the artist's legacy.

Social Organisation

Assuming responsibility for their cultural memory, Macuto's community gathered to promote an initiative to recover El Castillete. This enterprise has its origin in the social organisation of this community during the last quarter of 2006. As a response to the political shift and proposal for social empowerment during Chávez's government, cultural institutions encouraged organised communities under the scheme of *consejos comunales* (communal councils) to express their needs and expectations in a communitarian diagnostic which later would serve to identify priorities and fields in need of attention and investment from state institutions.

These socio-political changes occurred in the context of Hugo Chávez's consolidation of a socialist government that envisaged community organisation as playing a substantial role in the construction of a new social order and in which issues such as rights, equity and justice, shifted from a universal narrative to more local ones. This shift was enshrined in a discourse of the political participation of citizens in the running of public affairs, which implied a redefinition of the role of communal organisations within the state and acted as a cornerstone for the inclusion of *el pueblo* (the people) in the new constitutional order. Communal organisations are thus paramount to understanding the present and its current manifestations of an epochal change, in which the people and the state are forces that complement one another. Greater participation of civil society and the reduction of the social duties

Figure 8. *Untitled*, Circa 1954, Victoriano de los Rios, Gelatin Silver Print.

Source: Galería de Arte Nacional (GAN) Collection – Fundación de Museos Nacionales (FMN). Ministerio del Poder Popular para la Cultura.

of the state have been explained as a way of balancing the overwhelming presence of the modern welfare state in every aspect of society. In this sense, people can regain control over issues that concern them because they are able to satisfy their own needs and also to participate in the management of public affairs (Ochoa, 2000).

Since 1999, the notion of social organisation in Venezuela has been strength-ened by the Asamblea Nacional (National Assembly), the Bolivarian Con-stitution, political reforms, and by the introduction of the term *poder pop-ular* (social empowerment) into various pieces of legislation. 'Participation' or 'social empowerment', which are recurrently invoked in political discus-sion and legal terms, imply a process of mutual transformation of the person taking on a role or responsibility within the community. Participation encom-passes various spaces and structures, from informal groups of social work to the formal organisation of community councils (*consejos comunales*), which after completing a series of legal requirements established by the govern-ment, can request and access public funds to manage and carry out their own projects in every field of social interest.

In December 2006, Macuto's organised community voted for El Castillete to be included in their *diagnóstico participativo* (participatory diagnostic) on the basis that, since its disappearance in 1999, the site had been totally abandoned by the local authorities, cultural institutions and heritage management bodies and, what was worse, was being used as a truck car park by some neigh-bours (Noriega, 2013). In this process, after the identification of priorities and needs in the diagnostic, different governmental bodies, depending on their field of work, would encourage the activation of projects that would tackle those aspects in need of development. At that stage, El Castillete was clearly a central element of the community's cultural memory, a landmark charged with events and images that meant a great deal for three generations. As a result, the will to create a commemorative site of some sort was born out of the Macuto's community awareness of its significance and their need to dig-nify the site. Taking charge of their own cultural heritage and opposing the authorities' apathy, the community gathered together to create a platform of discussion in which all visions and wishes surrounding El Castillete would be revealed.

Community Museums

Community museums constitute a means for communities to get involved in the appreciation, preservation and fostering of their cultural memory. Such museums therefore contribute to the integral development of the community and, above all, to enhancing the quality of life and strengthening the sense of belonging and awareness of community identity. From this perspective, thinking about a community museum as a nucleus can only be achieved by connecting it to the past, present or future of its community. According to the principles of socio-museology, communal organisation and participa-tion are fundamental to creating a local museum's own discourse and, in turn,

Figure 9.   Community Gathering for a Working Session in Callejón San José, Macuto.

Source: Ángel Rizo.

the museum can respond to the community's own needs and expectations (Moutinho, 2010). Indeed, the promotion of social participation, accompanied by legislation inviting stakeholders to assume responsibility, care and appropriation of their heritage, set the grounds for an active and enthusiastic community to take part in the development of such a project. This, in turn, is the basis for a long-term and sustainable relationship based on the grounds of remembrance, inclusion and training.

The above ideas provided the theoretical and methodological starting point for the fieldwork underlying this chapter, which in turn was part of a broader project in which my role was to coordinate the production of a sensitive project for the site where El Castillete once stood. By request of the Fundación de Museos Nacionales (National Museums Foundation, FMN), the body governing all national museums, the fieldwork was designed around the delivery of a series of theoretical workshops ranging from history, anthropology, architecture, to art history and museology, with the aim of guiding the community of Macuto in their decision-making process and towards the conceptualisation of a holistic project for the recovery of the site (Fig. 9). The notion of intangible heritage served as the bedrock to create a project that would enhance and embrace the vision and interpretation of the cultural heritage embedded in El Castillete.

Since its loss as an element of immovable heritage, the site technically should be classified as 'intangible heritage', in accordance with Article 2.1

of UNESCO's 2003 Convention for the Safeguarding of Intangible Cultural Heritage, which states that '"intangible cultural heritage" means the practices, representations, expressions, knowledge, and skills – as well as the instruments, objects, artefacts and cultural spaces associated therewith – that communities, groups and, in some cases, individuals recognise as part of their cultural heritage' (UNESCO, 2003). To carry out the project, it was essential to provide the community with the necessary knowledge to debate the various museological possibilities available for commemorative sites, while bearing in mind the diverse and complex levels of memory inscribed in El Castillete, so as to make the right decisions for the future of the site. As a ruin, the site itself served as a testimony of the tragedy and trauma that had befallen Macuto ever since 1999. According to the material and information provided, members of the community were able to discuss notions of cultural spaces and, moreover, the delicate subject of the replica, using valid and informed arguments. The challenge of the final project was to fulfil three major objectives: (1) to foster the life and work of Armando Reverón; (2) to be a vivid depiction of his very peculiar habitat; and (3) to rebuild a museum.

The starting point of the project's conceptualistion was a shared need among members of the Macuto community to see El Castillete spatially recontextualised. This generated a need to create a working platform in collaboration with the local community, to envisage the incorporation of those willing to participate actively by gaining training during and for the site's conceptualisation, and for running the project once it materialised. Based on this premise, we gathered a very heterogeneous group including elders with very vivid memories of the original El Castillete, middle-aged people who had worked in El Castillete when it was a museum, and other members of the community, including young people willing to participate and learn more about their local history.

This process of sharing Macuto's cultural memory was initiated by a display of visual, archival and architectural material that would trigger discussions, anecdotes and memories revolving around El Castillete. This material would also be crucial for establishing a methodology for the construction, or not, of a full replica or, as was proposed, a site-museum with a replica of the *caney*, Reverón's studio. This material was studied in detail with the group in order to define to what extent the replica should emulate the original El Castillete, given that since the site underwent transformations after Reverón's death. The process of rediscovering the original – the version of El Castillete last seen by Reverón – conjured in the group members' minds the image of a site that was transgressed to accommodate new needs and uses by those who remained related to it after 1954.

The organic process of building up this image created a common sense of responsibility for respectfully redeeming El Castillete with its original aspect. Two major considerations were taken into account when drafting the methodology: first, El Castillete's original architectural features; and, second, the assistance of Reverón's neighbours in the site's original construction, as recorded in Edgar Anzola's documentary (1934). These two factors informed the proposal to carry out the construction of the replica of the *caney* as an architectural workshop aimed at fostering the knowledge of traditional construction techniques, conceived as a form of traditional knowledge and intangible heritage in need of safeguard and transmission.

The conceptualisation of a commemorative site for El Castillete was an empirical process in which the elements to be musealised gradually brought to the discussion the theoretical arguments to evaluate the project, as well as the technical means for its materialisation and interpretation. The premise of this initiative was to incorporate the community of Macuto in all phases of the project and in return to provide them with advice from professionals in the field to assure a successful enterprise from research and conceptualisation, through to planning, development, design, musealisation, communication and management. This bridge was essential to breed a new cultural life of its own through the bond established between the community and the site of El Castillete. The entailment phase between community members of different ages and the space, as well as the articulation with non-members of the community through the transmission of knowledge and the sharing of experiences, was considered vital for weaving a new relationship with the space as a relational network from which the future museum would emerge.

Instrumentalised Heritage

The case study of El Castillete provides real insights into the different levels of social negotiation involved when a community takes on the role of mediator and cultural promoter. In the context discussed experience has proved that most arts, culture and heritage projects presented by communal councils over the last decade have not received the necessary funds for their completion. This is due in most cases to bureaucratic obstacles posed by funding applications, which in turn postpone the process of social empowerment that underpinned the Chávez government's broader policies. The aim of creating a community museum for El Castillete was to realise a project that could become a model for shared and sustainable management between public institutions and local communities. The proposal depended on a series of institutions coming to an agreement and taking a proactive attitude, yet the project was thwarted when the Ministry of Culture failed to assign financial resources to it.

Paradoxically, in the face of this grassroots initiative, since 2014 there has been a rise of references in official political discourse that claim Armando Reverón and El Castillete as national heritage. On 10 May 2014, Armando Reverón's cultural legacy was declared national cultural heritage via a televised speech and the Ministry of Culture and the local government of Vargas state were tasked with producing a project to build a memorial that would incorporate a replica of El Castillete. The fact that the announcement followed a period of deep social discontent exemplified by the student protests of February that year means it could be interpreted as a political manoeuvre devised to raise the population's spirits by the fostering the spirit of *venezolanidad* enshrined in Article 8 of the *Ley Orgánica de Cultura* (2014) (National Culture Law):

> It is the duty of the State to protect and promote the constitutive popular cultures of Venezuelan identity [*venezolanidad*] according to the principle of interculturality and diversity through public policies, plans, projects programmes and initiatives aiming at fostering the creative and critical capacities of the people, with special attention to the ethnic groups in the country's borders to preserve and protect Venezuelan cultural sovereignty.

Although the legislation created a legal duty of interaction between the central government and *consejos comunales* (communal councils) for the care of cultural heritage, the case of El Castillete undermines this ideal. As the government of Nicolás Maduro, Chávez's successor after his death in 2013, claimed to become the redeemer of the memory of El Castillete by creating a project indisputably associated with the current administration by presidential decree, it ignored the grassroots work that an active community had carried out over a decade. In turn, the announcement had major physical and political implications for the management of Armando Reverón's cultural heritage. Admittedly, for the community of Macuto, its neighbours and mourners, the news came as a relief, but the governmental moves had serious outcomes. Not only did they foster a rushed reconstruction of a site with a very particular architectural character and museological features, they revealed the instrumentalisation of the cultural heritage linked to Armando Reverón and its use to create political momentum.

The aftermath of the decree was an impressive media follow-up across newspapers, online media and even Caracas's underground train network as part of a plan to 'socialise' Armando Reverón's legacy (Fig. 10). In line with Nava Muñoz's (2007) definition of 'socialisation' as the sharing of knowledge, results and processes and an acknowledgment of the need to open up to new audiences, this campaign was devised to orchestrate a massive impact on the

Figure 10. An Underground Train in Caracas with a Campaign Entitled *Arte en el Tren* (Art on the Train), 2014.

Source: Verónica Agustí.

general public by turning the tribute to Reverón into a media spectacle, and in so doing providing support for the government's vindication of this important artist's cultural memory.

The government adopted a paternalistic approach to heritage, posturing as the figure that shares, protects, provides access to Reverón's cultural heritage, while at the same time instrumentalising the artist as a flagship of *venezolanidad*. This gesture of bringing cultural heritage to the streets not only sent out the implicit message that there was no need any longer to visit a museum to be in contact with the arts; it also followed the historical precedent set by other socialist revolutions that, as Almond (1983) contends, have developed powerful cultural strategies and staged grandiose commemorations of the country's historical or cultural memory to strengthen the emotional bonds between the people and the state. In the case of Armando Reverón, the instigation to consume his imagery through media platforms and public space updated the longstanding socialist precept of removing art and culture from the museum – the elitist institution *par excellence* – and taking it to the wagons of the underground. Without entering into a discussion on the aesthetics of the campaign, the government's strategy to enter the public cultural sphere from various directions does not elucidate its formulation of a thoroughly planned and conceptualised agenda regarding Reverón and El Castillete, as much as the instrumentalisation of the cultural heritage attached to the artist as a political strategy.

The ultimate expression of the appropriation of Reverón's cultural memory was manifested in the transferral of the artist's bodily remains to the National Pantheon. Rather than the Ministry of Culture, it was the highly politicised institution of the National Assembly that mandated the transfer (Prensa Asamblea Nacional, 7 April 2015). Given that a political institution discussed and made this decision without an open discussion including art historians or Reverón's biographers, it is reasonable to conjecture that the ultimate aim was also political. Indeed, the grandiose commemoration might be construed as proof of a broader desire to create monumental sites of memory, such as Reverón's tomb, that align cultural figures and heritage with the Bolivarian Revolution. Yet the dangers of such monumentalising strategies, as cultural theorist Huyssen has pointed out, are manifold:

> The monumental is aesthetically suspect because it is tied to nineteenth century bad taste, to kitsch and to mass culture. It is politically suspect because it is seen as a representative of nineteenth century nationalisms and twentieth century totalitarisms. It is socially suspect because it is the privileged mode of expression of mass movements and mass politics. It is ethically suspect because in its preference for bigness it indulges in the larger-than-human, the attempt to overwhelm the individual spectator. It is psychoanalytically suspect because it is tied to narcissistic delusions of grandeur and to imaginary wholeness. Andreas Huyssen (1996: 191-206)

The instrumentalisation of culture as a political tool is, and will remain, a potent option for any type of government, since it has the potential to reach mass audiences. Armando Reverón, who transcended the small town where he lived on the coast to circulate in museums worldwide, fits very well into this strategic use of heritage. Ultimately, the determination of cultural heritage and its value is apt to fall into a political game. Here, the central government's discourse centred on the appropriation of Reverón's cultural memory as a flagship of a socialising process, this time in the cultural field, serves as a reminder of the power of culture as an identity constructor, since identity goes hand-in-hand with patriotism and nationalism (Kaplan, 2006: 153).

Besides the ethical issue of what would be a more suitable resting place for Reverón, according to his personality and wishes, the government's urgent move to commemorate Reverón's legacy was more than an overdue response to the loss of El Castillete: it suggests a move to eternalise a political project rendered monumental by usurping the artist's memory. With the passing of time, monuments associated with governments ought to portray their relevance in history, in the same way that when we stop experiencing memory spontaneously from within, we begin to 'design' memory, to create its external signs, and traces, such as monuments and historic buildings (Nora, 1989: 10). Seen in this context, the recent commemorations of Reverón signal not so much the wish to perpetuate *his* memory, but to leave the imprint of the current government in the collective memory of times to come.

Conclusion

By contrast to the enduring cultural memory unearthed during fieldwork in Macuto and the long-term community-centred project presented here, the recent spotlight cast on El Castillete has subjected the site to a compulsive reconstruction that, in its intention to recreate it as a whole, has simultaneously compromised its uniquely ephemeral characteristics. Evidently, the rushed nature of the presidential decree governing this recent decision not only generates uncertainty as to the outcome of the memorial, it also stands in direct antagonism to the methodology of the community museum, thus endangering the ethical treatment of the site reconstruction.

The discussion of the most appropriate and ethical approaches to recovering El Castillete have breached the bounds of discussion of museum practice to fall into politicised discourses. Besides the ups and downs of years of institutional apathy, the project to reconstruct Reverón's dwelling place with community stakeholders was an invaluable experience that confirms the importance of social participation as an important guarantor of the sustainability of a cultural project. Cultural promoters ought to foster integration, taking into account the voices of the community and incorporating them into their decision-making process and placing communities at the core of development. For their part, governmental institutions are under the obligation to provide serious training and know-how to ensure an ethical transfer of responsibilities to communities that are willing to undertake the care of their cultural heritage.

For the purpose of this research and as the restoration project was publicly announced, an inquiry was made in June 2014 about the ethical considerations of replicating El Castillete and plans to rebuild it. However, neither cultural institution in charge of the project (Instituto de Patrimonio Cultural, Institute for Cultural Heritage, IPC,) and the Instituto de la Imagen, las Artes y el Espacio (Institute for the Arts, Image and Space, IARTES) gave a reply. Now the replica of Armando Reverón's El Castillete has been fully built and the results are visible: there is no evidence of use of traditional construction

Figure 11.   El Castillete in 2017.

Source: Cruz Alejandro Sojo.

techniques and, on the contrary, the use of cement has erased the fine lines between the few existing ruins and the new additions to the site (fig. 11).

There is discrepancy in the terminology used to depict the project in the media (*El Nacional,* 2015) since official statements speak alternately of 'recreation', 'reconstruction' and 'replica', each of which entails a different approach to the site's authenticity and integrity. In terms of the relevance of replication as a way of solving historical and social needs, the replica may itself acquire use-value, especially in the case of the loss of the original. However, this requires a clear basis for its conceptualisation and justification on the part of the curator or researcher (Barassi, 2007).

Today, El Castillete awaits the construction of a purpose-built building that will serve as a visitor services centre. Besides the completion of the architectural works, the rebuilt site is yet to depict the details of each its spaces, that is, a museographical project that would shed light on the objects that inhabited it, and the uses and atmosphere of El Castillete. Even as the local community expresses satisfaction with the reconstruction of Reverón's studio as a commemorative site, the challenge remains to portray El Castillete's original function as a dwelling place and studio.

   This complex terrain serves as a reminder that social changes cannot be addressed without also tackling the problem of cultural heritage, fostering a real understanding of it and providing the necessary training to local communities to ensure that all considerations are met during a decision-making process in which they are active stakeholders. If the focus on the relevance of cultural heritage wanes, modern society can easily fall prey to the instrumentalisation of cultural memory and identity by political discourses. As Venezuelan intellectual Mariano Picón Salas (1949) put it: 'The paths of culture tend to be more silent, whispering and confidential than those that lead towards politics; the latter are more bustling and full of collective agitation [...] to invent the future, it is necessary to rethink the past; to rethink the past, we need to visit it'.

Acknowledgments

I am deeply indebted to the community of Macuto for their contribution to this research, in particular to B Reyes and D García. My deepest acknowledgement to Professor Calzadilla for sharing his knowledge and memories of El Castillete. I want to express my gratitude to G Colmenares and all active staff at the GAN for allowing me access to invaluable material and resources.

In memoriam Elba García (1926–2017).

References

Almond, G. (1983) 'Communism and political culture theory'. *Comparative Politics* **15**(2): 127-138.
Armando Reverón: 4 Testimonios (1996) Film (40 min.). Directors: Edgar Anzola (1934), Roberto Lucca (1945), Margot Benacerraf (1951). Cinemateca Nacional: Caracas.
Assmann, J. (1995) 'Collective Memory and Cultural Identity'. *New German Critique* 65: 128.
Assmann, J. (2008) 'Communicative and cultural memory' in A. Erll and A. Nünning (eds) *Cultural Memory Studies. An International and Interdisciplinary Handbook*. Duke University Press: Berlin and New York: 109-118
Maduro anuncia que obra de Armando Reverón es declarada patrimonio cultural de la nación (2014) 10 May. [Online]. Available at: https://www.youtube.com/watch?v=qEzFeLeTOpQ [accessed 7 July 2016].
Bal, M. (1999) 'Introduction'. *Acts of Memory: Cultural Recall in the Present*. University Press of New England: London, vii.
Barassi, S. (2007) 'The Modern Cult of Replicas: A Rieglian Analysis of Values in Replication'. *Tate Papers* **8** (autumn). [Online]. Available at: http://www.tate.org.uk/research/publications/tate-papers/08/the-modern-cult-of-replicas-a-rieglian-analysis-of-values-in-replication [accessed 28 October 2017].

Batallan, L. (1966) 'La arquitectura vegetal del Castillete amenaza en desplomarse en escombros'. *El Nacional*, 19 June.

Brunskill, R. W. [1971] (2000). *Illustrated Handbook of Vernacular Architecture* (4th ed.). Faber and Faber: London, 27-28.

Burelli, G. (2009) 'Graziano Gasparini: el historiador de la arquitectura colonial venezolana'. *Prodavinci*, 29 September. [Online]. Available at: http://prodavinci.com/2009/09/23/artes/testimonios-inmigrantes/ graziano-gasparini-el-arquitecto-el-historiador-de-la-arquitectura-colonial- venezolana/ [accessed: 10 December 2014].

Calzadilla, J. (1990) *Reverón, voces y demonios*. Monte Ávila Editores: Caracas.

Calzadilla, J. (2013) Personal interview with the author at the Galería de Arte Nacional.

Desvallées, A. and Mairesse, F. (2009) *Key Concepts of Museology*. Musée du Louvre/Armand Colin: Paris.

El Castillete de Armando Reverón. (2016). Film (3.53 min.). Instituto de Patrimonio Cultural. [Online]. Available at https://www.youtube.com/watch?v=Yq_ 85AaqlC8 [accessed 25 October 2017].

El Nacional (2015) 'El Castillete busca la luz' 23 August. [Online]. Available at: http://www.el-nacional.com/noticias/historico/castillete-busca-luz_ 46002 [accessed 20 September 2017].

García, E. (2013) Filmed interview with the author.

Garrido, S. (1978) 'Castillete de Armando Reverón'. *El Nacional*, 9 May.

Gasparini, G. (1986) *Arquitectura popular de Venezuela*. Armitano Editores: Caracas.

Gasparini, G. (2008) Telephone interview with the author.

Hernández, A. (1974) 'En Centro Museográfico de Evaluación de las Artes Plásticas será convertido Catillete de Armando reverón en Macuto'. *El Nacional*, 16 June.

Huyssen, A. (1996) 'Monumental Seduction' in M. Bal, J. Crewe and L. Spitzer (eds) *Acts of Memory: Cultural Recall in the Present*. University Press of New England: London, 191-206.

ICOFOM (1995) *Originals and Substitutes in Museums*. Symposium proceedings: Zagreb, October 1985.

Kaplan, F. (2006) 'Making and Remaking National Identities' in S. Macdonald (ed.) *A Companion to Museum Studies*. Blackwell Publishing: Oxford, 152-169.

Lancini, D. (1967) 'Prisioneras en cajas de madera las muñecas de Armando Reverón'. *La República*, 8 March.

Meneses, G. (1966) 'El Castillete de Reverón'. *El Universal*, 16 June.

Ministerio del Poder Popular para la Cultura de la República Bolivariana de Venezuela (2004) *Catálogo del Patrimonio Cultural Venezolano: Estado Vargas*. Instituto de Patrimonio Cultural: Caracas, 39

Ministerio Público de la República Bolivariana de Venezuela (2014) *Gaceta Oficial # 6154, 19 Noviembre*. Imprenta Nacional: Caracas.

Moutinho, M. (2010) 'Evolving Definition of Sociomuseology: Proposal for Reflection'. *Cuadernos de sociomuseologia* **38**(27). Available at: http:// revistas.ulusofona.pt/index.php/cadernosociomuseologia/article/view/ 510 [accessed 6 July 2016].

Nava Muñoz, R. (2007) 'Socialización del conocimiento académico con el uso de tecnologías de información y comunicación'. *Revista venezolana de información, tecnología y conocimiento* **5**(1): 65-78. Available at: http://www.scielo.org.ve/

scielo.php?pid=S1690-75152007000300004&script=sci_arttext [accessed 26 June 2014].

Nora, P. (1989) *Les lieux de mémoire*. University of California: Stanford.

Noriega, N. (2013) 'El Castillete de Armando Reverón es usado como estacionamiento'. *El Universal*, 11 May [Online]. Available at: http://www.eluniversal.com/caracas/130511/el-castillete-de-reveron-es-usado-de-estacionamiento [accessed 7 January 2015].

Ochoa, A. (2000) 'Community organisations in Venezuela: Toward the Disintegration of the Modern State and the Emergence of a "Community Organised" Society?' *Systemic Practice and Action Research* 13(2). [Online]. Available at: http://link.springer.com/journal/volumesAndIssues/11213 [accessed 10 May 2010].

Oramas, L. E. (2001) 'Armando Reverón: la gruta de los objetos y la escena satírica' in *El lugar de los objetos*. Galería de Arte Nacional: Caracas.

Picón Salas, M. (1940) *Cinco discursos sobre pasado y presente de la nación venezolana*. Editorial La Torre: Caracas.

Ponti, G. (1954) 'Reverón a la vita allo stato di sogno'. *Domus* **296** (July): 33-39.

Prensa Asamblea Nacional (2015) 'AN aprueba traslado de los restos de Armando Reverón al Panteón Nacional'. *Alba Ciudad*, 7 April 2015. [Online]. Available at: http://albaciudad.org/2015/04/an-aprueba-traslado-de-restos-de-reveron-al-panteon-nacional/ [accessed 9 September 2015].

Sanoja, M. (1978) 'Patrimonio histórico y desarrollismo' *Papel Literario, El Nacional*, 26 March, 4.

UNESCO (2003) *Convention for the Safeguarding of the Intangible Cultural Heritage*. World Heritage Centre: Paris. [Online]. Available at: http://www.unesco.org/culture/ich/en/convention [accessed 7 July 2016].

7

El Helicoide and La Torre de David as Phantom Pavilions: Rethinking Spectacles of Progress in Venezuela

LISA BLACKMORE

University of Essex

Outsize buildings cast the shadow of their own destruction before them
– W. G. Sebald, *Austerlitz*.
Han pasado siglos y todavía me parece vivir en un campamento.
(Centuries have passed and I still feel like I'm living in a campsite.)
– José Ignacio Cabrujas, *El Estado del disimulo*. (1987).

Spatial arrangements that herald national development are more than bricks and mortar or concrete and steel. As they shape space into specific forms, they build 'a framework for a worldview and a carcass for futurist dreams' in tune with the prevailing political and economic ideologies of their times (Boym, 2010: 64). Yet for these prospects to hold sway monumental constructions must be more than paper architecture; they must be completed and used according to plan. This raises the question of what happens when this is not the case. What can lapsed buildings tell us about the way progress is conjured through built space? And how can we think through the presence of truncated constructions on the urban landscape without reducing them to dystopian sites or aestheticised ruins? This chapter addresses these issues by examining a couple of constructions in Caracas whose grand designs were conceived as signs of unstoppable development, but whose curtailment saw them yield to precarious uses and collective amnesia.

The first is El Helicoide Shopping Centre and Exhibition of Industries (1955), a spiral-shaped modernist mall conceived and designed by Jorge Romero Gutiérrez, Pedro Neuberger and Dirk Bornhorst during the oil-rich military dictatorship of Marcos Pérez Jiménez, whose construction stuttered after the post-1958 transition to democracy. Under state control since 1976, it underwent numerous failed transformations and even became a refuge for landslide victims. In 1985, Venezuela's intelligence police took over the site and since 2010 it has been both a jail and a police training academy. The

Previously published in BLAR Volume 36, Issue 2 [05 March 2017].

second building is the Confinanzas Financial Centre (1989), better known by the moniker La Torre de David, which was designed by Enrique Gómez y Asociados for banker David Brillembourg as an icon of Venezuela's finance sector. The construction of the 45-storey tower and adjacent buildings halted after just four years amid the fall-out from the violent disturbances of the 1989 *Caracazo*, the 1992 coup attempt and the ensuing financial crisis; and after it had languished for years under state control, in 2007 squatters set up home in its concrete carcass, only to be extricated by the government four years later, leaving the building's future hanging in the balance.

Despite – or perhaps because - of their dramatic stories, El Helicoide and La Torre de David inspire impassioned reactions. But instead of probing the sites' complexities or considering their passages from blueprint to truncated monument, discussions about them tend to remain ensnared in reductive framings. Showcased in celebratory publications (Bornhorst, 2007) and high profile exhibitions like the Museum of Modern Art's recent *Latin America in Construction: Architecture 1955–1980*, El Helicoide has largely been cleansed of its problematic afterlife and merely consecrated as modernist heritage. For its part, even as the media frenzy around La Torre de David's occupation drew the building out of obscurity, as it was filtered through the polarised lenses of contemporary debates about Venezuela it was either cast as cipher of gener-alised ruin (Wilson, 2012; Anderson, 2013) or proof of governmental capacity for national renewal (TeleSUR, 2014). In such settings these problematic sites risk becoming blind spots in the nation's cultural, historical and political consciousness. Even as such buildings remain in public view, their roles as testaments to modern history are 'masked and distorted by layers of amnesia and hysteria', as Alejandro Velasco has pointed out. (Velasco, 2015: xiii).

The complexity of El Helicoide and La Torre de David's rise and fall calls for a critical framework in which political, economic and social history dovetails with aesthetic and cultural criticism. In this regard, my aim in this chapter is to develop a method that builds on analyses of architectural design, recognises the buildings as testaments to political and economic upheavals, but also as 'structures of feeling' whose aesthetic remediation offers routes to rethinking national development, urban transformation, and crisis (Williams, 1977: 132-133). Specifically, this approach entails approaching El Helicoide and La Torre de David as remnants of the 'dazzling spectacles of national progress' and boom-and-bust cycles that Fernando Coronil uncovered at the heart of Venezuela's 'magical state' and experience of modernity (1997: 1-5). More broadly, by engaging the buildings as curtailed and precarious structures, I draw on related inquiries into ruination and monumentality that have emerged alongside the current boom of 'ruin lust' (Dillon, 2014), which risks aestheticising abandoned or unfinished buildings as melancholic wreckage and thus muting their complex 'afterlives'. (Draper, 2012).

As scholars (Hell and Schönle, 2010) currently engaged in this field contend, the challenge is to approach problematic sites in such a way that they shed light on shared histories and enduring challenges. Excavating their unfinished forms and ruptured materiality thus offers a means to uncover the political, economic and social conflicts embedded in them (Gordillo, 2014). Incidentally, similar proposals are found in recent debates that call for a re-envisaging of monumentality to account for, rather than overshadow, political and social complexities. Engaging Deleuze's criticisms of conventional links between monumentality and commemoration, and the former's monolithic and intransigent postures, Jacques Rancière (2010) proposes aesthetic mediation as a means to refigure monumentality and thus attest to conflictive realities.

To this end, the discussion below establishes a framework to liken El Helicoide and La Torre de David to 'pavilions'; that is, symbolic encapsulations of national progress. Next, I leverage this conceptual tool in two interconnected directions. First, I use it to retrace the stories of the buildings' conception and curtailment through the boom-and-bust cycles of Venezuela's modern history. Second, I analyse how recent artworks develop productive engagements with these buildings' histories to refigure their vocations as pavilions and monumental contours to make room for the unpredictability of a future in a constant 'process of becoming'. (Deleuze and Guattari, 1994: 177).

The Pavilion as Spectacle of Progress

The long-standing bonds between architecture, nationhood and spectacle offer a means to bring El Helicoide and La Torre de David onto common ground. On a global level, and especially amid the quest to consolidate Latin America's emergent nation-states in post-independence, a number of spatial typologies have served as 'galleries of progress' to demarcate national identity, herald future development and to attract local and foreign capital (Andermann and González Stephan, 2006). Since the late nineteenth century, pavilions, museums, conventional monuments and constructions of monumental proportions have all served as more than architectural forms. They are discursive and exhibitionary spaces that marshal certain ideas of nationhood and forms of social and political order. (Bennett, 1995)

It is on the first of these typologies that I will draw to elucidate the two buildings under discussion here. Since its inception, the pavilion has been tasked with encapsulating ideal models of nationhood through its combination of architectural design, technologies of display, and formative itineraries (Bennett, 1995). When deployed in a prospective mode to project future development, it conjures optimistic horizons as preordained realities, forecasting guaranteed progress in line with specific economic models, usually through modes of capitalist and industrial production. As Timothy Mitchell has shown, to gain purchase for this idea the pavilion summons a 'reality effect', where forward-looking aesthetics and optimistic itinerary are presented as seamless continuations of the real world, rather than aspirational conjectures. (1989: 236)

As across Latin America, this edifying way of depicting national development swiftly gained traction in Venezuela. After 1889, successive governments commissioned pavilions to construct a 'self-portrait' to buttress the nation-state, cohere its imagined community, and legitimise models of development (Marin, 2006: 268; González Stephan, 2008). Later, Venezuelan pavilions became imbricated with the dreams of instantaneous development that the oil economy engendered as they played out the shift from traditional agricultural economy to modern oil nation. At the 1937 Paris World Fair, Venezuelan architects Luis Malaussena and Carlos Raúl Villanueva designed a neocolonial pavilion that celebrated Venezuela's Hispanic heritage and agricultural production. Just two years later, though, at New York's World of Tomorrow Fair, this traditional 'self-portrait' was replaced by a glass-walled pavilion designed by the American firm Skidmore and Owings. As it left behind pastoral and colonial heritage, the forward-looking design reinvented the nation as a key contender in global oil markets. Even though the pavilion's modish International Style bore no relation to Venezuela's architectural vernaculars at the time, the commissioners enthused about its 'absolute identification [...] [of a] burgeoning country that has already taken its path to modernisation and left its past behind' (Calvo Albizu, 2002: 331). Evidently what mattered was not that the building resembled the existing landscape, but that it heralded a nation on the up.

Literally speaking, the grand scale of El Helicoide and La Torre de David's designs surpass the pavilion's typically smaller size. The buildings were conceived as markers of Venezuela's development and economic growth at home, not abroad. Even so, the analogy I propose here is not beholden to a literal notion of the pavilion, but draws on it as a paradigm of the way spectacles of progress are staged by architectural means. The way the pavilion attempts the affective capture of its public not because its aspirational conjectures are the truth, but because 'such a notion of the real, such a system of truth, continues to convince us' (Mitchell, 1989: 236), dovetails with the function of El Helicoide and La Torre de David's forward-looking architecture as a buttress for the spectacles of progress that Coronil associates with Venezuela's modern history. It is this parallel that informs the redefinition of the two buildings as 'pavilions' and which the next section will address as it traces their conception and design through the upheavals that reduced both to phantasmal forms: sites haunted by promises of development that did not materialise as planned.

Figure 1.   Photograph of model of El Helicoide. Anon. (undated).

Source: Dirk Bornhorst Archive/ Proyecto Helicoide.

Retracing Histories of Boom and Bust

It is no coincidence that Romero, Neuberger and Bornhorst's dreamed up the idea of building El Helicoide at precisely the same time that *Time* magazine described Venezuela as the 'dreamboat' of South America: an economy buoyed up by rising oil revenues and foreign investment. Intoxicated by this boom time climate, in 1955 the three architects began designing a building that served multiple ends. It was a speculative enterprise for the firm; another foothold for Venezuela on the global map of architectural modernism; and confirmation of national development all at the same time (Fig. 1). El Helicoide's construction site was located at the Roca Tarpeya, an undeveloped outcrop located close to downtown Caracas, reached by the Avenida Fuerzas Armadas and connected to the new arteries that headed east. The rock was bulldozed into shape and clad with dual helix reinforced concrete ramps that echoed Frank Lloyd Wright's Guggenheim Museum (1943). Along with the ramps, the design featured four street-level elevators that were to provide vehicular and pedestrian access to more than 300 stores, offices, a hotel, multi-room movie theatre, television studios, car showrooms and a gas station. At the summit, a 2300 m² trade fair of oil, petrochemical, gas, iron, aluminium, and agriculture industries would be set up under a Buckminster Fuller dome to present Venezuela as an industrialised powerhouse of global proportions. (Villota, 2014: 420)

The building's audacious design and incorporation of automobile culture even earned it a place at the Museum of Modern Art's 1961 exhibition

Roads; its colossal scale and its modernist style tapped directly into debates about modern monumentality that occupied critics and architects in the mid-twentieth century. Indeed, even though it was not a state commission, El Helicoide adds weight to Gregor Paulsson's assertion in the *Architectural Review*'s seminal symposium 'In Search of a New Monumentality' that '[g]enuine monumentality can only arise from dictatorship' (Paulsson *et al.*, 1948: 123). Sixty years on, many still attribute the building to dictator Coronel Marcos Pérez Jiménez (1952–1958), since its daring style chimed with the military mandate to deliver instant modernity by channelling the nation's rising wealth into high-speed construction.

For all the impetus put behind modernist architecture during the period in which El Helicoide emerged, the period was one of significant upheavals. Military rule had intercepted the tentative process of liberalisation and democratisation that followed the protracted dictatorship of Juan Vicente Gómez (1908–1935), on whose watch oil extraction began. The late 1930s and 1940s marked a shift to centralised urban planning and investment in public works, which cemented the equation between built space and progress (Frechilla, 1994), yet for some military officers the speed of development was not fast enough. In 1948, after a military junta toppled national novelist Rómulo Gallegos, the first president voted into office through universal suffrage, a poorly masked dictatorship was installed that lasted ten years. Although the leaders promised free elections in 1952, a fraudulent count of votes installed defence minister and coup leader Marcos Pérez Jiménez in power.

As Castillo (1990) shows, the initially 'soft' dictatorship (*dictablanda*) was built on the promise of a New National Ideal: the developmentalist ideology that advocated the transformation of the physical environment to expunge the 'backward' trappings of rural life, trigger rapid development and propel Venezuela to modernity. A combination of curbed civic rights and soaring state revenues caused by the post-war demand for petroleum, the closure of the Suez Canal and the Iranian crisis of 1954 secured the dictator's seat in power (Karl, 1987: 71). The state increased regulation of oil, minerals, and private enterprise, and controlled strategic sectors of growth, like steel and electricity. Armed with an open chequebook, the regime equated nation building to the rapid construction of mass housing and infrastructure – a correlation that official propaganda entrenched by equating large-scale modernist architecture to extant modernity.

Its conception as an exponent of modern monumentality in Caracas's changing urban landscape and an exhibition centre to showcase the nation's industrial might, El Helicoide synthesised the political mandate for modernisation delivered at a spectacular speed and on a colossal scale. The speculative mode of investment behind the architects' method of selling space off plan to fund round-the-clock construction tapped into the ranking Venezuela reached between 1950 and 1957 as the country with second highest amount of foreign exchange in the world (Karl, 1987: 71). Moreover, as a cutting-edge shopping mall, the building was perfectly in tune with the ideology of capitalist growth and lifestyle trends inflected by oil culture in the 1940s and through the 1950s, which advocated social clubs, modern hotels and an expanding marketplace chock full of novel goods, imported mainly from the United States as markers of modernity (Vicente, 2003; Tinker Salas, 2009: 181- 189). Briefly put, El Helicoide was the ultimate national 'pavilion' of its time: spectacular proof that Venezuela could live up to the reports that dubbed it *The New El Dorado*. (Ward, 1957)

But when the political and economic tides changed, El Dorado did not materialise as planned. The spectacle of progress built on military rule and escalating public spending turned out to be unsustainable, as did El Helicoide's round-the-clock construction. As Karl (1987) points out, since the dictatorship had risen to power by stunting processes of democratisation cultivated between 1946 and 1948 that were leaving behind military authoritarianism, the emergence of a new crisis was just a matter of time. By 1957, the dictatorship's extravagant construction projects deepened the incipient economic and fiscal crisis. However, instead of placating Venezuela's increasingly disgruntled industrialists, the regime isolated them further by shutting them out of strategic sectors. The upshot was that conservative economic elites sided with outlawed parties like Acción Democrática, joined in calls for regime change voiced increasingly by the church, restless military officers and members of society eager to play a more active part on the political stage.

On 23 January 1958, Pérez Jiménez fled and the dictatorship came to an end. El Helicoide's architects attempted to ride out the storm over the next ten months as the political landscape was prepared for elections, leading to the Pact of Punto Fijo signed by the three main parties. In it they pledged to secure national stability and democratic rule by initiating a political truce and respecting the results of the upcoming election, but just as democracy was gaining a foothold, construction on El Helicoide stuttered. The climate of uncertainty over these transitional months had made the architects' risky sell-to-build strategy unfeasible. Despite assistance from commercial banks and the provisional post-dictatorship government, funds began to dry up, building slowe, and investors sued the architects (Bornhorst, 2007: 17-18). By 1961 the firm had gone bankrupt amid the climate of austerity advocated by newly elected president Rómulo Betancourt and the unfinished project ground to a definitive halt. The 12,000 blueprints that projected unstoppable industrial and capitalist expansion came tumbling down to earth, turning the spectacular pavilion of progress into a phantom haunted by dictatorial hubris and economic crisis.

Over the ensuing years, as Acción Democrática (AD) and the Comité de Organización Política Electoral Independiente (COPEI) took turns in power, stop-start construction stumbled along, but the unfinished spiral was overshadowed by a new megaproject: the 59-storey twin-tower residential, cultural and commercial complex of Parque Central (1970), designed by Daniel Fernández-Shaw and for a long time the tallest building in Latin America. The complex befitted the renewed spectacle of progress associated with Carlos Andrés Pérez's first term as president from 1974 to 1979. Bolstered by quadrupling revenues produced by the 1973 oil crisis, Pérez heralded a 'Great Venezuela', reviving 'the illusion that instantaneous modernisation lay at hand […] that oil money could launch the country into the future' (Coronil, 1997: 237). As the economy soared, so too did buildings and the Parque Central 'pavilion' shaped the nation up to its moniker *Venezuela saudita* – a kingdom in South America like its oil-rich counterpart in the Middle East. The state increased financing and management of extractive industries, nationalising oil and steel, encouraging import substitution, and funding the world's third-largest hydroelectric dam. Meanwhile, the private sector benefitted from high-yield investments in real estate, commerce and construction (Coronil, 1997: 246, 286). Flush with wealth, the state purchased El Helicoide in 1976, proposing numerous projects, from a cultural centre to an environment ministry and a cemetery. (Olalquiaga, 2014)

However, as Luis Herrera Campins took over from Pérez in 1979, the still empty building did not rise from the ashes, but slid further into obscurity. As heavy rains left hundreds destitute and the state turned the building into a temporary refuge, storm clouds also gathered in the economy. Boom turned again to bust as consumption outran production, foreign debt rose, oil plunged and the bolivar's Black Friday on 18 February 1983 brought an unprecedented devaluation against the dollar (Coronil and Skursi, 1991: 293). As this new crisis played out, the precarious community squatting in El Helicoide grew to some 12,000 people, who were only evacuated six years later when a local government realised the gravity of conditions on the site. After the police-led clearance in which residents were paid to demolish homes and erase traces of their dwelling, the project leaders celebrated that it had effectively 'domesticated' the building and laid out detailed plans to create a Museum of Anthropology there. (Gobernación del Distrito Federal, 1982: 7)

The museum's construction did not last long, however, but stopped a year later. It was then that the intelligence police stepped into the void and moved into El Helicoide. Still, even amid the economic downturn in which, as debt repayment overtook state-funded development, Pérez's spectacular promise of the 'Great Venezuela' lingered. Although El Helicoide was pushed from the spotlight, construction on the Parque Central towers continued during the mid-1980s and private banks invested in building new skyscrapers. It

Figure 2.   Portrait of David Brillembourg with a model of La Torre de David

Source: Ricard2 (c. 1989).

was amid the recent memories of economic boom and the enduring faith in renewed growth that investor David Brillembourg commissioned plans for La Torre de David and launched his banking group's slogan *Confinanzas: renace la confianza* (Confinanzas: confidence is reborn). Venezuela would rise again, onwards and upwards with the skyscraper's 45 storeys.

La Torre de David also sketched out the contours of an imagined nation, both developed and prosperous (Figure 2). Much as El Helicoide's architects had invested in the endurance of spectacular growth, Brillembourg gambled on a return to economic boom, projecting continued growth in the banking sector and demand for luxury office space. Albeit in a different architectural vernacular, this new 'pavilion' of prospective development was also designed to monumental proportions. As well as housing the Confinanzas financial group, the 45-storey main tower and four additional buildings would feature 30,000m2 of office space, a luxury hotel, 81 apartment suites, a twelve-storey car park, swimming pool and helipad (Urban-Think Tank, 2013: 70-73). Engaging the architectural idiom of corporate luxury and global finance, the main tower was to be decked out with a 30-metre high glass atrium and covered by a glass curtain manufactured by the same firm that had clad the ill-fated World Trade Centre (Urban-Think Tank, 2013: 87). Its location near the Miraflores presidential palace, Capitolio building, government ministries, and Central Bank would situate La Torre de David at the centre of political and economic power.

Despite the dogged optimism associated with its design, when construction started in the late 1980s the economic crisis deepened. Venezuelans' election of Carlos Andrés Pérez to a second term in 1989 suggested that the population was still invested in his promise of the Great Venezuela, but hopes of its renewal were soon shattered. In an attempt to restore confidence among foreign creditors, the *Gran Viraje* (Grand Turnaround) Pérez promised ended up replacing state-protected business with an austerity package that engendered panic among Venezuelans (Coronil and Skursi, 1991; López Maya, 2003). As the state withdrew subsidies on basic goods, ended price controls and freed up interest rates, violent protests and looting broke out in the *Caracazo* of 27 February 1989, shattering the rebirth of confidence in which Brillembourg had invested. In 1993 Pérez was impeached for embezzlement, the finance sector buckled a year later, and the Confinanzas group went down with it, turning La Torre de David into another a phantom pavilion of unrealised promises.

Over the following years, the abandoned building stood by as another sea change occurred in Venezuelan politics. The cumulative impacts of Black Friday, the *Caracazo*, and a further austerity package introduced in 1996 all exposed fractures in the two-party system and the model of democratic representation, state-led development and social and economic wellbeing that had marshalled Venezuela from dictatorship to democracy after the Pact of Punto Fijo was concluded (Cicciarello-Maher, 2014). Although, as David Smilde argues (2011: 3-6), the model had brought manifest gains in health, literacy and prosperity, its gradual weakening created room for the alternate promises of national renewal that Hugo Chávez offered voters. After leading an unsuccessful coup attempt in 1992, Chávez's election to office in 1998 brought pledges of the dawn of a new Venezuela. Out of the rubble of the conflictive 1990s, he promised to draw up a reformed Constitution that would deliver greater social justice, equity, popular participation and economic reform. (López Maya, 2005: 40-60)

Despite initial consensus, support waned amid growing radicalisation, and the national strike and coup of 2002 divided the nation into polarised groups of *chavistas* and *oposición*, whose animosities continued over later struggles for recall referendums and constitutional reforms to extend presidential terms and re-election (Cannon, 2004: 293- 298). It was in the midst of this tempestuous political climate, a particularly bad bout of torrential rains, and the continual pressures of a long-standing housing deficit that in 2007 a few hundred people took shelter in La Torre de David. Over the next few years, the population grew to nearly 4500 people, who improvised sewerage, electricity, and water systems, and replaced the glass curtain with red brick walls, living in precarious conditions against all the odds.

Suddenly, La Torre de David returned to the forefront of public debates. The state turned a blind eye to the squat until 2012 but amid media attention and confronted with one of its occupants on live television (Sarabia, 2012),

Chávez ordered an inquiry into living conditions, which led to its evacuation in July 2014. Under National Guard supervision, residents boxed up belongings and boarded buses to new government housing outside Caracas. As the evacuation advanced, government websites celebrated internal demolition work (Oficina Presidencial de Planes y Proyectos, 2014a, b) and President Nicolás Maduro declared La Torre de David a ruin of the pre-Chávez era (TeleSUR, 2014). With that the spotlight was shifted onto the horizon of a reborn socialist nation whose dawn Chávez predicted in 1999. On television Maduro handed ex-residents keys to a 'new socialist city' produced by *Constructores del Socialismo* – Builders of Socialism. (GMMV, 2013)

When the global media frenzy and government speculation about La Torre de David's transformation (Agencia Venezolana de Noticias, 2015a, b) had died down, the building slipped back into obscurity. Just a few kilometres away across the Caracas valley, El Helicoide remained embroiled in contradictions. Although a training academy had been installed there in 2010 to enact 'comprehensive police reform' (Humphrey and Valverde, 2014: 162), the site continued to serve as an improvised prison for high-profile detainees implicated in political conflicts and violent crimes. (Fernández: 2015)

Spectres Past, Challenges Present: Phantom Pavilions in Contemporary Art

This historical overview shows that as 'phantom pavilions' both El Helicoide and La Torre de David are as much haunted by the past as they are embroiled in present conflicts. Given their propensity to slip in and out of public debates, it bears asking by what other means these problematic sites might become topics of more productive, critical discussions. Through research-led websites, exhibitions and public events, Proyecto Helicoide (2013), founded by cultural historian Celeste Olalquiaga, and La Torre de David (2010), developed by artists Ángela Bonadies and Juan José Olavarría, have contributed to encouraging public engagement in the buildings they study. The artworks drawn from these projects for analysis here are significant because by summoning their roles as 'phantom pavilion', they manage to work through their complex histories, at the same time as they engage with calls for revised notions of monumentality and critical representations of ruination highlighted at the start of this chapter.

The installation *Melancolía de Roca Tarpeya. Homenaje a la traición* (Melancholy of Tarpeian Rock. Homage to Treason), by artists Rodrigo Figueroa, Marjiatta Gottopo, Federico Ovalles-Ar and Gerardo Rojas was created in 2014 for the exhibition *Helicoides posibles: visiones fantásticas* held at the Centro Cultural Chacao in Caracas and curated by Proyecto Helicoide to bring the building back into public debate (Fig. 3). In one half of the exhibition, an

Figure 3.   Installation View of *Melancolía de Roca Tarpeya. Homenaje a la traición*

Source: Rodrigo Figueroa, Marjiatta Gottopo, Federico Ovalles-Ar and Gerardo Rojas (2014).

illustrated timeline charted the history of El Helicoide, while the other displayed works by artists invited to reconceive the building in fantastical forms.
In *Melancolía* the artists used El Helicoide's truncated promises of development as a departure point to design a speculative monument, which was displayed as a scale model in the gallery alongside materials from their research
process. As Figure 4 shows, the monument was framed as a 'cenotaph' of El
Helicoide's monumental prospect and promise of development. The artists
appropriated as the structural framework for this hypothetical construction
the solid form that appears in Albrecht Dürer's iconic engraving *Melancholia
I* of 1514 (Fig. 5). Set amid a scene depicting abandoned tools and a frustrated
creator, this solid form – also known as the 'magic square' – connotes architectural failure and truncated endeavour.

Redeployed half a century later in *Melancolía*, it stands as a double of
El Helicoide: a melancholic commemoration of the Tarpeian Rock from
which the building was carved out. Although the use of Dürer's solid as an
allegorical tomb for El Helicoide's modern utopia mobilised a conventional
monumental idiom to commemorate the past, *Melancolía* did not indulge in
the 'restorative nostalgia' that reconstructs a 'lost home' as a locus of 'truth
and tradition' (Boym, 2001: 41). On the contrary, the installation literally
emptied out the causal connection between monumentality and progress.
As Figure 6 shows, Dürer's monumental 'magical square' was not rendered
anew as a spectacular or monolithic volume; it was first pared down to
its skeletal framework and placed in dialogue with El Helicoide and the
informal urban fabric in which it is embedded.

Figure 4.   Design for *Melancolía's* Cenotaph of El Helicoide

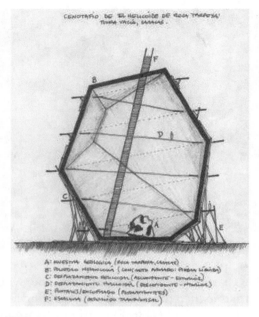

Source: Figueroa *et al.* (2014).

By stripping the 'magical square' down to its bare bones, the artists countered both the spectacular valences of the pavilion's promise to depict and encapsulate the nation, and the solidity with which monumental structures purport to embody nationhood in edifying and durable forms. In turn, the artists applied this action of voiding spectacular display and solid mass to the new monument they conjured. As can be seen in Figure 6, the 'cenotaph' is a rudimentary framework supported by scaffolds, whose spiral walkways revive a spectre of El Helicoide's optimistic itinerary. However, while the design envisaged users ascending the apparently solid monument using its walkways, they would not reach a triumphant summit but a descent into its cavernous interior. In this 'tomb', the phantom of El Helicoide's dream of instant modernity was replaced by a piece of concrete rubble. To be sure, this 'monument' was a solid mass, but one entirely out of step with the linear trajectory of progress: its reinforced concrete was supposed to connote construction, not destruction.

While these aspects focused on the unstable foundations on which El Helicoide was originally built, the hypothetical monument presented in the installation also established a dialogue with conflicts and crises of the present. The artists proposed that it be erected on the recently levelled site

Figure 5. Albrecht Dürer (1514) *Melancholía I*

Source: British Museum, Creative Commons.

of a jail called La Planta, built in 1964 only a few hundred metres from El Helicoide. Over the preceding years, La Planta had become a landmark of the deterioration, deadly riots and overcrowding that characterise Venezuela's penitentiary system (Morais, 2009) and the rising crime rates (United Nations Office on Drugs and Crime, 2012; Zubillaga, 2013) that interfere with optimistic narratives of national rebirth associated with Chávez's rise to power. Using similar methods of media coverage to those deployed during the evacuation of La Torre de David two years later, in 2012 the government ordered the prison's demolition and brought in bulldozers to reduce it to rubble on live television. As the prison was destroyed, ministers wearing hard hats announced the Bolivarian Revolution's plans to replace this site of 'horror' with a 10,000m2 communal park where life would prosper (Venezolana de Televisión, 2012). In spite of the upbeat messages that framed the clearance of space as a triumph of life over horror, its erasure simply moved the architecture of incarceration from view in order to put another large-scale – and as yet unfinished – construction in its place.

Figure 6.   Photograph from *Melancolía* showing model opposite El Helicoide

Source: Figueroa *et al.* (2014).

By summoning the jail's demolition and positing an alternate occupation of its vacant site not with a funereal 'cenotaph' but with a life-affirming park, *Melancolía* confronted the logic of erasure and reinscription that was synonymous with modernist planning and that endures today. By merging La Planta and El Helicoide's respective trajectories from jail to park, and utopian mall to police headquarters, the new public space would host past spectres. In so doing, it posited a way to look at conflictive landmarks in dialogue, rather than in isolation. Against the amnesia on which the new park was proposed, in the hypothetical site conjured by *Melancolía* architectures of development and incarceration would overlap in the sediments and rubble left by spectacles of progress, their construction and ruination. In sum, the installation experimented with an alternate mode of monumentality, that promised neither spectacular display nor intransigent postures. Instead, as *Melancolía* revived El Helicoide as rubble on the site of the demolished jail, it looked forward, positing a site in the urban landscape where the gathering of their 'afterlives' could allow 'a mode of experiencing the echoes of a past that is lost to history but that has the potential to be heard and made legible'. (Draper, 2012: 5)

Figure 7.   *Estudio fachada este*

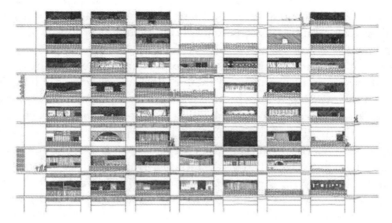

Source: Ángela Bonadies and Juan José Olavarría (2010).

Figure 8.   Installation view of *La prueba*

Source: Ángela Bonadies and Juan José Olavarría (2010).

The phantom pavilion as a site of productive encounters rather than collective amnesia is also the core of Bonadies' and Olavarría's project on La Torre de David. Their works, exhibited in Venezuela and internationally, from Germany to Mexico and Dubai, raised awareness about the building before it became a media sensation that drew accusations of misery porn (Hancox, 2014), an urban laboratory showcased at the 2012 Biennale di Venezia (Urban Think Tank, 2013; Kallipoliti, 2013), a topic of academic comment (Gordillo, 2014), or a ruin of the pre-Chávez era worthy only of demolition, as President

Nicolás initially suggested. Bonadies and Olavarría's works engage La Torre de David as a specific site shot through with structural and social challenges, and a departure point that afforded them a long view of urban design that created enduring links between architectural form and promises of national development.

In a series of meticulous pen drawings of sections of the building's façade, the artists appropriate the trope of the architectural blueprint only to problematise it by inverting its prospective temporality. As Figure 9 shows, rather than use the grid form of rational planning to propose an ideal space, *Estudio fachada este* (Study of Eastern Façade) uses it as a means of recording in detail the improvised dwellings implanted in the failed tower. Beyond the immediate depiction of La Torre de David, the façade's irregular lattice brings to mind the simple grid map of Caracas sketched out in 1567 to entrench the structure of colonial power, as well as the Monumental Plan drafted by Maurice Rotival in 1939, whose expansion of the colonial grid is credited with originating urban modernisation but whose grand designs also entailed problematic sites – like the insalubrious El Silencio area – being reduced to rubble in the name of progress (Fraser, 2000: 103-110). This potential to summon a *longue durée* of urban transformations from a fragment of the building displaces the limiting focus on its decaying monumental contours as a stimulus for ruin lust and polarised judgments. Instead, the work calls forth an imaginary of intermittent promises of spatial – and national – order from Venezuelan history, to make connections between the persistent quests devised to induce development through spatial arrangements.

While this strategy illuminates urban history, Bonadies' and Olavarría's works do not eschew the contingencies and particularities of the building's occupation. Indeed, their frequent use of installation assembles an archival scene, composed of documents charting the building's origins, photographs of its recent occupation and the objects they present – fictitiously – as vestiges of the real site, which give the materiality of the precarious structure a tangible presence. This strategy is significant precisely because it avoids reducing the building to a merely symbolic phenomenon or dystopian postcard. Instead, it brings into focus its occupation as a real human problem and in so doing pushes back against the blind eye the state initially turned to the building's perilous conditions and, more broadly, the tendency to aestheticise ruinous sites as picturesque scenes cast through romantic or apocalyptic lenses.

It is in this context that Bonadies and Olavarría's installation *La prueba* (The Test) garners particular significance. As Figure 10 shows, *La prueba* is a simple installation comprising a life-size tent of tarnished fabric. The work restages the conditions in which La Torre de David's first occupants settled there and the latter method implemented to put aspiring residents to the test referenced in its title; only if they could live amicably in a tent for a set period would newcomers be given a space to build their own apartments.

Alongside this compelling factual dimension of the work, which fabricates the tent to signal a real, material problem, the installation educes another illumination. As it privileged a provisional shelter over the building's monumental and now iconic contours, *La prueba* directly engages the spectres of precariousness this chapter has unearthed as the scaffolds for spectacle and monumentality. In so doing, it exposed other valences in the concept of the term 'pavilion', bringing to mind its etymological roots in *papillio* – the Latin word for butterfly and tent, both of which epitomise flux and provisionality. This semantic bridge elucidates the contradictory space staged in *La prueba*: monumental contours that have become a makeshift tent – stained fabric marked by a vulnerable community, in place of a glass curtain providing grand views for bankers.

Through this reading, the installation can be conceived as a renewed staging: one that puts the spotlight on the engrained indeterminacies that lurk amid the monumental buildings whose rise and fall mirrors the boom-and-bust of modern Venezuela. Much like *Melancolía*, this artwork also refigures monumentality to counter its intransigent forms by foregrounding a site that speaks to the way unstable experiential and material horizons happen gradually. While Deleuze (1994) imagined an alternate monument emerging from piles of rocks left by walkers as testimony to their common passage on a shared path, here it is the tarnished fabric of the tent in *La prueba* that conjures residual traces left by fictional inhabitants. By giving presence to provisional living conditions, the work strips the monument of its commemorative function and monolithic form, reconfiguring it instead as 'a sensible element torn from the sensible': a fissure in the grand aspirational 'pavilion', now rendered a makeshift tent. (Rancière, 2010: 173)

Conclusions

Much as Sebald wrote that monumental contours and grandiose constructions 'cast shadows of their destruction before them', the curtailment of El Helicoide and La Torre de David elucidates the shaky scaffolding that propped up the spectacles of progress that shaped Venezuela in the mid-twentieth century and that continue to inform the present. Instead of diverting the gaze from these lapsed buildings or fixating on them only during momentary media frenzy, the concept of 'phantom pavilions' brings their shadows and spectres back into focus. Revisited in historical context and remediated through aesthetic practice, truncated sites and their problematic afterlives take on a more productive presence: they stand as testaments to the discontinuities between hubristic imaginaries of progress and enduring social, economic and political challenges.

The aesthetic of provisionality that is found in *La prueba* and *Melancolía* suggests that attempts to secure development by uprooting the nation and remaking it in monumental forms are recurrent features of Venezuela's modern history. Indeed, this idea evokes the oft-cited comments of José Ignacio Cabrujas (1987) in the wake of economic crisis and not long before the upheavals of the *Caracazo*. As he pondered the prevailing model of progress and statecraft, he conjured Venezuela as a provisional camp transformed into a grand hotel, administered by a state permanently incapable of securing its guests' comfort and welfare. In this image of an indeterminate nation caught between provisional sites and aspirational buildings, boom-and-bust cycles and periodic occupations and clearances emerge as coetaneous features of spectacles of progress, whether conjured as a New National Ideal or a Great Venezuela.

While bulldozers and demolition continue to serve promises of instant transformation, sites like El Helicoide and La Torre de David stand as challenges to amnesia and as apt starting points for critical debates about much more than architectural design. When looked at carefully, without hysteria, these buildings' curtailment and modified functions alert us to the enduring dangers of boom-and-bust cycles that set the oil nation lurching between definitive forms and makeshift contingencies. Reconfigured through artworks that invite public engagement, El Helicoide and La Torre de David begin to plot a history of the spectacles of progress that informed their rise, and the socio- economic challenges that brought their demise. When they find ways into public discussions these critical dimensions create opportunities to rethink architectural remnants and also to conceive alternate monumental forms that allow shadows and spectres to gather to remind us that they are as much a thing of the past as persistent features of the present.

Acknowledgements

I am grateful to Á. Bonadies, J. J. Olavarría, R. Gómez Pérez and R. Jiménez (Ricard2), C. Olalquiaga,and G. Rojas for providing images for this chapter.

References

Agencia Venezolana de Noticias (2015a) 'Prevén usar temporalmente Torre Confinanzascomo centro de atención de emergencia de la Gran Caracas'. *Agencia Venezolana de Noticias*, 20 April [WWW document] URLhttp://www.avn.info.ve/contenido/prev%C3%A9n-usar-temporalmente-torre-confinanzas - como-centro-atención-emergencia-gran-caracas [accessed 20 August 2015].

Agencia Venezolana de Noticias (2015b) 'Torre Confinanzas se convertirá en un Centro de Derechos Urbanos Socialista'. *Agencia Venezolana de Noticias*, 29

May [WWW document] URL http://www.avn.info.ve/contenido/torres-confinanzas-se-convertir%C3%A1-centro-derechos-urbanos-socialista [accessed 5 April 2016].

Andermann, J. and González Stephan, B. (eds) (2006) *Galerías del progreso: museos, exposiciones y cultura visual en América Latina*. Beatriz Viterbo: Buenos Aires.

Anderson, J. L. (2013) 'Slumlord: What has Hugo Chávez wrought in Venezuela?' *The New Yorker*, 28 January. [*WWW document*]. URL http://www.newyorker.com/magazine/2013/01/28/slumlord [accessed 5 April 2016].

Anon. (undated) *Photograph of model of El Helicoide*. Dirk Bornhorst Archive/Proyecto Helicoide.

Bennett, T. (2010) '(1995) *The Birth of the Museum: History, Theory, Politics'*. Routledge: London.

Bonadies, A., and Olavarría, J.J., http://latorrededavid.blogspot.com.

Bonadies, A. and Olavarría, J. J. (2010) *Estudio fachada este*.

Bonadies, A. and Olavarría, J. J. (2010) *Installation view of La prueba*.

Bornhorst, D. (2007) *El Helicoide*. Carsten Todtmann: Caracas.

Boym, S. (2001) *The Future of Nostalgia*. Basic Books: New York.

Boym, S. (2010) 'Ruins of the Avant-garde' in J. Hell and A. Schönle (eds) *Ruins of Modernity*. Duke University Press: Durham and London, 58–88.

Cabrujas, J. I. (1987) *'El estado de disimulo'. Heterodoxia y estado: 5 respuestas (special edition of Estado & Reforma)*. COPRE: Caracas, 7–35.

Cannon, B. (2004) 'Venezuela, April 2002: Coup or Popular Rebellion? The Myth of a United Venezuela'. *Bulletin of Latin American Research* **23**(3): 285–302.

Castillo, O. (1990) *Los años del buldózer: ideología y política 1948–1958*. Ediciones Tropykos: Caracas.

Cicciarello-Maher, G. (2013) 'We Created Chávez: A People's History of the Venezuelan Revolution' in Duke University Press: Durham and London.

Coronil, F. (1997) *The Magical State: Nature, Money and Modernity in Venezuela*. University of Chicago Press: Chicago.

Coronil, F. and Skursi, J. (1991) 'Dismembering and Remembering the Nation: The Semantics of Political Violence in Venezuela'. *Comparative Studies in Society and History* **33**(2): 288–337.

Deleuze, G. and Guattari, F. (1994) 'What is Philosophy?'. *Trans. G. Burchell and H. Tomlinson. Verso: London*.

Dillon, B. (2014) *Ruin Lust*. Tate: London.

Draper, S. (2012) *Afterlives of Confinement: Spatial Transitions in Postdictatorship Latin America*. University of Pittsburgh Press: Pittsburgh.

Dürer, A. (1514) *Melancolia I. [WWW document]*. URL http://www.britishmuseum.org/research/collection_online/collection_object_details.

(March 2015) *aspx?objectId=1363679&partId=1 [accessed. , 31*.

Fernández, A. (2015) 'Habla la hija de "El Aviador"'. *Contrapunto* (25 March). [WWW document]. URL http://www.contrapunto.com/index.php?option=com_k2&view=item&id=18238%3 Alissette-gonzalez-mi-papa-y-yo-siempre-tuvimos-una-vision- politica-muy- distinta&Itemid=264 [accessed 31 March 2015].

Figueroa *et al.* (2014) *Installation view of Melancolía de Roca Tarpeya. Homenaje a la traición*.

Fraser, V. (2000) *Building the New World: Studies in Modern Architecture of Latin America 1930–1960*. Verso: London.

Gobernación del Distrito Federal (1982) Proyecto Helicoide. Gobernación del Distrito Federal: Caracas.

González Stephan, B. (2008) 'Tecnologías para las masas: democratización de la cultura y metáfora militar (Venezuela siglo XIX)'. *Iberoamericana* **8**(30): 89–101.

Gran Misión Vivienda Venezuela (2013) *Constructores del Socialismo.* [WWW document]. [WWW document]. URLhttp://www.mvh.gob.ve/index.php?option=com_content&view=article&id=476&Ite   mid=584 [accessed 21 August 2015].

Hancox, D. (2014) 'Enough Slum Porn: The Global North's Fetishization of Poverty Architecture Must End'. *Architectural Review* (12 August).

[WWW document]. URL http://www.architectural-review.com/enough-slum-porn-the-global-norths-fetishisation-of-poverty-architecture-must-end/8668268.article [accessed 25 April 2015].

Hell, J. and Schönle, A. (2010) 'Ruins of Modernity' in *Duke University Press: Durham and London.*

Humphrey, M. and Valverde, E. (2014) 'Hope and Fear in Venezuelan Democracy: Violence, Citizen Insecurity, and Competing Neoliberal and Socialist Urban Imaginaries' in L. F. Angosto-Ferrández (ed.) *Democracy, Revolution and Geopolitics in Latin America: Venezuela and the International Politics of Discontent.* Routledge: London, 147–176.

Kallipoliti, L. (2013) 'Torre David / Gran Horizonte'. *Journal of Architectural Education* **67**(1): 159–161.

Karl, T. L. (1987) 'Petroleum and Political Pacts: The Transition to Democracy in Venezuela'. *Latin American Research Review* **22**(1): 63–94.

López Maya, M. (2003) '*The Venezuelan Caracazo of 1989: Popular Protests and Institutional Weaknesses* '. *Journal of Latin American Studies* **35**(1): 117–137.

López Maya, M. (2005) 'Del viernes negro al referendo revocatorio'. *Alfa: Caracas.*

Marin, O. (2006) 'Construir la nación, construir sus imágenes: Los pabellones de Venezuela en las exposiciones internacionales' in T. Straka (ed.) *La tradición de lo moderno: Venezuela en diez enfoques.* Fundación para la Cultura Urbana: Caracas, 312–313.

Martín Frechilla, J. J. (1994) *Planes, planos y proyectos para Venezuela: 1908–1958. Fondo Editorial Acta Crítica: Caracas.*

Mitchell, T. (1989) 'The World as Exhibition'. *Comparative Studies in Society and History* **31**(2): 217–236.

Morais, M. G. (2009) *Situación actual de los derechos humanos en las cárceles en Venezuela.* Instituto Latinoamericano de Investigaciones Sociales: Caracas.

Oficina Presidencial de Planes y Proyectos (OPPE) (2014a) 'Arranca fase cuatro de la Operación Zamora con clausura de dos pisos de la Torre Confinanzas'. *OPPE.* 30 July. [WWW document]. URL http://www.opppe.gob.ve/2014/07/30/arranca-fase-cuatro-de-la-operacion-zamora-con-clausura-de-dos-pisos-de-la-torre-confinanzas/ [accessed 11 March 2015]

Oficina Presidencial de Planes y Proyectos (OPPE) (2014b) 'Demolidas estructuras precarias en pisos clausurados de la torre Confinanzas'. *OPPE* 17 August. [WWW document]. URL http://www.opppe.gob.ve/2014/08/17/demolidas-estructuras-precarias-en-pisos- clausurados-de-la-torre-confinanzas/ [accessed 11 March 2015].

Olalquiaga, C. (2014) 'Tropical Babel'. *Cabinet* **52**: 50–55.

Paulsson, G. *et al.* (1948). 'In Search of a New Monumentality'. *Architectural Review* **104**(62): 117–128.

Proyecto Helicoide (2013) [WWW document]. URL http://proyectohelicoide .com [accessed 18 May 2016].

Rancière, J. (2010) . *Dissensus. On Politics and Aesthetics. Trans. S. Corcoran. Bloomsbury: London.*

Ricard2 (c. 1989) *Portrait of David Brillembourg with a model of La Torre de David.*

Sarabia, I. (2012) 'Chávez dijo desconocer de invasores en Confinanzas'. *Últimas Noticias*, 8 August. [WWW document]. URL http://www.ultimasnoticias .com.ve/noticias/ciudad/ambiente/chavez-dijo-desconocer-de-invasores-en-confinanzas.aspx [accessed 11 February 2015].

Smilde, D. (2011) 'Introduction. Participation, Politics, and Culture – Emerging Fragments of Venezuela's Bolivarian Democracy' in D. Smilde and D. Hellinger (eds) *Venezuela's Bolivarian Democracy: Participation, Politics, and Culture under Chávez.* Duke University Press: Durham and London, 1–27.

TeleSUR (2014) *'Estudiamos el proyecto más viable para la Torre de David: Maduro'.* 23 July. [WWW document]. URL http://youtube/ZdPCLZK65CQ [accessed 19 August 2015].

Tinker Salas, M. (2009) *The Enduring Legacy. Oil, Culture, and Society in Venezuela.* Duke University Press: Durham and London.

United Nations Office on Drugs and Crime (2013) *Global Study on Homicide* 22. [WWW document]. URL http://www.unodc.org/documents/gsh/pdfs/ 2014_GLOBAL_HOMICIDE_BOOK_ web.pdf [accessed 13 March 2015]

Urban-Think Tank (2013) *Torre David: Informal Vertical Communities.* Lars Müller: Zurich.

Velasco, A. (2015) *Barrio Rising: Urban Politics and the Making of Modern Venezuela.* University of California Press: Oakland.

Venezolana de Televisión (2012) *Con demolición de La Planta, inicia fase de construcción de Parque Comunal Cipriano Castro.* [WWW document]. URL http://www.vtv.gob.ve/articulos/2012/09/01/con-demolicion-de-la-planta-inicia- fase-de-construccion-de-parque-comunal-cipriano-castro-8025.html [accessed 19 August 2015].

Vicente, H. (2003) 'La arquitectura urbana de las corporaciones petroleras: Conformación de "distritos petroleros" en Caracas durante las décadas de 1940 y 1950'. *Espacio Abierto* **12**(3): 391–414.

Villota Peña, J. (2014) *The Hyper Americans! Modern Architecture in Venezuela during the.* Unpublished doctoral dissertation, University of Texas at Austin: Austin, 1950s.

Williams, R. (1977) *'Marxism and Literature.* Oxford University Press: London.

Wilson, P. (2012) 'How Hugo Chávez Built a Squatter City in his Backyard" in *Foreign. Policy,* 6 January. [WWW document]. URL http://foreignpolicy.com/ 2012/01/06/the-skyscraper- slums-of-caracas/ [accessed 15 July 2015].

Ward, E. (1957) *The New El Dorado.* Robert Hale: London.

8

Queering the *Barrios*: The Politics of Space and Sexuality in Mariana Rondón's Film, *Pelo malo* (2013)

REBECCA JARMAN
University of Leeds

Pink Wave Cinema

Many of the authors contributing to this volume have voiced concerns with the nature of state influence exercised over cultural production in Bolivarian Venezuela, whether in constitutional legislation that speaks to partisan values, in the selective financing of projects that align with Bolivarian visions, or with the spectacular public commemorations of political narratives and historical figures that overshadow the work of authors and artists who do not participate in the 'officialist' sphere of culture. Writers and artists have claimed that this has stifled cultural projects starved of publicity or financial backing, exacerbated by recent shortages of the raw matter required for artistic production, for example, ink and paper. Despite this, the private gallery and independent editorial sectors have seen significant growth and innovation during the Chávez era. The same can be said of new Venezuelan cinema, produced with and without state assistance. During the past fifteen years, Venezuela has seen an increase in the number of films produced and a rise in ticket sales, as noted in this volume in the chapters by Silva-Ferrer and Kozak, and elsewhere by Alvaray (2013) in her illuminating account of state-sponsored production under Chávez (see also Silva Ferrer, 2014). Several of these filmic offerings have been successful in the international arena, at least where success is measured according to the number of accolades collected by film-makers at international festivals and positive reviews in commercial media outlets like The Observer and NPR, or the billing of Venezuelan films at European and North American box offices (Garsd, 2014; Kermode, 2015). Until the past year or so, however, even the most substantial of volumes dealing with Latin American cinema as a regional movement have failed to account for Venezuelan productions, some unwittingly contributing to the common misconceptions that these films are 'not being made' or 'not being distributed beyond national borders' (Shaw, 2007: 3; see also Shaw,

2003; Hart, 2004; Shaw and Dennison, 2005; Dennison, 2013). By offering an analysis of Mariana Rondón's third feature-length production, *Pelo malo* (Bad Hair) (2014), this chapter contributes to an incipient body of work on Bolivarian film-making that, in turn, serves to address a significant lacuna in Anglophone scholarship on contemporary cinema from Latin America (see Delgado, 2017; Jarman, 2017; Alvaray, 2018; Shaw, Duno-Gottberg, Page and Prado, 2018: 50-52).

Aside from prompting questions as to how and why Venezuelan cinema has, in recent years, gained prominence, the selection of new Venezuelan films celebrated by journalists and critics also shares a thematic interest. Contemporary Venezuelan cinema has demonstrated a marked preoccupation with sexualities and genders that deviate from heterosexual norms, sometimes featuring characters who undergo a process of sexual awakening, or, more often, who find themselves in social contexts unaccepting of sexual behaviours that deviate from heterosexual coupling. Several of these productions have received financial assistance from state-funded programmes, including the Centro Nacional Autónomo de Cinematografía (CNAC, National Autonomous Centre for Cinematography), and production support from Villa del Cine, the film studio inaugurated in 2006 by the Chávez government (El Universal, 2013; Silva Ferrer, 2014: 257; Peña Zerpa, 2015). The 'queer' films that have lately come out of Venezuelan studios, in addition to *Pelo malo*, include Miguel Ferrari's *Azul y no tan rosa* (My Straight Son) (2013), awarded the Spanish Goya for Best Foreign Film in 2014, and Lorenzo Viga's *Desde allá* (From Afar) (2015), a film that has had considerable exposure and acclaim on the European film circuit. These internationally distributed films add to a compendium of lesser-known productions, such as Eduardo Barbarena's *Cheila: una casa pa Maíta* (Cheila: A House for Ma) (2010) and Alejandro Bellame Palacios's *El tinte de la fama* (The Colour of Fame) (2008), both starring transgender protagonists who confront attitudes of intolerance and violence that are envisioned as prevalent in the poorer neighbourhoods of Caracas. These accompany an explosion of testosterone-driven films that perform hyperbolic masculinities: Jonathan Jakubowicz's high-grossing *Secuestro express* (Express Kidnap) (2005), Marcel Rasquin's *Hermano* (Brother) (2010), and Hernán Jabes's *Piedra, papel o tijera* (Rock, Paper, Scissors) (2012) are three of the most salient examples of the films that scan the relationship between poverty and violence through the lens of hypermasculinity.

The movement that I term the 'pink wave' of Venezuelan cinema is accompanied more broadly in Latin American cinema by what scholars have termed a turn to the queer, notable in millennial filmic productions. Alongside Gutiérrez-Albilla, I understand queer cinema to mean a loose body of work that poses a challenge to heteronormativity in form and content. This challenge is often (but not always) articulated by characters whose fluid mediations of sexuality and gender reveal the artificiality of heterosexist structures. This is channelled by a 'perversion' of structural cinematic discourse that might be seen to correspond to the Lacanian Real, revealing the master narratives of the libidinal-linguistic economy to be both fragile and restrictive (Gutiérrez-Albilla, 2008: 23-26). In a deconstructionist vein, Gutiérrez-Albilla argues that this dismantling of libidinal-linguistic systems is to be celebrated as a 'politics of perversion and of alterity pushed to the point of nihilism': it disturbs the boundaries that distinguish cinematic discourse from lived reality and the putative delineation of subjective identifications (2008: 20). To make this argument, he draws on the so-called antisocial thesis, elaborated by US-based queer theorists, where the death of the subject as social currency is celebrated as the end of negative differentiation and the detachment of sexuality from of its determination by social restrictions (see also Edelman, 2001: 4-5; Joseph, 2002: 21-25). Beyond film studies, however, this position has been refuted, particularly by those concerned with the positionality of knowledge and the importance of recognising the cultural specificities of sexual experience (Bond Stockton, 2009; Muñoz, 2009). Muñoz claims that the antisocial thesis posits queerness as susceptible to 'what some theorists seem to think of as the contamination of race, gender, or other particularities that taint the purity of sexuality as a singular trope of difference' (Muñoz, 2009: 11). Its promotion is thus, he implies, a marker of 'unmarked' privilege that takes hegemonic subject positioning (typically White, male and middle-class) as an unannounced universal signifier, without accounting for the geopolitics of theory or the materialism of subjectivity (see Dyer, 1997: 8-9). In the place of 'a faltering antirelational mode of queer theory' Muñoz endorses 'a queer utopianism that highlights a renewed investment in social theory (one that calls on not only relationality but also futurity)' that is not decoupled from an awareness of a political need for categorisations, especially in a postcolonial context (Muñoz, 2009: 10).

This chapter takes this polemic and applies it in reading *Pelo malo* to evaluate its mediation of queerness in one of Venezuela's most notorious high-rise housing projects by situating the film in the political context of the 'pink tide' movement. In the early 2000s, this saw the rise of left-leaning governments that proclaimed ideals associated with socialist principles, their red hue blanched by varying degrees of acquiescence to the interests of the global market and the values of liberal democracy that are seen to protect individual freedoms (Beasley-Murray, Cameron and Hershberg, 2009; Beverley, 2011; Coronil, 2011). The film's discursive complexities and aesthetic nuances makes it an ideal object of inquiry, suitable to be taken as a barometer of 'pink wave' cinema, while also developing scholarship on

1980s and 1990s queer Cuban cinema in a comparable political context. For some Cuban revolutionaries, as Foster puts it, homosexuality represented 'the most terrifying embodiment of bourgeois decadence' (Foster, 2003: 54), especially in the three decades prior to the 'special period'. After the fall of the Berlin wall, Gutiérrez Álea's (in)famous film, *Fresa y chocolate* (Strawberry and Chocolate) (1994), was, according to some film critics, a state-led attempt at a double-sided *rapprochement* with LGBTQ+ Cuban communities and free market economics, both of which had been explicitly condemned by the Revolutionary government (see Smith, 1994; Santí, 1998; Foster, 2003). Conversely, *Pelo malo* has attracted criticism for its putative politicisation of sexuality and gender, whereby its focus on queer sexualities has been interpreted as a subversive cinematic demonstration against the social and political values promoted by Bolivarian Socialism. The debate, to be discussed in further detail, prompts a series of interrogations about the politics of 'pink wave' cinema in Venezuela. Can it be said that *Pelo malo* instrumentalises non-heterosexual identities as a surreptitious form of dissidence, both against heterosexuality and the Bolivarian Revolution? Is queerness, instead, taken as a premise that might nuance understandings of marginality, power and politics, thus challenging hegemonic identities and fostering a more positive relation with difference? With the rise of identity politics that accelerated the left turn of 'pink tide' nations, have divergent sexual identities been fetishised for international audiences? Or is queerness the key to a fluid form of film-making that disturbs preconceptions and subjectivities, inviting an open and inconclusive relationship with the spectator, that finds renewed importance against a backdrop of political polarisation?

The Polemics of *Pelo malo*

Funded in part by the CNAC, with contributions from institutions in Spain, the US and Germany, *Pelo malo* was awarded the coveted Concha de Oro (Golden Shell) prize at the 2013 San Sebastián Film Festival, and was included in the official selections for BFI and Toronto (Alvaray, 2018: 252). It stars an androgynous, poor, Brown child protagonist, aged about 9 or 10, named Junior, played brilliantly by Samuel Lange, for whom *Pelo malo* is a debut in professional acting. Junior lives in a notorious inner-city *barrio* in Caracas, El 23 de Enero, deemed by anthropologist George Ciccariello-Maher, to be 'one of the most revolutionary spaces in all Venezuela' (Ciccariello-Maher, 2013: 69). He is daydreamer who enjoys singing and dancing; he appears to have a crush on an older boy in the neighbourhood, and prefers to straighten his thick, undulant hair that lends the film its title. The main narrative focus is on Junior's struggles against Marta, his domineering mother, who attempts to 'fix' Junior's sexuality – both in a corrective and a categorical sense – so that his appearance and behaviour is identifiably 'straight' and masculine. His paternal grandmother, at loggerheads with Marta, encourages Junior's preference for a more effeminate appearance, although her motivation for doing so is apparently to antagonise her daughter-in-law, with whom she has had a particularly troubled relationship since the death of her son, possibly in gang-related warfare. More broadly, the film articulates concerns surrounding a larger patriarchal order that propagates heteronormative dualisms, static gender constructs and a restrictive, class-inflected biopolitics, against the backdrop of a neighbourhood metonymic for leftist rebellion and resistance, in a city that has garnered an unfortunate reputation for being the world's capital of homicides (CCSPJP, 2015). Alongside this, Rondón draws attention to the racialised and racist ideologies that are imposed onto Junior's brown-skinned body: Marta, whose features are 'Whiter' than her son's, insists that Junior cuts his hair as symbolic disassociation from his Black lineage. A feasible, though reductive, reading of the film would cast Marta as a despotic figure of power who abuses her symbolic young son on account of his vulnerability and his sexual and racial difference. However, for reasons to become clear with close filmic analysis, Rondón's flirtations with national allegory do not permit such a straightforward conclusion; rather, she uses creative cinematography in an attempt to think beyond the romanticised and demonised projections of the neighbourhood that dominate public discourse.

Despite *Pelo malo*'s impressive performance at the global box office, in Venezuela the film attracted condemnation, particularly from commentators aligned with *chavismo*. Upon receiving the Concha de Oro at San Sebastián, Rondón commented that she was driven to make the film by the anguish of experiencing pronounced intolerance towards what she termed 'la diferencia' (difference) (Hernández, 2013), later suggesting in an interview with *El País* that such intolerance was exacerbated by the polarising discourse characteristic of the charismatic and contentious Chávez (García and Belinchón, 2013). The feature in the Spanish newspaper, known for its thinly veiled hostility towards the late president, generated something of a maelstrom back in Venezuela. The state media system and associated representatives released a series of statements that chastised Rondón's critiques of the state couched in a rhetoric of tolerance, recalling the assistance that she had received from Villa del Cine studios. Her most vocal critics interpreted the film as an appeal for the diversification of the national political landscape dominated by *chavismo*, or the return of neoliberalism as a technical political programme to the benefit of the business elites, where homosexuality was read implicitly as form of protest against Bolivarian Socialism. Similar criticisms were levelled at the filmic discourse of *Pelo malo*, understood by some as harbouring a hidden, reactionary agenda that capitalised on marginality and 'otherness' while perpetuating understandings of informal neighbourhoods as politically revolutionary but socially conservative, not to say overtly homophobic, racist and misogynistic. With the same sleight of hand, *Pelo malo* obscured its own intolerant discourse towards *chavista* constituencies whose racial and economic make-up largely matched that of the film's protagonist (see Duno Gottberg, 2003, 2011; Cannon, 2008), thus applauding diversity in theory but denouncing heterogeneity in practice. In essence, one critic argued, Rondón had fetishised 'otherness' in its intersectional inflections to appeal to international spectators, her empty calls for tolerance a White, middle-class lament of 'pink tide' progress (Salima, 2014). As Rondón told me in interview, this also led to personal abuse that targeted her on social media: she was accused of appropriating marginality, motivated by an allegiance with counter-revolutionary and anti-*chavista* forces.

Pelo malo was made at time of minor successes and major frustrations for LGBTQ+ organisations in Venezuela and across the Americas in general (I use this Anglophone acronym in the knowledge that it conceals internal struggles and cultural differences, but follow the lead of Perriam (2013: 1-13) in recognising its usefulness in discussions of globally connected political mobilisations). The 'pink tide' has left a mixed legacy in issues surrounding gender and sexuality: some countries, like Brazil, have implemented holistic programmes surrounding 'Homosexual Citizenship'; others, like Venezuela, have focused more efforts on instituting the long-term demands of the women's agenda (Friedman, 2009; Espina and Rakowksi, 2010; Fernandes, 2010). As Friedman puts it, '[f]eminist intervention in the 1999 constitutional convention resulted in the prohibition of gender discrimination and promotion of gender equality, illustrated by the use of gender-inclusive language throughout the constitutions' (2009: 421). For all this constitutional emphasis on gender inclusivity and equality, however, the Venezuelan political establishment is not always welcoming of sexual diversity in rhetoric or legislation. Prominent members of ruling party Partido Socialist Unida de Venezuela (PSUV, Venezuelan United Socialist Party), and opposition Acción Democrática (AD, Democratic Action), have repeatedly used homophobic jibes with reference to two-time presidential candidate Henrique Capriles Radonksi, while Capriles has tended to respond defensively as opposed to challenging the premise of their accusations (Meza, 2013; Vielma, 2014; El Nacional, 2016). Meanwhile, the National Assembly has rejected petitions to amend the Constitution to protect the basic human rights of LGBTQ+ groups, especially beneath the watch of pro-state Christian President of the Comisión de la Familia, Mujer, Niñez y Adolescencia (Commission for Family, Women and Children), Marelys Pérez (Merentes, 2010: 220). At the time of writing, same-sex marriage remains illegal in Venezuela, although some congressional steps have been taken in debating amendments to legislation thanks to lobbying from civil union groups beneath the banner of the Proyecto de Ley de Matrimonio Civil Igualitario (Project for Equality in Civil Marriage Law). These efforts have been supported by El Festival Venezolano de Cine de la Diversidad (FESTDIVQ, Venezuelan Festival for Diverse Cinema) that, in turn, has grown since 2011 both in political ambition and in audience (Peña Zerpa, 2015: 170): film-making is seen by this independent organisation as a creative but practical endeavour to influence policy-making.

Although the themes explored in *Pelo malo* resonate with the pragmatic concerns of FESTDIVQ, Rondón's primary objective is not to call for specific policy change or constitutional amendments. What is at stake is a critical look at identity politics that, as we shall see, takes queerness as a form of navigating relational difference by creating a shifting cinematic cartography of the complexities of social interactions, especially when shaped by sexual desire and underscored by political tensions. This complexity can be obscured by semiotic theory that situates hetero- and non-heterosexual subjectivities in mutually exclusive co-dependence. According to Foster, the queer is to be found in or between these signs and symbols or, as he puts it, 'between what lies inside or outside of the category that is privileged as the norm or the normal, where incoherencies, ambiguities, internal contradictions, and, quite simply, absurdities of meaning can be perceived to occur' (Foster, 2003: 21). In other words, as this school of thought would have it, the queer is that which escapes social labelling, at least in terms of its cultural intelligibility: it is related to the Lacanian concept of the Real, 'that which resists symbolization, a gap-in-knowledge that subverts or defeats the presumption to know it' (Gutiérrez-Albilla, 2008: 20). In cinema, queerness is channelled with 'perversions' of linear, cause-effect narrative structures (Gutiérrez-Albilla, 2008: 4), with devices such as the *mise-en-abyme*, the motif and the stylised disturbances of chronology and setting that '[frustrate] the spectator's desire for interpretation and [foreground] the constructedness of representation' (Gutiérrez-Albilla, 2008: 4). In this sense, queer film-making opens up the relationship between the film and its spectator. By inviting multiple interpretations and positing heterogeneous narrative possibilities, it deviates from the binary channels of desire that are often presupposed between the feature film and its box office audience (see Mulvey, 1989). For Gutiérrez-Albilla, this 'desubjectivization' is particularly powerful in forging a positive difference with marginal subjects in liminal spaces (Gutiérrez-Albilla, 2008: 20): rather than fetishise otherness, queer cinema seeks to foster sensitivity and open-minded approximations. This is applicable to gender and sexuality as much as it is to race, class, ethnicity, age and politics, or any other markers of social differentiation.

Liminal Spaces

It is this mode of film-making that drives *Pelo malo* and informs my reading of its interpretation of El 23 de Enero, as it screens social alterity and subversion in a polarised political context. Before exploring El 23 as it is interpreted by Rondón, both as an identity and a filmic setting, it is worth offering a brief account of its history since its construction in the mid-1950s. In his book-length study of the neighbourhood, Velasco argues that the social housing estate situated just above Miraflores Presidential Palace 'reflect[s] the history of modernizing and democratic governments and revolutionary projects' (Velasco, 2015: 7-8). The cluster of high-rises was built in the mid-1950s under the Marcos Pérez Jiménez military dictatorship, originally named 2 de Diciembre to mark the date of his presidential inauguration. Inspired in part by the Utopian urban visions of Swiss-French architect Le Corbusier and his Unité d'Habitation in Marseilles, the residential community was designed by prominent Paris-trained Venezuelan architect Carlos Raúl Villanueva (Fraser, 2000: 118). The finished complex was to house over 60,000 low-income residents, largely first- and second-generation rural migrants who, in a state-led mission known as the 'Battle against the Shanty', were to be evacuated from the unplanned communities that had mushroomed on the hillsides of Mount Ávila (Blackmore, 2017: 7). For urban historian Almandoz, the insertion of recent arrivals from the countryside into regimented patterns of modern urban living represented an attempt to convert rural migrants into 'improvised [urban] citizens' (Almandoz, 2012: 99). These patterns were articulated architecturally with the rectangular compartmentalisation of the modernist tower blocks that would superimpose a linear notion of order and development on the perceived chaos of the informal settlements. In this sense, the project was a concrete expression of the so-called New National Ideal instituted by military rule: 'its fundamental claim was that technological and architectural modification to the national territory would propel Venezuela towards a better future' (Blackmore, 2017: 34). Importantly, this development also hinged on biological reproduction, as such ideals were to be projected onto children as the symbolic beneficiaries of this progress. A look at the 1954 Banco Obrero plans for the Unidad Residencial 2 de Diciembre (reproduced in Velasco, 2015: 40) reveals a site that houses state-run familial institutions, such as the National Childcare Institute, as well as twenty kindergartens, twelve daycare centres, seven schools and sixteen playgrounds. Like much urban planning, the complex was designed for the small, heterosexual family unit; its architecture would, so it was thought, regulate the routine and behaviour of its occupants (see Bell and Valentine, 1995).

Towards the end of the 1950s, however, the military regime was confronted with an economic crisis, blamed by the private sector on Pérez Jiménez's overspending of petrodollars (Coronil, 1997: 201). On 23 January 1958, a joint civilian-military coup toppled the president that saw Pérez Jiménez flee to the Dominican Republic, later to be imprisoned on charges of embezzlement (Blackmore, 2017: 9). Still mostly uninhabited and partly unfinished, the *bloques* were forcibly occupied during the popular uprising that accompanied the *golpe* in Miraflores. 'In the span of the 48 hours following the coup', writes Velasco, 'nearly thirty thousand people had illegally occupied over 3,000 apartments in the western sectors of the housing project, units that remained vacant despite their formal inauguration weeks earlier' (2015: 52). These new inhabitants changed the name of the neighbourhood to commemorate the restitution of democracy. They also oversaw the arrival of extended family members whose low-lying *ranchos* filled the areas designed as leafy parks and wide open green spaces. Within a matter of weeks, El 23 grew into a rhizomatic *barrio*, placing high amounts of pressure on the provision of electricity and water, eventually generating protest movements that would lobby the government to improve urban services (Velasco, 2015: 133-159). Soon it became home to social activists, urban guerrillas and political dissidents who would struggle against the state establishment in its different guises, though it enjoyed a mixed reception among the neighbourhood's pre-existing inhabitants (Ciccariello-Maher, 2013: 69-87; Velasco, 2015: 87-110). More recently, it has become one of the urban *focos* for militant *chavista* activists such as the Units for Electoral Battle and, according to the most damning observers, armed paramilitary groupings or *colectivos* that have targeted political dissidents (Manwaring, 2012; Infobae, 2014). That one neighbourhood has acquired such visibility in politics and scholarship is thus thanks to more than its symbolic high-altitude location next to one of Caracas's major highways, although in 2002 this hilltop setting facilitated access to the presidential palace for the mass demonstrations against the coup attempt that attracted spectacular media coverage (Irazabel and Foley, 2008). For better or worse, it has often figured in public discourse as the home of a unified Bolivarian subject (Velasco, 2011: 158); the installation of the Chávez mausoleum at its outskirts has done little to detract from this partisan image.

This complex history has meant that the characteristics associated with El 23 are often contradictory in its contemporary representations, even when these present the site as a staunch *chavista* stronghold. The neighbourhood figures as a site of activism, rebellion and resistance, although it can also be said to be subject to governmental paternalism, a passive beneficiary of patriarchal politics. It is situated simultaneously at the margins of *caraqueño* society and, paradoxically, at the centre of the imaginary of Bolivarian state-making.

According to Ciccariello-Maher, the bipartisan political system that developed after the fall of Pérez Jiménez, known as *puntofijismo*, monopolised union affiliation and excluded the informal sectors from formal politics. This meant that the nexus of class struggle was to be found in everyday gatherings in low-income neighbourhoods, so that 'class demands have been subsumed to territorial, neighbourhood demands that manifest, above all, *politically*' (Ciccariello-Maher, 2013: 227, original emphasis), expressed electorally with the landslide victories of Chávez. El 23 is one of the neighbourhoods taken as a case study to evidence this argument. Ciccariello-Maher is not alone in placing emphasis on the importance of social collectives in 'pink tide' Venezuela, or in the Americas more broadly, during a two-decade period that has witnessed the rise of anti-establishment, left-leaning presidents across the region (see Beverley, 2011). The millennial turn to the left was, according to some observers, driven by discontentment with representative liberal politics, understood to be overly pliant to the IMF and its stringent readjustment programmes during the late 1980s and 1990s (Beasley-Murray, Cameron and Hershberg, 2009: 327). In a context of widespread suspicion towards democratic institutions that advocated neoliberal economic strategies, political parties were obliged to respond to 'a series of resurgent social movements' (ibid.) that were often organised around shared identities, single issues and broad-based policy agenda. As Kinsbury demonstrates in this collection, such identifications in Venezuela often speak to demands for decolonisation, or for the end of the underdevelopment that has accompanied the development of the oil economy, that take markers of race, territory and class as their master signifiers. This, in turn, feeds into presidential discourse that generated new partisan loyalties by celebrating race and class as 'central sources of identification' (Cannon, 2008: 741) with constituents disenchanted by conventional party politics. Although they congeal around certain issues and iconic figures, such territorial subjectivities are multi-layered entities that cannot be reduced to a single sign of partisan affiliation, much less restricted to dualistic camps divided by voting tendencies or ideological persuasion.

By employing a series of creative filmic strategies and scripting self-consciously intersectional characters who trouble dichotomous restrictions, Rondón attempts to project this multidimensionality as a form of cinematic queerness. At first glance, Rondón's visual framing of El 23 in *Pelo malo* does little to undermine received understanding of the neighbourhood as a site of unwavering support for the Bolivarian Revolution, where revolution is equated negatively with belligerence, gang warfare and violence. The opening sequence of the film includes pointed postcard shots of a removal truck adorned with severed dolls' heads and murals depicting Christ and the Virgin armed with Kalashnikovs, both visual hallmarks of the neighbourhood likely familiar to *caraqueños*, though perhaps somewhat uncanny to international audiences. The vehicle, known locally as the *camión de muñecas*, is driven by Jesús Poleo Díaz, a 64-year-old resident of El 23 who claims to have been arrested more than once on account of his eccentric mode of transportation (Zacarías, 2014). The polemical mural that is painted on the entrance to El 23, meanwhile, has become an emblem for the neighbourhood since it was designed in 2010 by community artist Nelson Santana, and executed in collaboration with local political collective, La Piedrita (Omaña, 2012). The religious figures are accompanied by revolutionary slogans, *¡La historia nos absolverá!* ('History will absolve us!') and *La Piedrita Venceremos* ('La Piedrita will be victorious'). The transcendental future tense resonates with Chávez's fusion of religious and Marxist tropes and his resource to Cuban political idiom, having incited condemnation from the church and the media for instilling *odio y muerte* (El Universal, 2012). Using these inflammatory symbols as her opening gambit, Rondón might stand accused of fetishising the neighbourhood for the viewing pleasure of box-office spectators. Taken together, the icons create a cinematic version of what journalists have called 'Revolutionary tourism' (Gould, 2006), revealing the underbelly of Bolivarian Socialism in the shantytowns and hinting at Caracas as it appears in headline-grabbing reports on the 'world's deadliest capital'. Indeed, such violence is channelled in Marta's abusive treatment of Junior, as well as in his off-handed references to shootings in the neighbourhood and his father's untimely death, suggestive of the normalisation of murder in the complex. But this branding of the *barrio* is also undermined with its cinematic exploration that rejects the political symbolism that imagines its inhabitants as a cohesive body of political activists. The film's aesthetics, for the most part, emphasises the excesses of El 23 that are obscured by the *parti pris* politicisation of the community in hegemonic discourse, by permitting fleeting access to the spaces beyond these signifiers, so as to refine depictions of the neighbourhood as a synecdoche of *chavismo*.

One of the ways in which Rondón contests the visions of political unity attributed to the neighbourhood is by using self-conscious filmic mechanisms to draw attention to its occupants as a disparate group of individuals. At times these are brought together in close, and often uncomfortable, contact; at other times they are segregated, particularly in the complex's communal spaces. The viewer is first exposed to El 23 from Junior's perspective. From the window of a bus, we are confronted with panoramic travelling shots of the seemingly infinite facades of the iconic buildings. The ominous and impersonal structures are juxtaposed with documentary close-ups of individual apartments in a sequence that includes stylised images of Junior and his friend, 'la niña', who play a version of 'I Spy' from the vantage point of his top-floor apartment. The second-long cropped shots of the rectangular flats visually replicate the spliced segments of a film reel, serving as a reminder that narratives of any kind – social, political or cinematic – are the sum of discrete units that, according to logic, must homogenise difference to garner cohesive meaning (see Foster, 2003: 19). The screen is taken up by endless towers of cramped apartments with faded paint and crumbling concrete exteriors, their windows barred with metal grills or haphazardly bricked up by their inhabitants. In their totality, the blocks are framed as the manifestation of an exhausted Utopian project, akin to the 'phantom pavilions' discussed here by Blackmore. In their faded grandeur, the blocks are ghostly remnants of a failure to deliver on the promises of modernisation and social inclusion that drove the construction of the complex, and that continue to operate in the visual codes of the murals that offer Bolivarian Socialism as a form of historical emancipation. In this way, the film summons multiple and overlapping temporalities as a means to deviate from teleological visions of history, whereby the unfulfilled pledges of past modernising projects hang over the present moment of the cityscape that also faces towards a perpetually receding future. This concords with Fernando Coronil's analysis of the temporal trajectories of the 'pink tide' that reboots emancipatory discourses and rekindles old nationalisms; its rhetoric protracts the political field between 'the malleable landscape of utopian imaginaries and the immutable ground of recalcitrant histories' (Coronil, 2011: 235). As such, the film also speaks to theorisations of queer temporalities, where deviations from heteronormative psychic processes to subjectification map out alternative modes of navigating time-spaces that are both elastic and palimpsestic, instead of linear and progressive (Muñoz, 2009; Stockton, 2009).

Divergent Sexualities

Rondón's choice of a child protagonist is, in this regard, significant. *Pelo malo* joins a list of prolific Venezuelan films that feature a child as its main character, including *Maroa* (2005), *Postales de Leningrado* (Postcards from Leningrad) (2007), *El chico que miente* (The Kid who Lies) (2007), *El rumor de las piedras* (The Rumble of the Stones) (2011), and *Brecha en el silencio* (Breach in the Silence) (2012). It also speaks to a broader trend in Latin American film-making that casts the child as 'a cinematic figure that invites or permits spectatorial mobility, and does so within a narrative in which such a mobility can be seen as a way of negotiating […] cultural tensions' (Martin, 2017: 189; see also Rocha and Seminet, 2014; Randall, 2017). In contemporary queer cultural studies, the figure of the child itself has become a site of tension, regarded either as vacant vessel for heteronormative ideals or a site of queer resistance. Writing prior to legislation surrounding equal reproductive rights, Edelman is highly sceptical about the proliferation of the symbolic figure of the child in cultural discourse. For him, the child is appropriated in the public arena to reproduce the conditions of social life that propagate conservative sexual politics; as the 'fantasmatic beneficiary of every political intervention', it is used to perpetuate discrimination against non-heterosexual practices (Edelman, 2004: 2-3). Conversely, for Bond Stockton, the child as it is mediated in fiction has the potential to permutate tropes that might otherwise homogenise otherness. She argues that the figure of the child, regardless of sexuality, is necessarily queer and necessarily ghostly: queer because the normative passages towards erotic maturity, even when these are bent towards heterosexuality, cast the child as 'not-yet-straight' (Bond Stockton, 2009: 7) before subjectification; ghostly because the fictional child is 'the act of adults looking back' (Bond Stockton, 2009: 5); it signifies the death of childhood as the child becomes an adult that, in turn, imagines childhood. Rather than 'growing up', she suggests that figurative child must be understood as 'growing sideways', whereby 'the width of a person's experience or ideas, their motives or their motions, may pertain at any age, bringing "adults" and "children" into lateral contact' (Bond Stockton, 2009: 11). In other words, the child prompts reflection in the adult about her own positioning relative to social constructs; the child is also troublesome as he channels a desire for incest not yet repressed by social conditioning.

Crucially, Junior's sexuality remains ambiguous throughout the duration of *Pelo malo*. This ambiguity is suggestive of the taboos surrounding child sexuality, as well as the psychoanalytical theories that understand childhood as a domain that precedes identification. The lack of any physical sexual interaction between Junior and another character makes it difficult to corroborate his sexual identity with any certainty (in interview Rondón revealed that she decided not to film the child naked, even in a bath scene, because Lange could not give adult consent, so any explicit physical intercourse was, in a practical sense, out of the question). At most, we see his subdued flirtations with the twenty-something male who works in the kiosk below his apartment, although this relationship, in the absence of Junior's father, could equally be read as a form of fraternal admiration that blurs the lines between homosexuality and what anthropologists have called 'homosocial' behaviour (see Foster, 2003: 24-25). Rather, his sexual identity is a predetermined subjectivity that is imposed upon him by his mother, Marta, who is a tragic and tyrannical figure somewhat reminiscent of Gallegos's Doña Bárbara. Having been dismissed from her job as a security guard, Marta spends much of her time policing Junior's actions, that she takes to be symptomatic of his future sexual preferences. She perceives Junior's homosexuality in much of his childlike behaviour, including the imaginary games he plays with his neighbours and his enjoyment of dance and music. In one particularly painful scene, she seeks medical advice on how to prevent her son from becoming 'gay' when he is older; this prophecy is self-fulfilling, as she blames her own failures as a mother for his not yet being heterosexual. The more Marta projects these homophobic fears onto Junior, the more he responds with prototypically *machista* behaviour. In their most disconcerting iterations, Marta's attempts to 'correct' Junior's sexuality verge on manifestations of incestuous desire, recalling Lacanian theory that takes the so-called mirror stage as an incomplete moment of filial separation, later determining sexual subjectification. One evening, Marta obliges Junior to watch her seduce her former employer in an attempt to win her job back (she has been dismissed for unspecified reasons). They have sex on the sofa in view of Junior's bedroom. The morning after, Junior orders Marta to cook plantain to his liking: the chauvinistic outburst shores up concepts of masculinity that are bound up with the violence associated with the *barrios*, as though heterosexual desire is premised on domestic aggression. These shifting positions of power between mother and son unsettle the stasis of gendered constructs, revealing instead the relativity that determines social actions. Simultaneously, they gesture to the unknowable sexuality of the child that summons the threat of incest, serving to undermine the fixity of the desiring individual and instil anxiety in the adult subject.

Given his indeterminable sexual identity, Junior's queerness is not merely or necessarily sexual. It is also in his creation and occupation of liminal spaces that distort the gendering of the cityscape identified by the self-denominating queer geographers (see Bell and Valentine, 1995; Johnston and Valentine, 1995; Ahmed, 2006). This begins on a micro-level with his occupation of his body that is projected outwards to the family apartment and beyond to the spaces of the neighbourhood that are segregated by gender. Junior's first act of rebellion, as suggested by the film's title, is to style his hair in a bob that reaches just above his shoulders. At home, he is most often found in the bathroom before the mirror in a neurotic hair-combing ritual, using domestic products like oil and mayonnaise to style his tight black ringlets. This infuriates Marta, who wears her own hair tied back and bothers little with clothes or make-up; she responds with a similarly obsessive campaign against what she sees as his feminine appearance. Eventually, Marta resorts to force to remove him from the bathroom: this is, for her, a place for women and so inappropriate for Junior, who is designated a special chair in the kitchen, as though a change in his positioning in the house might positively determine his sexual orientation. Still Junior insists on wearing his hair according to his preferences, and struggles against Marta's ultimatum that he shave his head or leave home to live with his grandmother. Junior's use of long hair as a sign of adolescent rebellion against authority has historical precedence in El 23, especially in the context of the police-led raids that targeted the *barrio* in the late 1960s. Then, writes Velasco, 'long-haired young men, at the time pejoratively referred to as *melenudos*, reported having their heads shaved on their way to or from school' by armed police officers (Velasco 2015: 148). In Bolivarian Venezuela, this surveillance is reasserted, especially in the spectacular realm of embodied political performance that is explored in the chapters by Bonet and Vásquez (see also Ochoa, 2014), where the focus on the shaved head also gestures towards preoccupations surrounding the militarisation of the social fabric. Seeping into Rondón's fictional construction of the neighbourhood are snapshots of life in the wider city, often captured in the television images that seem part of the furnishings in most of the apartments. Notable is the reconstructed news clip that shows a group of men and women shaving their heads 'in solidarity' with Chávez as he underwent chemotherapy during his treatment for cancer, suggested here to be a Foucauldian form of self-sacrifice in inflections of sovereign power articulated as biopolitics (Foucault, 1977: 24-31). The forces that work to determine Junior's bodily behaviour are thus revealed to be multiple and pervasive; they are not unique to the present moment but rather are undercurrents to a history of corporeal discipline in the neighbourhood and in the nation. These also seek to erase appearances of the stereotypical Black phenotype from Venezuelan lineage, where hair seemingly lends itself most easily to manipulation (see Gackstetter Nichols, 2013).

If Junior is seen to transgress the limits placed on the body as an articulation of spatial stratification, he also crosses the boundaries that cut across the neighbourhood as a community. El 23 is shown to be divided along the lines of gender: the spatial dynamics of the buildings gravitate towards the perpetuation of patriarchal lineage, whereby '[the] straight line would be that which moves *without any deviation* towards the "point" of heterosexual union or sexual coupling' (Ahmed, 2006: 78, original emphasis). The communal areas are dominated by the presence of men who publicly enact prototypical masculinities, whether fixing motorbikes on the rooftops, breakdancing along corridors or congregating in the basketball courts situated in between the buildings. The women, meanwhile, are usually confined to the interiors of their apartments: shots at the door frames show domestic hair salons, female-only séances, and young girls gathered around televisions to watch the latest round of the Miss Venezuela contest, that pseudo-national institution that privileges 'a particular form of hyperfeminine coroporeality' (Ochoa, 2014: 8). By and large, the lines that divide men and women are transgressed only at moments of (hetero)sexual excitement: Junior's mother enters a mechanic's workshop in pursuit of a love interest, who later enters her apartment for sex and leaves immediately afterwards. On a structural level, then, El 23 of *Pelo malo* is erected and maintained on the premise of a heterosexual family unit, even if the prominence of extra-marital relations means that this unit overspills the self-containment of the apartments.

Vacillating between the spaces designated and inhabited either side of the architectural masculine/feminine divide, Junior subverts the gendered segregation that otherwise characterises the complex in movements that are not channelled by heterosexual desire or gendered performance. He spends time with the girls watching television and outside, watching the boys playing basketball. This fluid occupation of the spatial organisation of El 23 is often portrayed with corresponding cinematic devices: these are moments that are unscripted, improvised and out of character. One such scene sees Junior watch a group of young break dancers take over a top-floor corridor, as he dances alone and out of sync with the aggressive electronic music. Lingering at the periphery of the filmic frame, Junior appears as a haunting and haunted ephemeral presence; he is a stubborn reminder of desire that does not conform to the Freudian psycho-sexual trajectory, and of the divergences that are disavowed by broader identity constructs. Emanating from this, Junior's unsettling presence in El 23 undermines territorial concepts of a unified political subject that can be said to work according to a similar logic of polarised thinking and dichotomous structures. This is echoed in another song that floats through the film, Henry Stephen's 1969 *Limón, limonero*, affording Junior a kitschy element meaning that he is out of time, as well as space and gender categories.

Such cinematic strategies mean that *Pelo malo* is situated self-referentially at an angle to symbolic signification. Writing on melodrama in the context of 'Golden Age' Mexican cinema, scholars have theorised the site of the working-class family as a microcosm of social relations, where state forms of authority are incarnate in dominant patriarchal figures and controlling fathers, symbolising the exercise of sovereign power over women and children as vulnerable citizens (Franco, 1989; Hershfield, 1996). Correspondingly, the matriarchal characterisation of *Pelo malo* might be understood as an allegory of twenty-first-century Bolivarian politics, where Junior is at the behest of the regime that his mother upholds in the apartment. The final sequence of *Pelo malo* sees Junior give in to his mother's demands: he eventually shaves his head in the film's understated, uncomfortable climax. In a drawn-out sequence that sees Junior seated in the kitchen, he takes an electric razor to his head. He watches his mother defiantly, and tells her that he does not love her. She returns the sentiment, and ensures he does the job correctly. Moments like these in the film leave Rondón open to criticism for infantilising the urban poor and demonising the late president, whose absence in the film is notable, but is also omniscient in its visual coding. Yet like many of the film's events, the sequence lends itself to several interpretations, purposefully summoning a spectrum of meaning that is intra- and extra-diegetic to the film's narrative construction. This is a moment of self-sacrifice that recalls the televised ritual for the sick president, and a victory for the tyranny that is embodied by

Marta. Here Junior would be the victim of coercion with minimal autonomy or independence who eventually submits to his tormentor. But it is also an act of self-harm that sees Junior mediate the death drive; he is, in this regard, self-effacing. His grip on the phallic razor can be interpreted, with Edelman, as resisting the reproduction of the dominant social order. Finally, it is an act of love that will prolong his proximity to his mother, whether incestuous or affective, who promises that he can stay at home as long as he keeps his hair short. The episode is preceded by Marta's humming of the Miss Venezuela theme tune: this is Junior's favourite song and the aural motif of the production that she constantly seeks to silence. That Marta unthink-ingly sings a melody that she loathes is suggestive of an approximation, if not of a reconciliation, between two seemingly polar forces that are also co-dependent. Junior's queerness is channelled subconsciously by Marta's 'growing sideways', blurring the lines between individual subjects. In this sense, Junior's relenting can be read, with Muñoz, as an investment in the future; or as 'a kernel of political possibility within a stultifying heterosexual present' (Muñoz, 2009: 49) that summons an alternative reality from close proximity to lived experience. This openness is an invitation to the audience to think differently, and individually, but in collective.

Conclusion

In the pages above, I have sketched out some initial answers to the questions that seek to distinguish queer Hispanic cinema in the context of the 'pink tide' from the queer Hispanic cinema that has been conceptualised predominantly in relation to neoliberal administrations (Foster, 2003; Perriam, 2013; Subero, 2014; Hoff, 2016). Refusing to essentialise sexuality or territorially-rooted subjectivities, *Pelo malo* attempts to foster a more intimate understanding of the inhabitants of its fictional world as a heterogeneous community, as opposed to a collective political protagonist united in partisan subscription. It does so with recourse to a cinematographic mode that opens up to liminal spaces, diverse histories and personal stories, channelled by Junior and his imaginative occupation of his body and his neighbourhood that defies facile categorisation. In this regard, it is a film that is sceptical of identity politics: it highlights the reductions that often accompany the reproduction of social ciphers associated with subjectivity and exacerbate conflict based on race, age, sexuality, class, politics and gender. Such reductions have informed much of the political polarisation that has characterised the 'pink tide' period. Simultaneously, however, it does not set out to undermine or erase subjective positions or relational difference; it does not seek to disavow structural inequalities from an 'unmarked' perspective. Rather, it recognises the role of these in the creation of a richly textured social field that contains within it plural possibilities for open-ended, divergent futures. It is, in this sense, a film that is highly aware of the moment and the place of its creation, undeserving of accusations that it fetishises marginality from an anti-*chavista* perspective. Its investment is not in a specific ideology, but rather in the particularities of place-making and of existing in togetherness that generate social narratives that cannot be said to collapse into a vacuous celebration of intersectionality or multiculturalism. A film such as this that seeks to nurture thoughtfulness, sensitivity and care amid heightened political tensions is worthy of commendation.

So much is evident in the film's closing sequence that sees Junior return to school for the beginning of a new semester. It opens with a final panoramic shot over a schoolyard in El 23 de Enero that is flanked by the iconic towers as its domineering backdrop. Two groups of students sing an atonal version of the national anthem; they are divided by a concrete canopy that runs between two playgrounds. The camera mingles between the rows of students until it focuses on Junior with his uneven haircut. Junior stands in line obediently, although he refuses to sing along with his classmates. This parting act of silent resilience projects El 23 in its various expressions and contradictions. Junior's character is not appropriated because it is never fully offered to the audience; instead, he nuances concepts of marginality by inviting inquiry from spectators who are offered multiple lines of interpretation. Might this refusal to sing the anthem signal a line drawn in libidinal investment in state-making in the twilight years of the 'pink tide' phenomenon? Is this privileging of the child another form of Utopianism that promises community integration on the basis of future cooperation and mutual understanding, a moment to come that is perpetually postponed in the present? Or does Junior's disobedience reject categorical grouping on principle and in practice, indicating a need to think differently of and about socially liberal politics? These questions highlight areas for further research on 'pink tide' gender politics and film-making both in and beyond twenty-first-century Venezuela, including queer films from Ecuador, Brazil, Chile, Bolivia and Argentina. In the meantime, *Pelo malo* asks viewers to consider the subtleties in social relations and cultural discourse that are obscured by political polarisation and heteronormative categories of sexuality and gender, as each of these inform attitudes towards 'la diferencia' in a specifically Bolivarian environment. In this sense, *Pelo malo* indicates a tendency in 'pink wave' cinema that seeks to nuance positional relations towards queerness and selfhood in their multiple and multiplying variations, cutting across temporal and geographic limitations and political subscriptions. Thinking otherwise about *chavismo*, with Rondón's Junior, demands a collective 'growing sideways', laying the ground for an alternative set of cultural narratives that mediate the complexities of social conflicts, hopes and desires as we look back at the Venezuela of the Chávez era.

References

Ahmed, S. (2006) *Queer Phenomenology: Orientations, Objects, Others*. Duke University Press: Durham and London.

Almandoz, A. (2012) 'Modernidad urbanística y Nuevo Ideal Nacional' in A. Almandoz (ed.) *Caracas, de la metrópoli súbita a la meca roja*. Quito: OLACCHI, 95-104.

Alvaray, L. (2013) 'Claiming the Past: Venezuelan Historical Films and Public Politics'. *Cultural Dynamics* **25**(3): 291-306.

Alvaray, L. (2018) 'Transnational Networks of Financing and Distribution: International Co-Productions' in M. D'Lugo, A. López and L. Podalsky (eds.) *The Routledge Companion to Latin American Cinema*. Routledge: London, 251-265.

Beasley-Murray, J., Cameron, M. and Hershberg, E. (2009) 'Latin America's Left Turns: An Introduction'. *Third World Quarterly* **30**(2): 319-330.

Bell, D. and Valentine, G. (eds.) (1995) *Mapping Desire: Geographies of Sexualities*. Routledge: London.

Beverley, J. (2011) *Latinamericanism After 9/11*. Duke University Press: Durham and London.

Blackmore, L. (2017) *Spectacular Modernity: Dictatorship, Space and Visibility in Venezuela 1948–1958*. University of Pittsburgh Press: Pittsburgh.

Bond Stockton, K. (2009) *The Queer Child, or Growing Sideways in the Twentieth Century*. Duke University Press: Durham and London.

Cáceres, O. (2009) 'Aproximación cualitativa a los modos de vida e intersubjectividades de las minorías sexuales en las urbes venezolanas: la eficacia material del imaginario colectivo y sus implicaciones simbólicas' in C. Colina (ed.) *Sabanagay: disidencia y diversidad sexual en la ciudad*. Editorial Alfa: Caracas, 209-237.

Cannon, B. (2008) 'Class/Race Polarisation in Venezuela and the Electoral Success of Hugo Chávez: A Break with the past or the Song Remains the Same?' *Third World Quarterly* **29**(4): 731-748.

Consejo Ciudadano para la Seguridad Pública y la Justicia Penal (CCSPJP) (2015) 'Caracas, Venezuela, la ciudad más violenta del mundo del 2015'. *Seguridad, justicia y paz*, 25 January. [WWW document]. URL http://www .seguridadjusticiaypaz.org.mx/sala-de-prensa/1356-caracas-venezuela-la-ciudad-mas-violenta-del-mundo-del-2015 [accessed 19 December 2017].

Ciccariello-Maher, G. (2013) *We Created Chávez: A People's History of the Venezuelan Revolution*. Duke University Press: Durham and London.

Coronil, F. (1997) *The Magical State: Nature, Money and Modernity in Venezuela*. University of Chicago Press: Chicago.

Coronil, F. (2011) 'The Future in Question: History and Utopia in Latin America (1989–2010)' in C. Calhoun and G. Derluguian (eds.), *Business As Usual: The Roots of the Global Financial Meltdown*. New York University Press: New York, London, 231-264.

Delgado, M. (2017) '"Meeting Points": An Interview with Mariana Rondón and Marité Ugás' in M. Delgado, S. Hart and R. Johnson (eds.) *A Companion to Latin American Cinema*. Wiley Blackwell: Oxford, 487-498.

Dennison, S. (ed.) (2013) *Contemporary Hispanic Cinema: Interrogating the Transnational in Spanish and Latin American Film*. Tamesis: Woodbridge.

Duno Gottberg, L. (2003) 'Mob Outrages: Reflections on the Media Construction of the Masses in Venezuela (April 2000–January 2003)'. *Journal of Latin American Cultural Studies* **13**(1): 115-135.

Duno Gottberg, L. (2011) 'The Color of Mobs: Racial Politics, Ethnopopulism and Representation in the Chávez Era' in D. Smilde and D. Hellinger (eds.), *Venezuela's Bolivarian Democracy: Participation, Politics, and Culture under Chávez*. Duke University Press: Durham and London, 271-297.

Dyer, R. (1997) *White*. Routledge: London.

Edelman, L. (2004) *No Future: Queer Theory and the Death Drive*. Duke University Press: Durham and London.

Espina, G. and Rakowski, C. (2010) 'Waking Women Up? Hugo Chávez, Populism, and Venezuela's "Popular" Women' in K. Kampwirth (ed.) *Gender and Populism in Latin America: Passionate Politics*. Pennsylvania State University Press: University Park, Pennsylvania, 180-201.

Fernandes, S. (2007) 'Gender Agenda of Pink Tide in Latin America'. *Economic and Political Weekly* **42**(39): 3900-3901.

Fernandes, S. (2010) 'Gender, Popular Participation and the State in Chávez's Venezuela' in K. Kampwirth (ed.) *Gender and Populism in Latin America: Passionate Politics*. Pennsylvania State University Press: University Park, Pennsylvania, 202-221.

Friedman, E. (2009) 'Gender, Sexuality and the Latin American Left: Testing the Transformation'. *Third World Quarterly* **30**(2): 415-433.

Foster, D. (2003) *Queer Issues in Contemporary Latin American Cinema*. University of Texas Press: Austin.

Foucault, M. [1977] (1991) *Discipline and Punish: The Birth of the Prison*, trans. by Alan Sheridan. Penguin: London.

Franco, J. (1989) *Plotting Women: Gender and Representation in Mexico*. Verso: London.

Fraser, V. (2000) *Building the New World: Studies in the Modern Architecture of Latin America 1930–1960*. Verso: London.

Gackstetter Nichols, E. (2013) '"Decent Girls with Good Hair": Beauty, Morality and Race in Venezuela'. *Feminist Theory* **14**(2): 171-185.

García, R. and Belinchón, G. (2013) 'Chávez nos sentenció a la guerra'. *El País*, 29 September. [WWW document]. URL http://cultura.elpais.com/cultura/2013/09/28/actualidad/1380390514_383994.html [accessed 30 October 2016].

Garsd, J. (2014) '"Pelo Malo" Is A Rare Look Into Latin American Race Relations'. *NPR*, 10 December. [WWW document]. URL http://www.npr.org/2014/12/10/369645207/pelo-malo-is-a-rare-look-into-latin-american-race-relations [accessed 30 Oct 2016].

Gutiérrez-Albilla, J. (2008) *Queering Buñuel: Sexual Dissidence and Psychoanalysis in his Mexican and Spanish Cinema*. Tauris: London.

Hart, S. (2004) *A Companion to Latin American Film*. Tamesis: Woodbridge.

Hernández, G. (2013) 'The Curious Case of Mariana Rondón'. *Caracas Chronicles*, 9 October. [WWW document]. URL http://www.caracaschronicles.com/2013/10/09/the-curious-case-of-mariana-rondon/ [accessed 30 October 2016].

Hershfield, J. (1996) *Mexican Cinema/Mexican Woman, 1940–1950.* University of Arizona Press: Arizona.

Hoff, B. (2016) *Reprojecting the City: Urban Space and Dissident Sexualities in Recent Latin American Cinema.* Legenda: Cambridge.

Irazábal, C. and Foley, D. (2008) 'Space, Revolution and Resistance: Ordinary Places and Extraordinary Events in Caracas' in C. Irazábal, C. (ed.) *Ordinary Places/Extraordinary Events: Citizenship, Democracy and Public Space in Latin America.* Routledge: London, 144–169.

Jarman, R. (2017) 'Bolivarian Landslides? Ecological Disasters, Political Upheavals and (Trans)National Futures in Contemporary Venezuelan Culture'. *EcoZon@* **8**(1): 22-41.

Johnston, L. and Valentine, G. (1995) 'Where I lay My Girlfriend, That's My Home: The Performance and Surveillance of Lesbian Identities in Domestic Environments' in D. Bell and G. Valentine (eds.) *Mapping Desire: Geographies of Sexualities.* Routledge: London, 99-113.

Joseph, M. (2002) *Against the Romance of Community.* University of Minnesota Press: Minneapolis.

Manwaring, M. (2012) *Gangs, Pseudo-Militaries, and Other Modern Mercenaries: New Dynamics in Uncomfortable Wars.* University of Oklahoma Press: Oklahoma.

Martin, D. (2017) 'What Is the Child for Latin American Cinema? Spectatorship, Mobility, and Authenticity in Pedro González Rubio's *Alamar* (2009)' in M. Delgado, S. Hart and R. Johnson (eds.) *A Companion to Latin American Cinema.* Wiley Blackwell: Oxford, 187-200.

Merentes, J. (2010) 'Gay Rights in Venezuela under Hugo Chávez, 1999–2009' in J. Corrales and M. Pecheny (eds.) *The Politics of Sexuality in Latin America.* University of Pittsburgh Press: Pittsburgh, 220-223.

Mulvey, L. (1989) *Visual and Other Pleasures.* Macmillan: Basingstoke.

Muñoz, J. (2009) *Cruising Utopia. The Then and There of Queer Futurity.* New York University Press: London, New York.

Ochoa, M. (2014) *Queen for a Day:* Transformistas, *Beauty Queens, and the Performance of Femininity in Venezuela.* Duke University Press: Durham and London.

Omaña, J. (2012) 'En Caracas el imagen es un arma'. *Ejéricito Comunicacional de Liberación R.L.,* 'PLOMo #1' [WWW document]. URL http://issuu.com/revistaplomo/docs/plomo_uno [accessed 8 May 2012].

Peña Zerpa, J. (2015) 'Arcoíris documental: tejido del activismo sexodiverso en Venezuela'. *Questión* **1**(48): 168-187.

Perriam, C. (2013) *Spanish Queer Cinema.* Edinburgh University Press: Edinburgh.

Randall, R. (2017) *Children on the Threshold in Contemporary Latin American Cinema: Nature, Gender and Agency.* Lexington Books: Lanham.

Rocha, C. and Seminet, G. (eds) (2014) *Screening Minors in Latin American Cinema.* Lexington Books: Lanham.

Salima, P. (2014) '"Pelo malo" y la enfermedad infantil del antichavismo'. *Aporrea,* 6 January. [WWW document]. URL https://www.aporrea.org/actualidad/a179595.html [accessed 30 October 2016].

Santí, E. (1998) '"Fresa y Chocolate": The Rhetoric of Cuban Reconciliation', *MLN* **113**(2): 407-425.

Shaw, D. (2003) *Contemporary Cinema of Latin America: Ten Key Films.* Continuum: New York.

Shaw, D. (2007) 'Latin American Cinema Today: A Qualified Success Story' in D. Shaw (ed.) *Contemporary Latin American Cinema: Breaking into the Global Market*. Rowman & Littlefield: Plymouth, 1-10.

Shaw, L. and Dennison, S. (eds) (2005) *Latin American Cinema: Essays on Modernity, Gender and National Identity*. McFarland: London.

Shaw, L., Duno-Gottberg, L., Page, J. and Prado, I. (2018) 'National Cinemas (re)ignited: Film and the State' in M. D'Lugo, A. López and L. Podalsky (eds.) *The Routledge Companion to Latin American Cinema*. Routledge: London, 44-61.

Silva-Ferrer, M. (2014) *El cuerpo dócil de la cultura: poder, cultura y comunicación en la Venezuela de Chávez*. Iberoamericana: Vervuert.

Smith, P. (1994) 'The Language of Strawberry'. *Sight and Sound* **12**: 30-33.

Subero, G. (2014) *Queer Masculinities in Latin American Cinema: Male Bodies and Narrative Representations*. Tauris: London.

Velasco, A. (2011) '"We Are Still Rebels": The Challenge of Popular History in Bolivarian Venezuela' in D. Smilde and D. Hellinger (eds.) *Venezuela's Bolivarian Democracy: Participation, Politics, and Culture under Chávez*. Duke University Press: Durham and London, 157-185.

Velasco, A. (2015) *Barrio Rising: Urban Popular Politics and the Making of Modern Venezuela*. University of California Press: Oakland, California.

Vielma, F. (2014) 'La homosexualidad de Capriles'. *Misión Verdad*. 30 September. [WWW document]. URL http://misionverdad.com/columnistas/la-homo sexualidad-de-capriles [accessed 18 December 2017].

Viga, L. (2015) *Desde allá*. Factor PH Producciones, Malandro Films, Lucia Films: Caracas.

Zacarías, G. (2014) 'El chófer del camión de muñecas: más que un personaje caraqueño'. 29 January. [WWW document]. URL https://palabraindeleble .wordpress.com/2014/01/29/el-chofer-del-camion-de-munecas-mas-que-un-personaje-caraqueno/ [accessed 30 October 2016].

Newspapers

El Nacional (2016) 'Capriles respondió a mensajes homofóbicos de Jorge Rodríguez'. 17 May. [WWW document]. URL http://www.el-nacional .com/noticias/politica/capriles-respondio-mensajes-homofobicos-jorge-rodriguez_32720 [accessed 18 December 2017].

El Universal (2010) 'Altos prelados rechazan murales de imágenes sagradas con fusiles'. 5 May. [WWW document]. URL http://www.eluniversal.com/ 2010/05/05/pol_ava_altos-prelados-recha_05A3863371.shtml [accessed 30 October 2016].

El Universal (2013) 'Artículo del Sibci'. 1 October. [WWW document]. URL http://www.eluniversal.com/arte-y-entretenimiento/131001/articulo-del-sibci [accessed 30 October 2016].

Gould, J. (2006) 'Venezuela's Revolutionary Tourists'. *Time*. 17 May. [WWW document]. URL http://content.time.com/time/world/article/0,8599,1195004, 00.html [accessed 30 October 2016].

Infobae. (2014) 'Bandas armadas en Venezuela: un monstruo creado por el *chavismo*'. 15 February. [WWW document]. URL http:// www.infobae.com/

2014/02/15/1543947-bandas-armadas-venezuela-un-monstruo-creado-el-chavismo [accessed 30 October 2016].

Kermode, M. (2015) 'Pelo Malo Review – Coming of Age in Caracas'. *The Observer*. 1 February. [WWW document]. URL https://www.theguardian .com/film/2015/feb/01/pelo-malo-review-mariana-rondon-samuel-lange-zambrino-samantha-castillo-caracas [accessed 30 October 2016].

Meza, A. (2013) 'Polémica por los insultos homófobos de un diputado chavista a Capriles'. *El País*, 16 August. [WWW document]. URL https://elpais.com/ internacional/2013/08/16/actualidad/1376629192_431773.html [accessed 18 Dececember 2017].

Films

Azul y no tan rosa, 2012. Film. Directed by Miguel Ferrari. Venezuela: Plenilunio Film & Arts; Centro Nacional Autónomo de Cinematografía.

Brecha en el silencio, 2012. Film. Directed by Andrés Eduardo Rodríguez and Luis Alejandro Rodríguez. Venezuela: Fundación Villa del Cine, TMI Proyect.

Cheila: Una casa pa Maíta, 2010. Film. Directed by Eduardo Barbarena. Venezuela: Fundación Villa del Cine.

Desde allá, 2015. Film. Directed by Lorenzo Viga. Venezuela: Factor PH Producciones, Malandro Films, Lucia Films.

El chico que miente, 2011. Directed by Mariana Ugás. Venezuela: Sudaca Films.

El rumor de las piedras, 2011. Film. Directed by Alejandro Bellame Palacios. Venezuela: Centro Nacional Autónomo de Cinematografía.

El tinte de la fama, 2008. Film. Directed by Alejandro Bellame Palacios. Venezuela: Totem Films.

Maroa, 2005. Directed by Solveig Hoogesteijn. Venezuela: Alta Films.

Pelo malo, 2013. Directed by Mariana Rondón. Venezuela: Sudaca Films; Centro Nacional Autónomo de Cinematografía.

Piedra, papel, tijera, 2012. Film. Directed by Hernán Jabes. Venezuela: Factor RH Producciones, Centro Nacional Autónomo de Cinematografía.

Postales de Leningrado, 2005. Film. Directed by Mariana Rondón. Venezuela: Sudaca Films.

Secuestro express, 2005. Film. Directed by Jonathan Jakubowicz. Venezuela: Tres Malandros.

9

Chronicles of Disenchantment: Rethinking Venezuelan National Identity in Eduardo Sánchez Rugeles's *Los desterrados*

MARÍA TERESA VERA-ROJAS

Universitat de Lleida

In the midst of the Venezuelan publishing boom of the last fifteen years, Eduardo Sánchez Rugeles has stood out as one of the most prolific writers. He is the author of a trilogy comprised of the novels *Blue Label/Etiqueta azul* (2010), *Transilvania Unplugged* (2011) and *Liubliana* (2012), of a brief and illustrated novel narrated from a child's perspective, *Julián* (2014), and of a crime novel, *Jezabel* (2013). His work breaks with the trend of fiction about Venezuelan national identity (in Spanish, *venezolanidad*), by focusing on twenty-first-century middle-class Venezuelan experiences of migration. His texts speak to a generation of readers who recognise themselves not only in their use of Venezuelan idioms (*venezolanismos*) but moreover in the allusions to Venezuelan popular media culture from the 1980s and 1990s. These factors have come together to form a literary project that conceives of displacement as the starting point for the life experiences of his characters, whose identities are shaped in a 'radical disagreement with the imaginary of rootedness' (Rivas Rojas, 2013: 199; all translations are the author's own).

Sánchez Rugeles's characters undertake identity quests that evidence their disagreement with the national fictions inherited from twentieth-century Venezuelan nationalist discourses. By exploring his characters' experiences of youth and adulthood, his narrative manages to penetrate the conflictive reality experienced by a minority middle-class population of Caracas. Such characters – and the social class they represent – express their disagreement with the imposition of a sense of national belonging that is articulated by institutional discourses with recourse to nationalist symbolism, as well as through the collective recognition that is forged through everyday bonding.

The compilation of chronicles entitled *Los desterrados* (*The Uprooted*, 2011), the text that criticises this symbolism most directly, is Sánchez Rugeles's most explicit enactment of the confrontation between the middle-class Venezuelan readership and the experiences of uprooted subjects. It does so not only by tracing geographic displacements, but moreover those positions in society that engender a feeling of social and historical estrangement in twenty-first-century Venezuela. As I shall explain, this is accomplished through the projection of a 'telescopic – although close – gaze on the country of origin, from the perspective of displaced subjects; it is a compilation of texts of a hybrid genre that is placed within the boundaries of the journalistic chronicle and autobiographical fiction' (Valladares-Ruiz, 2013: 116).

Following these ideas, in this chapter I seek to explore some of these chronicles so as to reflect on disenchantment as one of the experiences that define the failure of hegemony in Venezuelan democratic discourses. Embodied in nationalist ideologies, this failure involves not only the Bolivarian nationalism of the period denominated the Fifth Republic but also that which preceded it. Both of these nation-building projects had recourse to the spell of the 'magical state', that is, a form of governance that, according to Fernando Coronil:

> [A]stonishes through the marvels of power rather than convinces through the power of reason, as reason itself is made part of the awe-inspiring spectacle of its rule. By manufacturing dazzling development projects that engender collective fantasies of progress, it casts its spell over audience and performers alike. As a 'magnanimous sorcerer', the state seizes its subjects by inducing a condition or state of being receptive to its illusions – a magical state. (Coronil, 1997: 5)

The mode of disenchantment encountered in these stories responds to the rationalisation of a national Utopia, the perpetually postponed endpoint of collective fantasies of progress, and to the desacralisation of the enchantment exerted by the Venezuelan magical state, a petro-state that 'came to hold the monopoly not only of political violence but of the nation's natural wealth' (Coronil, 1997: 4). As such, this petro-state 'has exercised this monopoly dramaturgically, securing compliance through the spectacular display of its imperious presence – it seeks to conquer rather than persuade […] the Venezuelan state has been constituted as a *unifying force by producing fantasies of collective integration into centralised political institutions*' (Coronil, 1997: 4; emphasis added) in ways that breach ideological differences.

Using this framework, my analysis of Sánchez Rugeles's chronicles argues that in *Los desterrados*, the notion of disenchantment goes hand in hand with the awareness of its middle-class citizens of the failure of the magical state and its perpetual nation-building projects. These are engendered by historical figures as the embodiment of state power wielded to bind together its population with a cultural imaginary of heroic deeds and the fantasies of development. This scenario has repeatedly re-enacted a Manichean foundational discourse that sees a confrontation between civilisation and barbarism – i.e. sovereignty vs. imperialism, *pueblo* vs. oligarchy. Here disenchantment does not acknowledge the Utopian possibility of redemption, but instead recognises the mental and ideological restrictions that it can entail, in this case, at the hands of the Bolivarian Revolution.

Lastly, with reference to these chronicles, I consider disenchantment as an expression of dissidence that works through the desacralisation of nationalist fictions, as well as through the idea that the representations of displaced subjects in contemporary Venezuelan literature are an expression of the irreversibility of the myth of national unity. Within this context, the nostalgia that permeates Sánchez Rugeles's writing constitutes one of the means linked to the love-hate relationship of its characters with their national origin, as well as to the critical gaze that from a distant perspective is able to dismantle the fictions of origins through which identity and a national sense of belonging are imposed.

From a broader perspective, through the analysis of these texts I seek further to propose the idea that this disenchantment cannot be detached from the emergence of new literary projects, writers and publishing houses that have come to problematise the traditional influence of the petro-state in the construction of Venezuelan national discourse and its literary intelligentsia.

Under the Spell of Oil: Venezuelan State and Its Fictions of National Belonging

Conceived from the border or 'stateless' place where chronicle and fiction meet and clash with each other, *Los desterrados* is a group of texts, the main character and writer of which is Lautaro Sanz, a 'character who, by way of *alter ego*, was created [by Sánchez Rugeles] to express with determination the disenchantment of being Venezuelan in the twenty-first century' (Yslas Prado, 2011: 10). These chronicles offer us a personal account of displacement, which, as the title itself reveals, seeks to emphasise its 'evident rejection to any nationalist tie' (Yslas Prado, 2011: 11). Lautaro's ironic and irreverent tone performs, as we will see, a way of writing bound to banishment – that of the character, but also of the readers – not only from the country, but particularly from the boundaries of the national imaginary. This is a writing that, imbued with records of Venezuelan media culture of the last few decades, demands of us the redefinition of the myths and fictions concerning Venezuelan national identity faced with the failure of happiness and prosperity that were promised.

These assertions are part of the introduction to *Los desterrados*, written by Venezuelan writer Luis Yslas, in which he sets up the framework that

contextualises Lautaro Sanz's life and political position, while simultaneously acknowledging displacement and estrangement as one of the subjects
of contemporary Venezuelan literature: '[T]his prose of exile may be the
reproduction, in a sarcastic register, of the existential discomfort increasingly
universal to Venezuelans in the twenty-first century, which is the same hostility that reveals that, in fact, the country does not abandon Lautaro, even if he
carries it as a corrupted fondness, as an open wound' (Yslas, 2011: 14). Even
if Yslas lucidly suggests the idea that in these chronicles the nation is also
the creation of a transnational and desacralised cartography, their characters'
reluctance to commit to ideas of the nation could be read as an expression of
the failure of the magical state in its promise to construct a solid discourse of
national belonging.

Although apparently different in their nationalist aims, both the Fourth
and the Fifth Republics made use of the spell of oil to project their illusions
of a national community. The social democratic state shaped its nationalist
discourse by means of the inherited *criollista* and populist project of the 1930s
which found in *Doña Bárbara* '[a] foundational fiction that depicts the path
to nation building through an allegorical romance [...]. Marriage between
the elite and the pueblo will create, it promises, national historical progress.
The modern state, capitalism, and the bourgeois family will be harmoniously
wed' (Coronil and Skurski, 1991: 299). What cannot be overlooked is that 'This
hopeful view of national transformation became imaginable only with the
growth of the oil industry in the 1920s and with the progress it promised'
(Coronil and Skurski, 1991: 299–300). Meanwhile, *chavista* politics initially
re-appropriated such nationalist discourse by emphasising the oppositional
class binary of *pueblo* vs. oligarchy. This re-appropriation was not only with
respect to discourses of class divisions, but also in relation to the ideological
basis that gave shape to the Bolivarian Revolution in its beginnings, as Alicia
Ríos has pointed out:

> It was expected to begin from zero, to write a new history of the
> country where the participatory and leading place of *el pueblo* was
> acknowledged. However, the ideological bases of [Hugo Chávez's]
> project were anchored in the heroic beginnings of the nation, and
> he took as his model the military ideals that allowed its creation. It
> is in the intersection between the dominant, residual and emerging
> uses/manifestations of the Bolívar cult that Chávez has been able to
> give himself a new meaning as the representative, finally – and once
> again –, of Bolivarian values [...]. Thanks to the nation's access to oil,
> and to the advances of technology and communications, the new leader
> is able to undertake his liberating labor to new frontiers, beyond Latin
> American borders. (Ríos, 2013: 123)

However, Chávez's declaration of Venezuela as a socialist state some years after his election led him progressively to change his discourse towards a more revolutionary one that made of the bourgeois class its main domestic target. As Jonathan Eastwood clearly explains, both ways of referring to class coexist today:

> the distinction between the people and the oligarchy was well established in Venezuelan political culture before Chávez. This discourse cut across many social divisions and gained legitimacy by virtue of its close association with the idea of the Venezuelan nation, which resonated with the vast majority of Venezuelans. The 'bourgeoisie-proletariat' frame is potentially much more divisive (this is even true, though less so, of the hybrid 'bourgeoisie-pueblo' frame). *Perhaps for this reason, these two official discourses of class now exist alongside each other. Chávez himself weaves them together, despite the apparent contradictions between them.* (Eastwood, 2011: 4; emphasis added)

In addition, Chávez's attempt to implement a socialist state sought to transform the nationalist discourses through the rebuilding of a new fable of origins, where, although metamorphosed in Chávez and his endeavours, Simón Bolívar remained the only 'symbolic reference that unites, as an equivalent or at least approximated force, Venezuelan society as a whole' (Ríos, 2013: 19). This reinforced the fact that the cult of Bolívar is a:

> political category that, even at the beginning of the twenty-first century, still bears the weight of the national imaginary, and, on certain occasions, the continental imaginary as well. Thanks to a populist, anti-imperialist and militarist discourse, President Chávez has managed to strengthen a cult that casts itself once again, in its messianic nature, as the only path to follow for the complete development of a national identity. (Ríos, 2013: 19)

Sánchez Rugeles's chronicles criticise these overlapping discourses, as if the present itself were a reason to acknowledge that there is no nostalgic version of the past that is worth recovering at the expense of an awareness that one's personal identity begins with the rationalisation of the illusions of a 'natural' and 'common' bond among Venezuelans. It is an experience of uprooting that, as Magdalena López suggests when analysing twentieth-century Caribbean fiction, refers not only to a geographic or national dislocation, but to the 'loss of certainties, such as our relation to the past, upon which our conception of the world is based' (López, 2015: 22). In this sense, I am interested not in the cynicism of one who has lost the meaning of life, but in the possibility of conceiving of disenchantment as one of the experiences that allows us to question the homogeneous and univocal perspective with which narratives about Venezuelan national identity have been constructed. In this respect, Alicia Ríos quotes historian and political scientist, Luis Ricardo Dávila, who had critiqued these interrelated dimensions of Venezuelan nationalist discourses: 'Bolívar, the heroic "cult" and the Nation can be seen together as one of the most important ideological, political, and social articulations that unite Venezuelans; the other important articulation of our modernity was constructed around the notion of Venezuela as an oil nation' (quoted in Ríos, 2013: 48). According to Dávila, the impact of oil 'was symbolically related to the same independence process to construct a chain of equivalences that led to reinforce the unity of the Nation by means of its oil status' (ibid.).

Los desterrados: Experiences of National Uprooting

Los desterrados begins with a chronicle that describes the unexpected encounter in Madrid Barajas airport of two characters: Lautaro Sanz – a Venezuelan writer, reader, wandering subject and former high school teacher – and one of his ex-students, Felipe Garmendia, who has recently emigrated from Venezuela. This text, entitled 'El desarraigo imposible' ('The Impossible Uprooting'), collates the platitudes of those who reject their homeland and clichés that are offensive for the most patriotic followers of the country's nationalistic discourse. However stereotypical, it is through these curses against the concept of national origins voiced by the young Felipe that this text interrogates the dilemma of belonging to an imaginary of national rootedness while recognising the failure of the state in the nation-building project. Thus, while waiting for the flights that will take them to their destinations, a didactic scene unfolds, one in which a young Felipe full of hate, pain and confusion spits out his arguments, and in the midst of his efforts to move away from the nation and its signifiers, falls back into the emptiness and solitude faced by those who take the risk of withdrawing from its charms:

Yo, profesor, se lo digo honestamente, tengo más de un año promoviendo el exilio; persona con la que hablo que me comenta que tiene ganas de irse, le digo *lárgate, vete de esta mierda, esto no vale nada*. Sin embargo, dentro de mi espontaneidad apátrida no puedo evitar un sentimiento de culpa, una incomodidad ante el desarraigo, una especie de pesar por reconocer que una de las cosas más ridículas que he visto en mi vida es al tal Dudamel tocar *Pajarillo* con arreglo sinfónico […]. Usted, que siempre tuvo las respuestas, dígame cómo se puede sentir afecto por nuestra cultura de la mediocridad y la muerte. (Sánchez Rugeles, 2011: 22; original emphasis)

Professor, I honestly tell you this, I have been promoting exile for over a year; I tell each person I speak with who mentions that he or she is thinking of leaving the country *to leave, to go away from this shit, that this is worth nothing.* However, with this stateless spontaneity, I can't avoid feeling guilt, a discomfort before the uprooting, a sort of sorrow for acknowledging that one of the most ridiculous things that I have ever seen in my life is that guy Dudamel playing *Pajarillo* with symphonic arrangements [...]. You, you who always knew the answers, tell me how you can feel fondness towards our culture of mediocrity and death.

To Felipe's orphaned outburst, Lautaro Sanz reacts from the position of one who has lost the magic that brings together national subjects. His response contains a 'spoiler' of that which is to be discovered in these chronicles, that is, the awareness that there is no possible Utopia. The solitude that accompanies the experiences of exile has defeated the fictions that gather together the national community:

Sabes, Felipe, creo que si no tuviera tanto tiempo fuera de Venezuela no te diría lo que te diré ahora. He sido un errante, he llevado una vida sin destino, he estado en lugares que nunca me imaginé que podían existir. Al final, las cosas que se echan de menos no resultan visibles; creo que tiene que ver con el arraigo, es algo impalpable, telúrico [...]. Puede que haya cierta poesía en el despropósito, en lo mal hecho, en lo incompleto [...] creo que la falta de nobleza es la que nos permite reconocernos, la que nos da cierta identidad [...]. Esa desconfianza, esa visión paupérrima de la vida cotidiana, en el fondo, puede ser nuestro mayor atributo pero eso es algo que sólo puede verse desde lejos; estando inmersos en el caos sólo se percibe la vulgaridad y la miseria. (Sánchez Rugeles, 2011: 23–24)

You know, Felipe, if I hadn't been away from Venezuela for so long, I wouldn't tell you what I am about to say. I have been a nomad, I have had a life without destiny, I have been in places that I have never imagined could exist. In the end, the things that you miss the most are not the visible ones; I believe that it has to do with rootedness, it is something impalpable, telluric [...]. There may be a certain poetry in the nonsense, in what is poorly done, in what is incomplete [...] I think that this lack of greatness is what allows us to recognise each other, what give us a certain identity [...]. This distrust, this very poor perception of everyday life can be, deep inside, our greatest quality, but this is something that can only be seen from a distance; if you are immersed in the chaos you can only perceive vulgarity and misery.

From a position of sempiternal movement, Lautaro Sanz comes to be a chronicler of those uprooted subjects, the one who records, in his never-ending journey, their disenchantment with the accounts that have sought to bring together, imagine and shape the representations of Venezuelan nationalism. This is when the 'lack of greatness' turns into a source of rootedness. The bond that brings together the Venezuelan community lies in distrust, leading us to an oxymoron that defies the rootedness and magnificence that have reduced the representations of Venezuelan national identity to the adoration of national idols and to praise of the congeniality of their people. Moreover, this oxymoron emphasises the collapse of representations that aim to perpetuate the fiction of a national community produced through the myth of the Venezuelans as a happy people/nation. It is precisely this last premise which becomes the target of Felipe Garmendia's arguments, when he blurts out:

> Si me viene con el cuentico del Ávila, los panas, el pabellón, el Diablito o las hallacas, me pararé de aquí y lo insultaré; con todo respeto, créame que le caeré a coñazos. Yo no sé quién inventó esa ficción de que el venezolano es de pinga. Nunca he estado en un lugar en el que se tenga tanto desprecio por el prójimo. (2011: 23)

> If you come to me with the same old story about Ávila, the gangs, the *pabellón*, the *Diablitos* o the *hallacas*, I will stop here and I will insult you; with all due respect, believe me, I will hit you with my own fists. I don't know who invented that fiction that Venezuelans are cool people. I have never been in a place where people treat their compatriots with such contempt

Laurato Sanz and the other characters of these chronicles speak from a position that represents the hinge of this estrangement from memories of Venezuela over the years, calling into question the certainties of nationalist fictions, and expressing contempt for national figures and icons as an expression of the discursive nature of identity. But it especially rationalises and secularises the magical legacy of the Venezuelan petro-state, which has been recycled in the socialist Utopia of Chávez and his Bolivarian Revolution.

Lautaro is a wandering subject. A panoramic view of the chronicles that make up *Los desterrados* offers the image of a subject in perpetual movement that inhabits multiple places and realities. In his journey, he gathers losses, experiences and knowledge, in which friendship and emotions are the devices that trigger what Svetlana Boym has called 'reflective nostalgia', that is, the individual memory that understands that the recovering of signals and shattered pieces of memory does not mean the restoration of a lost home. Such nostalgia dwells in longing and loss; it does not reside in the evocation of national past and future, because it is about individual and collective memory, and although these may overlap in their references, 'they do not coincide in their narratives and plots of identity'. In fact, 'they can use the same triggers of memory and symbols, the same Proustian madeleine party, but tell different stories about it' (Boym, 2001: 49). In opposition to the 'collective pictorial symbols and oral cultures' and the reconstruction of 'emblems and rituals of home and homeland in an attempt to conquer and specialise time' (Boym, 2001: 49), which are orientations that define restorative nostalgia, reflective nostalgia 'cherishes shattered fragments of memory and temporalizes space […]. [It] can be ironic and humorous. It reveals that longing and critical thinking are not opposed to one another, as affective memories do not absolve one from compassion, judgment or critical reflection' (Boym, 2001: 49–50).

From this personal and critical place of memory, one of the chronicles entitled 'Redención. Encuentro en Oporto' ('Redemption. Encounter in Oporto') alternates memories of childhood and youth as these are experienced by Lautaro and his friend Cristina, with scenes of his encounter with Cristina's father, Don Marcelino García, who after the tragic death of his daughter in Caracas, decides to live his de-territorial condition in Oporto, the native home of his late wife. In their reunion, don Marcelino explains to Lautaro that in a black-out episode, when he was having a heart attack, Cristina asked him, among other things, to speak to Lautaro and to urge him to find a place for her among his memories:

> (Lo que quería decirte es que, tras la explosión del pecho, antes de que el corazón improvisara nuevos pálpitos, Cristina me habló de ti – Marcelino hizo una pausa de tos; tras el dilatado carrasposo continuó –: Viejo, dile por favor a Lautaro que, sin derecho a replica, revoco su renuncia') Sánchez Rugeles, 2011: 56.

> What I wanted to say to you is that, after my chest exploded, before my heart improvised new beats, Cristina spoke about you', Marcelino paused to cough; after the attack subsided, he continued: Dad, please, tell Lautaro that, without the right to reply, I revoke his renunciation.

This text aims to confront the reader not only with life and death, but especially with the temporality of shattered and individual memories, of those memories that belong to de-territorialised subjects who made their memories and remembrance the basis of their identity. To this end, Sánchez Rugeles

confronts the experiences of the Europeans who emigrated to Venezuela in
the twentieth century with those of the Venezuelans who have recently left
the country, not only to compare two experiences that mirror each other in
their confusion and solitude, but also to embrace the gap that distinguishes
one temporality from the other:

> No sabría decir de dónde soy, es complicado. Yo nací en un pueblo de
> Extremadura, un caserío sin nombre; viví toda mi vida en Caracas y
> moriré en Oporto. España ni siquiera es un recuerdo, es el país de mis
> hermanos mayores, es sólo el nombre de un barco. Mis primeros recuer-
> dos tienen olor a mar: La Guaira, miedo, sensación de paso. Durante
> toda mi vida eché de menos un pasado ficticio, un mar Mediterráneo
> inventado. Mi único Mediterráneo, a fin de cuentas, siempre fue el
> Caribe. No supe ser más que un hombre infeliz; un europeo en tierra
> caliente que siempre tuvo el afán de regresar a una patria falsa, a un
> hueco en el tiempo. (Sánchez Rugeles, 2011: 57–58)

> I couldn't say where I come from, it's complicated. I was born in a town
> in Extremadura, a small village without a name; I lived my whole life
> in Caracas and I will die in Oporto. Spain isn't even a memory; it is the
> country of my older brothers, it is only the name of a ship. My first mem-
> ories smell like the sea: La Guaira, fear, a feeling of just passing through
> life. All my life I longed for a fictitious past, an invented Mediterranean
> Sea. After all, my only Mediterranean was always the Caribbean. I didn't
> know better than to be an unhappy man; a European in warm land who
> was always eager to return to a fake homeland, to a hole in time.

In addition to revealing the estrangement and the contradictory position in
which uprooted subjects find themselves, this chronicle and the encounter
that it sets up enable an emotive reflection on the meaning of rootedness and
the role of individual memories in the construction of personal identity. This
is projected from the perspectives of two uprooted characters for whom the
nation and the homeland are no more than a background noise, a scant setting that vanishes away *vis-à-vis* the everyday experiences of their individual
memories:

> Todo está en la memoria – afirmó Don Marcelino –. Uno, finalmente,
> no pertenece a una cosa tan abstracta e insignificante como un país, ni
> siquiera a una ciudad. La vida, supongo, se construye en tu calle, en
> la ventana de tu casa o tropezando en el mercado con las personas de
> siempre; quizás la idiosincrasia no sea más que una cuestión de esquinas
> y paradas de autobús. Yo, por ejemplo, no sabría decir si soy venezolano

o portugués, mucho menos español, ni siquiera soy caraqueño. Lo que sí puedo decirte y lo que realmente siento es que soy de Los Chaguaramos […]. Porque, ¿qué es un hombre viejo, Lautaro? Al final, reales o ficticios, lo único que te queda son los recuerdos. (Sánchez Rugeles, 2011: 59–60)

Everything is in the memory – affirmed Don Marcelino –. One, in the end, does not belong to an abstract and insignificant thing such as a country, nor even to a town. Life, I guess, is built in your street, in the window of your house or by bumping into the regulars at the supermarket; perhaps idiosyncrasy is no more than a matter of corners and bus stops. Take me, for example. I couldn't tell if I am Venezuelan or Portuguese, much less Spanish. I'm not even *caraqueño*. What I can tell you, and what I really feel is that I am from Los Chaguaramos […]. Because, what is an old man, Lautaro? In the end, all that's left are memories, whether these are real or fictitious.

Regarding these re-encounters between Lautaro and different Venezuelan migrants in European geographies, I coincide with Patricia Valladares-Ruiz, who points out that:

[i]n his never-ending itinerary through different European destinations, Lautaro defines his country always in opposition to the recently discovered place. Nevertheless, perhaps one of the most suggestive aspects of the book are the episodes where Lautaro meets or re-encounters some Venezuelan emigrant, who tells him his/her reasons for his/her own departure as well as his/her passing of time abroad. (Valladares-Ruiz, 2013: 122–123).

In this sense, Valladares-Ruiz gestures towards the political backdrop of the migrations of these characters. She highlights a quotation from the chronicle 'El libero de Nicosia' ('The Bookseller of Nicosia'), perhaps the source of the leitmotif in *Los desterrados*:

No se preocupe, joven, las balas pasan, pero las palabras quedan. Eso de que los vencedores escriben la historia es falso, la verdadera historia la hace el perdedor. Busque testimonios, escriba, cuente las historias de los desterrados y hará honor a su oficio. Literatura mata ejércitos. Ahora vaya, lo dejará el autobús. (Sánchez Rugeles, 2011: 36)

Don't worry, young man, bullets fire, but words remain. That the winners write history is false, true history is made by the losers. Search for testimonies, write, tell the stories of the uprooted and you will bring honor to your work. Literature kills armies. Now go, the bus will leave you.

The experiences displayed in *Los desterrados* make private memories the basis of their characters' identity, but these texts also satirise the national heroes of Venezuela and, in their accounts, transgress the nation's cultural icons. That is because for Lautaro and the characters in these chronicles such symbols have lost the redemptive meaning that historical memory offers to explain the present (Magris, 2001: 10). This is the fate of Simón Bolívar in the text 'La conspiración' ('The Conspiration'), in which the discovery of a secret archive that supposedly revealed the homosexual relationship of Andrés Bello and El Libertador causes the intervention of the government in literary studies departments in the universities, in bookstores, and at the Ministry of Culture. Thus, in a conversation held between Lautaro and Inmanuel Barreto the mystery hidden behind the government censorship operation is disclosed:

'¿Qué es?,' pregunté alzando los hombros. 'Es la correspondencia erótica que mantuvieron Bolívar y Bello entre 1808 y 1812. El cuento es *heavy*; Bello era un bichito, la vaina en Inglaterra como que fue bastante *hardcore* [...]. El hecho es que en estas malditas cartas se describe, con retórica clásica y referentes ilustrados, cómo Andrés Bello le reventaba al culo adolescente de Simón.' (Sánchez Rugeles, 2011: 114–115)

'What is it?' I asked, shrugging my shoulders. 'It's the erotic correspondence that Bolívar and Bello exchanged between 1801 and 1812. The whole affair is pretty sordid. Bello was a rebel, the situation in England seems like it was quite hardcore [...]. The fact is that these damn letters describe, with classical rhetoric and erudite references, how Andrés Bello fucked Simón's teenage arse.'

Even today, and practically since his death, Simón Bolívar 'continues to have an overwhelming presence and constitutes one of the prevailing models of state policy, accompanied by an exacerbated nationalism' (Ríos, 2013: 58). Hence the transgressive nature of this chronicle that, in addition to its intentional desacralisation of the cult to Venezuela's founding father, seeks to dismantle the core beliefs of perpetual Venezuelan nationalism. In its rewriting of Venezuelan history, this chronicle not only makes evident the fictional nature of historical records, but moreover demonstrates the manipulation of the cultural representations and national icons instrumentalised by state institutions in the restoration of national memory and in the fictive consensus of national unity that revolves around Bolívar's adoration.

Furthermore, I would also like to point out the importance of sexuality highlighted by this chronicle as one of the discourses that define national identity in a country where machismo and militarism go hand in hand, as has been lucidly explained by Gisela Kozak (2008, 2012), where the body of the nation is incarnated in the untouchable and sacred figure of Simón Bolívar, the Father of the homeland – a topic also studied in depth by Javier Guerrero (2012). Along with another chronicle entitled 'Suite palermitana. Sobre una novela inédita y erótica de Rómulo Gallegos' ('Palermitan Suite. About an Unpublished and Erotic Novel of Rómulo Gallegos'), which also makes sexuality its main topic by mocking another hidden and erotic version of Rómulo Gallegos's narrative, in 'La conspiración' homosexuality is conceived by the author as a destabilising element, as a threat to the national order and the official discourse. However, and despite his critical intention, while trying to demystify the founding fathers of the nation by means of a parody of their presumed homosexuality, Sánchez Rugeles runs the risk of reinforcing homophobia and affirming the meanings of chaos and abnormality imposed on non-normative sexualities. That is, by means of this parody, mockery, violence and hatred against homosexuality could be seen in these texts as legitimate reactions that naturalise the normative and regulative power of heterosexual desire, identity and behaviour in the Venezuelan national imaginary – homophobic representations that also extend, somewhat unfortunately, to another of Sánchez Rugeles's books, his crime novel, *Jezabel*, whose main character is Alain: a bitter, narcissist, unhappy, lonely and homosexual character, who turns out to be an assassin with a twisted personality.

Another text, 'E-mail de Jamaica' ('Email from Jamaica'), has better luck in accomplishing this desacralisation. In this chronicle, Sánchez Rugeles rewrites Simón Bolívar's *Carta de Jamaica* ('Letter from Jamaica') not from the perspective of the patriotic writer, but from the position of a displaced subject who evaluates the state of Venezuelan intelligentsia, the poverty of their citizens, and the arbitrariness in which the charm of the revolutionary government is upheld. As it is represented in this text, the arbitrary nature of the Bolivarian Revolution reduces the nation to its conception of *el pueblo*, an identification that does not accept fissures and that condemns those who express dissidence toward its discourses as 'aliens':

> He llegado a pensar – con Inmanuel Barreto y otros desterrados – que tal venezolanidad no existe. Nuestra gran tara sociológica ha sido querer imponer por la fuerza una manera de ser, unas costumbres homogéneas e incuestionables, una manera común de interpelar el ocio o un estilo de música verdaderamente tradicional. Esa intuición de Briceño-Iragorry ha sido pervertida por los actuales gerentes de la cultura y llevadas a sórdidos extremos […]. La hibridación cultural ofende a la Revolución.

El eclecticismo, por lo tanto, ha sido proscrito. El venezolano, según esta gerencia, debe estar orgulloso de ser un individuo unidimensional. (Sánchez Rugeles, 2011: 104)

I have come to think – along with Inmanuel Barreto and other exiles – that this Venezuelan identity doesn't exist. Our major sociological flaw stems from this desire to forcefully impose one way of being, a set of homogeneous and unquestionable customs, one common form of leisure and one truly traditional style of music. Briceño-Iragorry's philosophical intuition has been perverted by the current administrators of culture and taken to sordid estremes […]. Cultural hybridisation offends the Revolution. Thus, eclecticism has been banned. According to this government, the average Venezuelan must be proud of being a one-dimensional individual.

Unlike the *Carta de Jamaica*, in which Bolívar's thoughts were part of his strategies to recruit followers for the cause of Independence, in the 'E-mail de Jamaica' disenchantment imposes itself upon the will to commit to the creation of a new Utopia for Lautaro. In this text, a consciousness of the arbitrariness that condemns dissident thinking in Venezuela takes precedence over conciliatory or redeeming myths. Hence, to the 'sociological flaw' of 'this desire to forcefully impose one way of being', Lautaro replies from a displaced position of estrangement, from which neither Utopias nor Utopian alliances are possible or desirable. In this way, in the origin of this disenchantment dwells the consciousness of the failure of the magical state, but also of its 'totalitarian' reinvention by Hugo Chávez and his Bolivarian Revolution:

Dices que deseas entender, en principio, la cuestión política. La verdad es muy simple, Henry: el llamado chavismo es un *proyecto totalitario*. Cualquier justificación de este despropósito no es más que mala literatura. Impera en estas tierras un *totalitarismo bailable, un bingo incompleto, un absolutismo circense, una raza híbrida de tiranuelos y sicarios*. Esta feria del mal gusto no aparece descrita en los ensayos de Arendt o Raymond Aron. La teoría, en este contexto, es inútil. (Sánchez Rugeles, 2011: 102; emphasis added)

You say that, first of all, you want to understand the political situation. The truth is very simple, Henry; the project known as *chavismo* is a totalitarian one. Any justification of this nonsense is not more than bad literature. In these lands there prevail *a dancing totalitarianism, an incomplete bingo, a circus of absolutism, a hybrid race of tyrants and hitmen.* This fair of bad taste is not described in the essays of Arendt or Raymond Aron. Theory, in this context, is useless.

According to this logic, the origin, formation and popularity of *chavismo* as nationalist authoritarianism, as well as the sanctification of Chávez by the state and his followers, have been practices linked to the need to maintain the rituals, mystery and magic that have been turned into failure. A continuity of such magic found in the mystery of Venezuelan wealth (i.e., oil) was re-signified by Chávez through the distorted humanist ideal of 'Supreme Social Happiness', the magical popular ingredient sought after to keep afloat the ritual of consensus and national community controlled by the state and its hegemony over the social, political, cultural and economic institutions. This was also his token to legitimate the arbitrariness of his government, to extend *el pueblo*'s investment and hope in the promise of happiness and in the promises of a future of social equality, as well as to administrate his kindness and the desirability of his project. Such is the importance of this concept for the imaginary of the Bolivarian Socialism of the twenty-first century, that supposedly in order to guarantee the fulfilment of social rights, in 2013 President Nicolás Maduro created the Vice-Ministry for the People's Supreme Social Happiness.

With respect to the 'totalitarian' project denounced by Lautaro (2011: 102), it is relevant to mention the observations that Claudio Magris proposes regarding Utopia and disenchantment, for they will help us to understand why an expression of dissidence resides in Lautaro's disenchantment:

> Utopia – Magris points out – means not giving in to things as they are and to fight for things as they should be; to know that the world, as a verse by Brecht says, needs to be changed and redeemed […]. Utopia and disenchantment, rather than oppose each other, have to modify each other reciprocally. The end of totalitarian Utopias is only liberating if it is accompanied by a realisation that the notion of redemption, both promised and postponed by those Utopian projects, has to be negotiated with patience and modesty. This must be done in the knowledge that there is no definitive formula for Utopia, but also without making a mockery of Utopia as a project […]. The disenchantment that mends Utopia reinforces its fundamental element, hope […] [which] is not born out of a reassuring and optimistic vision of the world, but of the laceration of lived and endured unveiled existence, which creates an irrepressible need for rescue […]. Disenchantment is an ironic, melancholic and courageous way to hope. (Magris, 2001: 12–15)

According to Magris it is not possible to conceive of Utopia without disenchantment or disenchantment without hope, because the fact of experiencing disenchantment means the acknowledgement of finding faith in a failed Utopia and in the promise of a future happiness. It is also true that hope rests not only in the future but in a past that has to be scrutinised and mended to make sense of life, not to praise triumphs or victories. In the case of *Los desterrados* and Lautaro Sanz, rootlessness is the end of Utopia, and disenchantment is the triumph of defeat. It is the failure of a nationalist project, the fissures of which became the cracks in the Bolivarian Revolution's re-appropriation of its narrations. For the characters of these chronicles there is no hope or possible future project, because displacement itself becomes the symptom of the failure of the redemptive promises made by the state, as well as of its will to mend its mistakes. This impossibility of creating a future becomes a desacralisation of representations of happiness, used in turn by official discourse to strengthen the ties of national identity.

Happiness relies on hope, on the possibility of an alternative that remains in the future, for hope 'is a thoughtful way of being directed toward the future, or a way of creating the very thought of the future as going some way. If happiness is what we hope for, when we hope for this or that thing, it does not mean we think we *will be* happy but that we imagine we *could be* happy if things go the right way' (Ahmed, 2010: 181–182; original emphasis). In the absence of a hope in which the notion of Utopia is upheld, the myth of happiness collapses because hope and happiness are irremediably oriented towards the anticipation of the future – a future in which the characters of the chronicles do not recognise their own parts –, that is,

> '[w]e have a certain confidence in outcome premised on the possibility that what comes out might be *just that*. If the future is that which does not exist, what is always before us, in the whisper of the 'just ahead', then hope also involves imagination, a wishfulness that teaches us about what we strive for in the present. Hope is a wish and expectation that a desired possibility is 'becoming actual'' (Ahmed, 2010: 182; original emphasis).

This is the double meaning of disenchantment that we find in these chronicles: disenchantment as rationalisation of the state's magical power, and disenchantment as subjective deception (Martín-Barbero, 1995). In these texts, both experiences are inseparable because they give shape to a subject – the uprooted, the displaced – whose truth is irreparably linked to the fracture with the nation, to the violence of a city, Caracas, that attacks and threatens its citizens, but most of all to the awareness that there is no possible emancipation for such wounds. In this way, the tragedy of displacement faces the failure of democratic Utopia in Venezuela, the victory of one-dimensional thinking. Faced with the memory and the signs of rootedness which bestow identity on citizens, Lautaro chooses anonymity, detachment, non-belonging. He expresses as much in 'El odio' ('Hatred'), a chronicle moved by his experience of mourning for the murder of his friend F. in Caracas:

> ¡Te maldeciré siempre!; me olvidaré de vivir; seré un infeliz hasta el fin de mis días consciente de la desgracia de haber nacido en tu miserable geografía [...]. Vivir en ti es padecer; nacer en ti es decirle a la vida que se equivocó. No, Caracas, no me intimidas, soy inmune a tu burundanga, he dejado de pertenecerte, renuncié, incluso, a mi condición humana. No tengo razón, ni corazón, ni pasaporte. Soy una fuerza bruta e invisible que, únicamente, logra sostenerse a través de palabras. Quiero que veas en mi pupila la sonrisa fugaz de todos tus muertos, de todo lo que has destruido a la sombra de tu triste montaña; ojalá fueras consciente del daño que haces, ojalá, al menos, tuvieras un sentimiento de culpa. Pero no te importa nada. Avanzas y me apuntas con una pistola sin marca ni serial. 'No me sorprendes, infeliz; la violencia sin sentido es tu único talento' [...]. Seguiré aferrado a la negación [...] La locura se ceba con mi nombre. El mundo ha dejado de ser una esfera; el oxígeno pica en la garganta; el sueño se fue y el alimento es un capricho innecesario. El sol dejó de ser fuente de luz. Soy un desertor de las tinieblas perdido en un lugar que no conozco ni entiendo. (Sánchez Rugeles, 2011: 48–49)

I will always curse you! I will forget to live; I will be an unhappy man until the end of my days, well aware of the disgrace of having been born in your miserable geography [...]. Living in you is to suffer; to be born in you is to say to life that it made a mistake. No, Caracas, you don't intimidate me, I am immune to your spell, I have stopped belonging to you, I have even renounced my human condition. I have no reason, no heart, no passport. I am a brute and invisible force that only gets to sustain itself through words. I want you to see in my pupil the fleeting smile of all your dead, of all you have been destroyed in the shadow of your sad mountain; I wish you were aware of how much you hurt, I wish, at least, you had a sense of guilt. But nothing matters to you. You move forward and hold a gun to me with no make or serial number. 'Wretch, you don't surprise me; violence without sense is your only talent' [...]. I will continue to take refuge in negation [...] Madness vents her anger in my name. The world has stopped being a sphere; oxygen itches in the throat; all dreams have disappeared and food is an unnecessary desire.

The sun has stopped being a source of light. I am a deserter from the
dark lost in a place I no longer know or understand.

By way of closure, and beyond offering concluding remarks, what I have tried
to reveal with my approach to Eduardo Sánchez Rugeles's *Los desterrados* is
that it is neither dialogue, nor Utopia, nor the promise of redefining the meaning of community that this writer seeks with his chronicles. Rather, he directly
acknowledges the awareness of disenchantment as a way to question the nor-
mativity that dwells in rootedness, particularly as a language with which to
articulate the fact that Utopia (democratic or socialist) reveals its failures when
the miseries of displacement become ingrained in the national imaginary.

References

Ahmed, S. (2010) *The Promise of Happiness*. Duke University Press: Durham and
    London.
Boym, S. (2001) *The Future of Nostalgia*. Basic Books: New York.
Coronil, F. (1997) *The Magical State: Nature, Money, and Modernity in Venezuela*. Uni-
    versity of Chicago Press: Chicago.
Coronil, F. and Skurski, J. (1991) 'Dismembering and Remembering the Nation:
    The Semantics of Political Violence in Venezuela'. *Comparative Studies in Soci-
    ety and History. An International Quarterly* **33**(2): 288-337.
Eastwood, J. (2011) 'Introduction: The Revolution in Venezuela?' in T. Ponniah
    and J. Eastwood (eds.) *The Revolution in Venezuela. Social and Political Change
    under Chávez*. Harvard University Press: Cambridge and London, 1-34.
Guerrero, J. (2012) 'Culturas del cuerpo: la *sagrada* familia venezolana'. *452°F.
    Revista de teoría de la literatura y literatura comparada* **6**: 17-38. [WWW doc-
    ument]. URL http://www.452f.com/es/javier-guerrero.html [accessed 1
    February 2012].
Jameson, F. (2005) *Archaeologies of the Future: The Desired Called Utopia and Other
    Science Fictions*. Verso: London and New York.
Kozak Rovero, G. (2008) 'El lesbianismo en Venezuela es asunto de pocas páginas:
    literatura, nación, feminismo y modernidad'. *Revista iberoamericana* **74**(225):
    999-1017.
Kozak Rovero, G. (2012) 'Política para machos'. *Tal cual digital,* 13 March. [WWW
    document]. URL http://www.talcualdigital.com/Nota/67525/politica-
    para-machos [accessed 14 March 2012].
López, M. (2015) *Desde el fracaso. Narrativas del Caribe insular hispano en el siglo XX*.
    Editorial Verbum: Madrid.
Magris, C. (2001) *Utopía y desencanto. Historias, esperanzas e ilusiones de la
    modernidad*. Editorial Anagrama: Barcelona.
Martín-Barbero, J. (1995) 'Secularización, desencanto y reencantamiento
    massmediático'. *Pre-textos. Conversaciones sobre la comunicación y sus contextos*.
    Editorial Universidad del Valle: Cali, 177-192.
Ríos, A. (2013) *Nacionalismos banales: el culto a Bolívar. Literatura, cine, arte y política
    en América Latina*. Instituto Internacional de Literatura Iberoamericana, Uni-
    versity of Pittsburgh: Pittsburgh.

Rivas Rojas, R. (2013) 'Ficciones de exilio o los fantasmas de la pertenencia en la literatura del desarraigo venezolano' in A. Tinajero (ed.) *Exilio y cosmopolitismo en el arte y la literatura hispánica*. Editorial Verbum: Madrid, 189-206.

Sánchez Rugeles, E. (2011) *Los desterrados*. Ediciones B Venezuela: Caracas.

Valladares-Ruiz, P. (2013) 'Desplazamiento y disenso político en la narrativa de Eduardo Sánchez Rugeles'. *Inti: Revista de literatura hispanica* **77-78**: 115-136.

Yslas Prado, L. (2011) 'El desarraigo militante'. Introducción. *Los desterrados*. E. Sánchez Rugeles. Ediciones B Venezuela: Caracas, 7-18.

Index